copywriting

j. jonathan gabay FRSA

For over 60 years, more than
40 million people have learnt over
750 subjects the **teach yourself**
way, with impressive results.

be where you want to be
with **teach yourself**

For UK order queries: please contact Bookpoint Ltd, 130 Milton Park, Abingdon, Oxon OX14 4TD. Telephone: +44 (0) 1235 827720. Fax: +44 (0) 1235 400454. Lines are open 9.00–18.00, Monday to Saturday, with a 24-hour message answering service. You can also order through our website www.madaboutbooks.com

For USA order queries: please contact McGraw-Hill Customer Services, P.O. Box 545, Blacklick, OH 43004-0545, USA. Telephone: 1-800-722-4726. Fax: 1-614-755-5645.

For Canada order queries: please contact McGraw-Hill Ryerson Ltd, 300 Water St, Whitby, Ontario L1N 9B6, Canada. Telephone: 905 430 5000. Fax: 905 430 5020.

Long renowned as the authoritative source for self-guided learning – with more than 30 million copies sold worldwide – the Teach Yourself series includes over 300 titles in the fields of languages, crafts, hobbies, business, computing and education.

British Library Cataloguing in Publication Data: a catalogue entry for this title is available from The British Library.

Library of Congress Catalog Card Number: on file

First published in UK 2000 by Hodder Headline Ltd, 338 Euston Road, London, NW1 3BH.

First published in US 2000 by Contemporary Books, a Division of the McGraw Hill Companies, 1, Prudential Plaza, 130 East Randolph Street, Chicago IL 60601 U.S.A.

This edition published 2003.

Typeset by Transet Limited, Coventry, England.
Printed in Great Britain for Hodder & Stoughton Educational, a division of Hodder Headline Ltd, 338 Euston Road, London NW1 3BH by Cox & Wyman Ltd, Reading, Berkshire.

Impression number   10 9 8 7 6 5 4 3 2 1
Year   2008 2007 2006 2005 2004 2003

iii

contents

how to use this book

Since the first edition of this book was published I have been inundated with requests to publish an updated version, taking into account the needs of the twenty-first-century copywriter and to be read in conjunction with *Teach Yourself Marketing*. Whether you are looking for some creative ideas for SOHO (Small Office Home Office) or Web business, working for a local charity or even working in advertising and want to dip in for extra hints and tips, this book is right up your street.

Throughout this book you'll find quick tips summarizing what you have read and exercises for you to do. If you want to brush up on all aspects of copywriting, then you should find something of interest in each section. If on the other hand you prefer to concentrate on one particular subject, simply look it up in the contents list or the index. At the end of the book, you'll find a practical glossary of terms along with useful addresses. You can also access a special website – www.gabaynet.com. If you are looking for only the basics on copywriting, I suggest you follow the flow chart below.

Have fun!

J. Jonathan Gabay
FRSA

COPYWRITING ESSENTIALS FLOW CHART

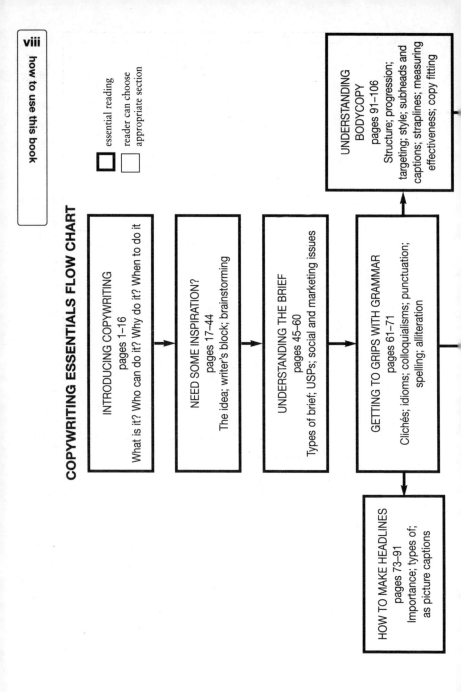

☐ essential reading

☐ reader can choose appropriate section

INTRODUCING COPYWRITING
pages 1–16
What is it? Who can do it? Why do it? When to do it

NEED SOME INSPIRATION?
pages 17–44
The idea; writer's block; brainstorming

UNDERSTANDING THE BRIEF
pages 45–60
Types of brief; USPs; social and marketing issues

GETTING TO GRIPS WITH GRAMMAR
pages 61–71
Clichés; idioms; colloquialisms; punctuation; spelling; alliteration

HOW TO MAKE HEADLINES
pages 73–91
Importance; types of; as picture captions

UNDERSTANDING BODYCOPY
pages 91–106
Structure; progression; targeting; style; subheads and captions; straplines; measuring effectiveness; copy fitting

HOW TO WRITE
GREAT OFF-THE-PAGE ADVERTISING

pages 138–48

Style; incentives; coupons;
telephone hotlines; premium rate lines

HOW TO MAKE CHARITY
MORE APPEALING

pages 186–91

Targeting donors; direct mail;
action lines; tone; emergency appeals

HOW TO WRITE
GREAT PRESS RELEASES

pages 255–67

Style and content; targeting;
dealing with 'bad' news

HOW TO WRITE GREAT
BUSINESS-TO-BUSINESS ADVERTISING

pages 124–38

Research; gaining attention; targeting;
corporate press ads; response; trade magazines

TARGETING DIRECT MARKETING

pages 149–85

One-to-one; direct mail; reply devices;
creative ideas; questionnaires; catalogues

THE INTERNET ESSENTIALS

pages 241–54

The Web; forums; IP address; HTML;
marketing

HOW TO WRITE
GREAT RECRUITMENT ADVERTISING

pages 118–24

Line ads; classified ads; display ads

HOW TO WRITE GREAT
TRADE DIRECTORY ADVERTISING

pages 237–40

Layout; approach

WRITING FOR BROADCAST MEDIA

pages 192–230

Script writing; targeting;
production techniques

With special thanks to Katie Roden, Catherine Newman,
Lesley Hadcroft and the Chartered Institute of Marketing.

To all the students I have taught and those from whom
I have yet to learn.

This edition is for Brenda who can no longer express in words
what she speaks with her heart.

introduction

Hello, I am a copywriter. Care to join me?

Thank you for buying this book. Over the next 320 pages or so, I hope to reveal and review the key aspects of copywriting.

> Hmmm. How does that opening paragraph sound to you? Well, it starts off with a positive statement – 'Thank you'. Next, it is relevant to this product and, finally, it is enticing. Could you do a better job? Perhaps you would redirect the approach? Instead of thanking the reader up front for buying this book (which, I suppose, may appear a little insincere), you could proceed directly to the benefits derived from reading it. Then, of course, you have to consider the type of person buying this book.

We haven't met face to face but based on research, I can make a few assumptions about you. Firstly, the obvious ones. Copywriting interests you. Next, you probably believe that, given the right guidance, you could pursue a career in advertising or creative marketing. Perhaps you already work in the industry, which means you may be interested in picking up some tips that would help to make your job more involving, rewarding and (let's face it) fun.

I will take you through all the main aspects of practical copywriting, starting from who makes an ideal copywriter and going on to the technicalities of awareness advertising, direct mail, sales promotion, the Web and so on.

Why advertise?

So, why advertise? More to the point, why spend and devote so much time and energy in getting the right mix of words and pictures to convey a message? The obvious answer is, to *sell*. This is indisputable. However, there is a much more pertinent answer. Advertising provides the consumer with the relevant information needed to make a purchasing *choice*. With so many brand names being simultaneously promoted you could argue that there is too much choice! That is where thoroughly planned copywriting comes into the picture.

Today's consumer is like a mollusc on a beach. Presented with so many advertised messages offering such great choice, the consumer only opens their guard to welcome marketing messages when those are entirely pertinent to specific needs.

Copywriting – supported by evocative images – explains the benefits of a product or service to an individual and then allows that person to make a considered buying decision based on facts, aspirations and associations.

From a professional viewpoint, the natural home of copywriters is the advertising agency. It has been so since 1809 when the first recorded freelance copywriter, the essayist Charles Lamb, worked on a lottery account for the James White agency. Incidentally, the Thomas Smith agency in London was the first – in 1889 – to employ full-time 'ad writers'.

Did you know?

The world's first known agency was based in London in 1786. It booked advertisements in the provincial press, charging a handling fee of 6d or 1s. The first international agency was Gordon & Gotch, which opened for business in Melbourne in 1855 and had its first overseas branch in London in 1867.

Involvement, reward and achievement

Before you write even the most carefully chosen words, consider your broader copywriting approach. If your approach is off course the reader will realize that you are not 100% committed to communicating an effective message.

Imagine a wooden stool. There are three supports to provide creativity stability to your copy. Remove one and your creative argument and integrity topples over.

- *Involvement* between the consumer and seller. (Usually achieved by creating empathy about a desired lifestyle.)
- *Reward* in terms of personal gain to a consumer for purchasing a product.

- *Achievement* is the third vital element. It concerns you, the writer, more than the consumer.

The basic ingredients for effective copywriting

It has often been said that great copywriting requires 50% information, 15% inspiration, 25% personalization and 10% perspiration!

The more balanced your approach, the greater will be your understanding of a targeted audience. Adapt your style and tone of voice to establish rapport and credibility with your intended reader, viewer, listener and so forth. It's by getting to know what makes people want to listen to/read/continue to watch what you have to say that you can write effective copy.

Keeping this introduction in your mind, please join me as we embark on our journey to the world of copywriting through a method that helps you to become your own best teacher.

Introducing ScotsdaleNorth.com and PenPod

At this point I want you to get acquainted with two fictitious companies. They typify organizations of their size and type. Throughout this book, we'll be looking at how each uses copywriting techniques to enhance their ongoing development plans. The first is ScotsdaleNorth.com

ScotsdaleNorth

com

This large multi-national food company supplies a vast range of fast-moving consumer goods (FMCG) via the Web. FMCG refers to goods that usually move off supermarket shelves quickly. Examples include tinned foodstuffs, toothpaste, ready-made meals and soft drinks. Stores need to keep fresh stocks of FMCGs to replace those that are sold.

A traditional retailer, ScotsdaleNorth has been established for 100 years. To celebrate their centenary, they are planning quite an extensive publicity and advertising campaign. This will also push their Web marketing drive.

They intend to launch several new products exclusively available on the Web, re-enforce their corporate awareness advertising and open a nationwide cyber-café chain.

4

introduction

PenPod is a small business. As yet, it hasn't been formally launched in the market. PenPod has two key company directors. One invented the PenPod. The other is the managing director in charge of sales.

The PenPod product is an ink pen encased in steel, used in a recent space mission to Mars. It is guaranteed to write underwater as well as at any angle. The real ingenuity of the PenPod is that its nib can be easily changed from a fountain-pen style to a ball-point style and even to a marker pen.

As in the case of ScotsdaleNorth, this is going to be a very important year for PenPod and much of the company's success will depend on effective advertising.

J. Jonathan Gabay FRSA

jj@gabaynet.com

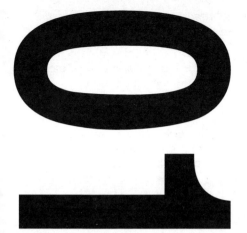

01

what is a copywriter?

In this chapter you will learn
- about the roots of copywriting
- how to write with conviction
- how to understand motives.

According to the *Bloomsbury/Microsoft Encarta World English Dictionary*, a copywriter writes the texts for advertisements or other promotional material.

Do you think that's accurate enough? Does it cover every aspect of the copywriting you do? Here's my own definition:

> A copywriter is a communicator who manipulates words/images and applies **creative strategies** within media. Those strategies are balanced to integrate the marketing and sales principles of a specific sector with a literary style that may be informative, persuasive, subliminal or a combination of all three. Through doing this, a copywriter communicates product or service *benefits*.

The tools of the trade

Did you know?

There are approximately 615,000 words in *The Oxford English Dictionary*. Whilst the French have around 100,000 words in common use, the British have over 200,000. There are around 2000 words with different English/American meanings. Each year around 5000 new words enter the language. Over 800 million people around the world speak English. It is the international language of airlines and the language of choice for the Web.

Given the information explosion, copywriting and everything associated with it is one of the most valuable tools for any business.

I have met scores of copywriters and even more would-be copywriters. The good ones share a remarkable ability to pinpoint, in words and pictures, key benefits of a particular product or service. So a copywriter interprets those benefits convincingly, concisely and with originality, through Webpages, text, pictures, sounds or images.

The top ten traits of a great copywriter

- Unstoppable curiosity about how things work.
- Fascination with images suggested by words.
- Enjoys every aspect of the media – and is not elitist.
- Recognizes both ends of an argument.
- Is a natural leader – either passive or dominant.

- Is totally interested in people and what makes them tick.
- Is sympathetic to people's needs.
- Has a vivid imagination.
- Takes a logical, lateral approach to technical matters.
- Has a good sense of humour – especially when, having worked all day long to craft a great piece of writing, someone returns their emailed copy with a green line through their favourite paragraphs!

Did you know?

If you want a job in copywriting, a first-class degree in English certainly will not be a disadvantage. Neither will attending a course on the subject at somewhere like the Chartered Institute of Marketing (www.cim.co.uk). A respectable qualification in commerce and marketing is also useful, as is a fair knowledge of history and social psychology. But even if you are not that academic – as this book proves – you can still become a brilliant writer.

How copywriting relates to sales

Copywriting is not just the art of inspired writing. It is often an English professor's nightmare. Take a billboard. The chances are high that the copy on it is grammatically incorrect (no full stops at the end of the headline, for example). Rather than thinking of copywriting as just creative writing, aim to use it as a selling skill. This applies even if you don't specifically want to sell something but rather want to encourage your audience to take the next step – such as donate some money to a charity.

All successful salespeople need the ability to think laterally. Original thinking is essential to assimilate various pieces of information into a finely tuned message.

You need to make your product or service:

Attractive Interesting Desirable Convincing Actionable (AIDCA)

In other words, turn

Features into Advantages and Benefits

Each of these elements will be examined in detail as we progress through this book.

Copywriting and subjectivity

Just because you like a piece of your creative writing, it doesn't necessarily follow that your target audience will be so appreciative of it that they will take the action which you seek.

Even when you think that you have correctly adjusted the balance of inspiration, imagination and personalization, you have to consider the tricky area of subjectivity. What one person finds interesting another may find irrelevant.

So, getting the message right is not as straightforward as you might at first think. But hang on, your very early creative writing and learning experiences may have already prepared you for a copywriting career.

From song writer to copywriter

From a very early age, creative writing plays an important role in your life. By understanding its role and influences, you can appreciate how it can be harnessed. From pre-school age, words accompanied by provocative images conjure powerful feelings and attitudes towards ourselves as well as the outside world. For example:

> Put in a historical context, nursery rhymes may not really mean all that much to toddlers. Their immediate attractiveness lies in their essential rhythm. Once their basic sentiments can be understood – even at the most fundamental level – their influence on children becomes tremendously powerful, specifically by drawing them in group play.

> That involvement enables a toddler to explore activities such as holding hands with others and then falling down to the ground on a key phrase (as in 'Ring-a-Ring-o'-Roses'), encouraging them to further explore the world through words.

> What may appear everyday sentences to you and me are potentially great adventures of discovery for the pre-school child.

Direction through words

The influence of the creative word through media such as books, videos, the Web and so on is that it trickle-feeds our subconscious. Take as an example tales from the Koran or the

Bible. They are retold time and time again. Through listening to them, we are intended to gain some kind of moral direction.

History has placed us in some sort of social chronology. Through it, we discover how, throughout time, people have handled key decisions – the very same judgements that may also affect us: to fight, to try to negotiate, to explore. It's not surprising that the written word concerning historical, religious or fictional characters – and, more significantly, what they represent socially – impresses us deeply.

Role playing and leading

Throughout adolescence, words in pop songs take on particular relevance to our lives. Love songs, for instance, can help us recover from a broken first romance while still at school. Other songs may even enable us to express feelings of rebellion against all the history that has preceded us and to declare our intention to redirect the course in a new, fresh direction.

Sometimes, the allure of songs and song writing is so strong that we form our own pop groups. For some, the creative lyric-writing process may turn what may be a boring English lesson into a voyage of self-awareness.

For others, just listening to songs, or maybe reading teen magazines about the singers, can provoke powerful images of empathy with the singer, whose words and performance often relate intimately to an adolescent's needs. This empathy with the singer often develops to such an extent that the pop fan's centre of attraction turns away from themselves to become a fascination with the singer and all that they represent. So begins a form of hero worshipping within which trends and ideals are set and followed.

I started to write songs when I was about 11 years old. They were meant only for me; unfortunately I never had the chance – or the voice – to become a pop hero! Others with creative instincts may turn to poetry or a variation on the theme such as Rap. Many keep a diary.

All these forms of creative writing are an ideal preparation for the future copywriter. However, the emphasis of this style of writing, about you and your world, needs gradually to shift from what is personally motivating to what touches an audience. More often than not – as happens in the case of the singer who is followed by adoring fans – this can be the same thing.

Your first steps in the copywriting thought process

You need to put yourself in someone else's shoes – those of the kind of person who would benefit from what you are writing. Then prioritize the pros and cons of your proposition.

The following example provides the initial cognitive steps for becoming a copywriter. Don't worry if you feel that the situation is a little far-fetched. At this stage the thought process behind the advert is more important than the actual circumstance. OK. Ready to explore? Let's go!

> Imagine yourself in the shoes of a teenage pop group leader. You need a pair of 150 Watt speakers for a rock gig which you eventually plan to offer as an MP3 clip on the Web. You don't kow where to find this piece of equipment and you are restricted to a limited budget.

You decide to pin up a notice on a local information board. It must be no larger than A4. What should you write? Here is your first attempt.

> ### WANTED
> A PAIR OF **150**-WATT SPEAKERS WITH DOLBY 'C' CONTROL AND AMPS.
> MUST BE CHEAP AND IN GOOD CONDITION.
> CALL **JJ** ON **0218 900 1234**

Well, that certainly gets the message across. However, does it cover *everything* you need? For instance, you are pretty desperate for this pair of speakers as the gig is on Friday night and your Web engineer is all Netted up to record. Ideally you will be ready by Wednesday at the latest. Next, what about that limited budget of yours? You only have £200 to spend; you can't be too choosy.

On the other hand, who would want to 'give away' a perfectly good pair of speakers below the going price? And let's consider your request that the speakers should be in good condition. Can you be a little more precise? Finally, what about the 'call to action' (how people can get in touch with you) – is it convincing enough? ('Convincing' is the 'C' in AIDCA.)

At this point you would be forgiven for thinking that if you were to include every requirement, you would need a lot more space than an A4 sheet stuck on a notice board! Consider the main restriction on your advert. It cannot cover more than an A4 sheet. If you use too many words it will become cluttered and difficult to read. Could you pep it up a bit with some colour in the headline?

Next, think about the type of people who are going to read this advertisement. It is being pinned up on the local community board. The readers may know you and if not they may assume that you live nearby. (This is important if they are expected to deliver the speakers.) Naturally, those interested will want to get as high a price as possible for their speakers. A factor in the bargaining would be the condition of the equipment.

Next, think about how the potential sellers will perceive you. Maybe they will assume you don't have much money. If you did, surely you would be advertising in a trade magazine?

Now, let's sort all of this information into sections:

Your needs	The ad space	Your prospect's needs
150-watt speaker.	A4 size.	Sell a speaker.
Dolby C Control.	Colour available.	Good price.
Good condition.	Not too many	Not too many delivery
Cheap.	words.	hassles.
Immediate availability.		

Now consider the motives behind this sale:

You	Your prospect
So that your band can be heard!	No need for an extra set of speakers.
So that you can be more creative with sound output.	Need to raise cash – quickly.
So that you can get more gigs ... ... and more experience.	Given up on music.
So that you can have more fun playing as part of a band.	Wants new, higher spec speakers.
So you can get your music on the Web.	Need the space that is taken up by the speakers.
So that the band can practise and perfect its act.	
So that your band doesn't become disbanded!	

Finally, imagine the speakers as a catalyst for emotions. In terms of feelings and tone of voice, how do they affect each interested party?

You	Your prospect
Happiness – as you can team up with your friends.	Nostalgia – for when they played in a band.
Confidence – as you can creatively express your feelings.	Happiness – when they recollect adventures that they had with the band.
Pride – when you consider what you and the band have already achieved.	Sadness – when they either: • had to give up with the band, or • recollect sombre times with the band.
Sadness – when you worry about what will happen to the band without the speakers.	Confidence – when they consider how playing with the band helped them develop their own character.
Optimism – that your band will be successful.	Regret – when they think about what the band was supposed to achieve and never did.
	Pride – when they recollect the achievements they enjoyed with the band.

Now that you have identified all your elements, consider revising the advert. A good copywriter gets to the heart of a proposition. In doing so they draw out a convincing set of motives for a prospect to discover more about a product or service. In this example, amongst the creative solutions you could try:

• Pampering to your prospect's nostalgia values.
• Addressing the practicalities of disposing of a cumbersome and bulky piece of equipment.
• Combining the approaches.

Your tone of voice could be:

• Serious
• Begging
• Irreverent
• Casual

• Humorous
• Challenging
• Formal
• 'Cool' and trendy

What do you think your prospect would want to hear?

Targeting your message

One way of targeting your message is to match mutual key motives.

You	Your prospect
Happiness	Happiness
Confidence	Confidence
Pride	Pride
Sadness	Sadness

I wouldn't think that this particular advert calls for an all-out negative approach. Creative propositions rarely do, except in notable areas such as charity and some aspects of general public information. For example:

> **DON'T DRINK AND DRIVE**
> **OR YOU COULD END UP**
> **IN A DEAD END STREET**

So, let's ditch the negative motive. What's left?

You	Your prospect
Happiness	Happiness
Confidence	Confidence
Pride	Pride

Now, imagine standing on a line on a graph which shows where your musical ambitions could take you. Then do the same for your prospect. This time, however, just summarize the emotions behind your prospect's experiences.

Advertiser's and prospect's ambitions

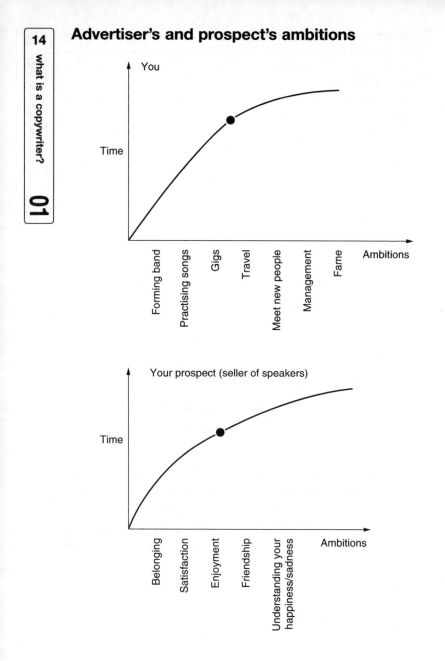

Now, return to your original catalyst list. There is one word for your prospect which connects all of these experiences: nostalgia.

Did you know?

The word 'nostalgia' derives from the Greek word *nostos* – meaning 'a return home'. Copywriting which directs itself at a subject's home truths is copywriting at its best.

If you rewrote the advert using nostalgia as the direction to take, you could incorporate all the powerful nostalgic feelings associated with an up-and-coming band:

- Challenging – like the motives behind the lyrics.
- Casual/easy going – like the key band members.
- Ambitious – as you are and as the then-younger prospect would probably have been when they originally purchased the speakers.
- Witty – like the band.
- Direct – like all youth.
- Intimate – like your songs.

Using the limited space available, let's give the advert another shot. My suggestion would be to connect your practical and emotional needs with those of your prospect.

CAN YOU HEAR US AT THE BACK?

They could with your help!

We need a pair of 150-watt speakers (inc. Dolby C and Amps).

We offer £100 ono + the chance to see our band playing live.

Please don't turn a deaf ear on us.

Call JJ on 0218 900 1234 ASAP – we're live this Friday!

Over to you

1 Basing it upon the author's advert, write an advert adopting the following approaches:

a serious
b practical.

2 Write another advert, this time from a person wishing to sell, rather than buy, speakers.

3 Think about the nursery rhyme 'Humpty Dumpty'.

> Humpty Dumpty sat on a wall,
> Humpty Dumpty had a great fall.
> All the King's horses
> And all the King's men
> Couldn't put Humpty together again.

a List four of the reasons Humpty Dumpty needs to be put together again.
b List three practical problems the King's men may have in putting Humpty Dumpty together again.
c Assuming Humpty Dumpty is the heir apparent to the throne and a father of two children, list three of his prime motives to be put together again.
d List three of the King's men's motives to put Humpty Dumpty together again.
e Finally, list the three main shared motives that Humpty Dumpty and the King's men have to put him together again.

the big idea

In this chapter you will learn
- how to unlock your creativity
- how to use copy formulae
- how to brainstorm effectively
- how to cross examine a creative need
- how to understand brands
- how to conduct a SWOT analysis.

How many times have you sat in front of the TV set and admired the clever combination of words and images in an advertisement? I've done just that many times. Often I ask myself, 'How and from where did they get such a good idea?'

The philosopher Plato (427–347 BCE) believed that the mind and body were made up of different things. Each followed separate sets of rules. He taught that the mind was the most important of the two and that the so-called 'body' (things you could see, touch and so on) formed the foundations for reality. 'Platonic ideas' came about through a process of reasoning, by drawing a general conclusion about something mainly based on experience or through experimenting with the facts available.

Plato maintained that ideas represented the genuine basis for reality. Why was this? Plato believed that once you had an idea about something, that idea was real. For example:

> You are walking by a coliseum. You think, 'Wouldn't it be great if the coliseum had a roof to protect everyone from the sun?' As far as your perception of the world is concerned, you have the ability to visualize the coliseum with a roof, and the roof might as well be there.

Some centuries after Plato left this earth for the great coliseum in the sky, a mathematician and philosopher called René Descartes entered the philosophical world. He extended Plato's theory by concluding that the processes that controlled the mind and soul were indivisible. On the other hand, the basic controls that govern the body could be divided and understood through mathematics and physical study. So, according to Descartes, ideas were directly perceived in the mind without any influence from the 'body'.

Today it is generally believed that an idea is a mental episode created in the mind and based on real experiences or known facts.

Unlocking your creative potential

John Locke (1635–1704) suggested that ideas are based solely on experience. According to Locke, a newly born baby can be likened to a blank sheet of paper. As the child develops, the sheet is filled with information acquired through experience.

The adult, according to Locke, experiences two kinds of ideas:

- Ideas of sensation (seeing, hearing, smell, sight, taste) – which he called *simple ideas*.
- Ideas of reflection (deliberation, construction) – which he defined as *complex ideas*.

Simple ideas are based on experience whilst complex ideas combine those experiences to create abstract concepts. You can read more about Locke and generating imaginative marketing ideas in *Teach Yourself Marketing*.

Did you know?
Agoraphobia – fear of public spaces – can also be interpreted as fear of the public marketplace. Words are your bridge to reach that market fearlessly.

The basic steps towards a new idea

How do we achieve a new idea? The seven basic steps are:

1 Specific experience.
2 Thought about that experience.
3 Other experiences – material facts (perhaps not directly related).
4 Consolidation of all the experiences.
5 Fresh opinion or insight relating to the original experience.
6 The formulation of a plan to implement a completely new experience.
7 The materialization of that plan – a completely new experience or material fact.

What to do if nothing brilliant comes to mind

Most people have heard of the expression 'writer's block'. It refers to that frustrating point in a creative writing project when no great ideas come to mind – at least none directly connected with the writing assignment itself. Every experienced writer faces this sometimes. There you sit, staring at the blank piece of paper, and there it rests lifeless.

So you make a token effort and start to concentrate on the project. Then you become distracted by something like whether you should have chips or baked potatoes with your dinner. Perhaps (if you are particularly distracted) you turn to considering how long it would take to type out every number from one to a million. (The answer is five years and 2473 sheets of US A4 size paper – with normal line spacing.)

Whatever the cause of your writing block, study this book and you will find that many excuses will become redundant.

To begin with, let's address the problem of the roving mind. At the start of this chapter, I outlined the main theories about how ideas are arrived at. Return to those. Understand the logical process behind thought association and you will be able to redirect the process back toward the specific task at hand.

Take a break

Writer's blocks may sometimes be your subconscious saying, 'This is tiring. Let's have forty winks and see if we can think of something else.' So relax, allow yourself to daydream for a while. Often that leads to a thought which is so different from your original line of thinking that it stimulates the innovative idea that you were looking for in the first place. This is the basis of Edward de Bono's practical books on lateral thinking.

Next, don't instinctively reach for the obvious approach to a copy assignment. Just the act of thinking laterally about a project is often enough to push out all the superfluous stuff in your head that's standing between you and your VDU or piece of paper.

Finally, and most importantly, remember Gabay's Golden Rule for eliminating writer's block: *Write – then get it right.*

If you don't write the first word, the second will never follow, however earnestly you dream about it.

Copywriting and lateral thinking

A few years ago I attended a course in problem solving. The tutor drew a box containing six crosses in two rows. He asked the class to connect six of the crosses by drawing no more than three strokes through them, without taking the pen off the paper. The class found this quite simple:

Then he drew a square box containing nine crosses. We were asked to draw through all the crosses in just four strokes, without lifting the pencil off the paper or retracing any line in any direction. The class started to scribble various lines. Most either retraced a line or drew more than the four lines permitted.

The solution was to think outside the box. Human nature being what it is, most people assumed that the box containing the crosses also held the parameters to work within for the solution. However, the tutor never actually said that the class should be restrained in this way.

The solution was to think laterally – to go beyond the predictable ways of looking at things and use creative initiative:

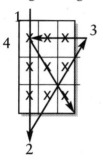

After this, the tutor asked the class to cross out sixteen squares within a square box using just six lines, without taking the pen from the paper. Eventually we arrived at the solution:

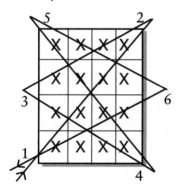

Again, the principle of thinking outside the box applied. Whilst many people in business are aimed-led thinkers, and many in the creative services industry are lateral-based thinkers, in addition to taking the broad view you also need to balance the two extremes.

Should you follow the formulae crowd?

Nowadays it seems that just about every industry sector likes to produce its own pet formulae for instant and guaranteed success.

Did you know?

The information technology industry uses mnemonics like GIGO (Garbage In, Garbage Out). Recruiters refer to QWL (Quality of Working Life), a holistic approach to careers that takes into account time spent on leisure and with the family as well as career progression.

In their favour, formulae help to impose a level of discipline. Think of them as reference points on a map. They suggest routes towards a destination. However, you should adapt these suggestions to help you reach your specific goal.

Perhaps, the most famous of all creative formulae is AIDA, created during the Roaring 1920s. It is derived from another formula that advocated the following:

All advertising must be:
Seen **R**ead **B**elieved **R**emembered **A**cted upon

The trouble with the original formula is that it is not well defined. For instance, it lists 'remembered'. How detailed should your memory be? And does 'read' mean that you should read every single word and think about it at length? Besides, how do you pronounce SRBRA (answers on a postcard, please).

Because it was inadequate, SRBRA begat AIDA and an entire nation of copywriting theories was born.

AIDA stands for:
Attention **I**nterest **D**esire **A**ction

AIDA's logic has stood the test of time:

- Attention leads to → Interest in the product or service
- Interest leads to → Desire to get hold of the offer
- Desire leads to → Action either to make a purchase or follow an instruction to take the next step, for example surf a website.

I prefer AIDA's cousin AIDCA – which we have already looked at briefly (see p. 10). Once your target audience desires what you are offering, you need to Convince them of your facts before they Act.

Once the word about formulae got around, just about everyone began to devise them.

Some classic formulae

Bob Stone's mail formula

Bob's formula is often quoted, notably in *Successful Direct Marketing Methods*. It is:

1 Promise the most important benefit.
2 Enlarge on it.
3 Specify the order in full.
4 Provide proof and endorsements.
5 Say what you might 'lose'.
6 Rephrase benefits.
7 Incite immediate action.

Reed's three Bs

This is included in Dick Hodgson's *Direct Mail and Mail Order Handbook*. The three Bs are:

• Benefits
• Believability
• Bounce

Sawyer's Seven Deadly Sins

The following list is based on Howard 'Scotty' Sawyer's checklist:

1 Never be a braggart. A lot of industrial advertising insists that one man is better than the next. Claiming superiority in itself is not necessarily wrong; it is wrong if little or nothing is done to substantiate the claim in a friendly, persuasive and convincing manner.
2 Stop talking to yourself. Direct your remarks towards the interest of the readers, not the company doing the talking.
3 Don't preach. Never look down upon the reader from way up high. Instead, invite the reader to do something.
4 Don't blow your bugle. You don't have to make a big noise to get readers to stand to attention.
5 Stop making a mess. Nobody likes anyone who is untidy. Equally, people don't like inconsiderate advertising.

6 Quit being cute. Deliver your story in as straightforward a manner as possible.
7 Ditch dullness – the worst sin of all. Instead feature crisp presentation of visual elements and some fast-moving copy. It's the least you can do.

Gabay's copy check

Before you reach for the mouse:

- Make sure you have an appropriate brief.
- If you don't, ask for one.
- Do you understand what is required of you?
- Do you have a convincing offer?
- Prioritize your benefits.
- Dismiss irrelevant ideas.
- Set the tone of your message.

Start as you mean to go on:

- Think about your three biggest features – choose appropriate words to reflect those ideals.
- Include the word 'you' in the first paragraph of your message.
- Make sure your introductory paragraph has some creative connection to your headline (proposition).
- Make sure you are sympathetic to your audience.

In the body text:

- Ensure your copy is appropriately structured.
- Keep the copy moving and your reader's interest alert.
- Use link terms: 'like', 'therefore', 'so', 'however'.
- At this stage, ask yourself if you would honestly want to read further.
- Have you covered every angle?
- Can you provide proof and endorsements?
- Have you reiterated your main benefits?

Close the deal:

- Know where and why you want the copy to end.
- Get there – either sell or invite an alternative response such as visiting a website. If you are selling off the page, make sure you include all relevant details, including when the reader can expect delivery.
- Review your presentation and content. Check the style is sympathetic to the medium in which the copy appears.

Copywriting and its influence on the mind

Ever since experiments on this took place in California during the late 1960s and early 1970s, neurologists have believed that each side of the human brain specializes in certain regions of consciousness. The brain consists of two hemispheres housed within a pleated casing some 2.5 mm thick, called the cerebral cortex. Each of the two hemispheres has lots of cavities called ventricles. Prior to modern scientific understanding, people thought that these ventricles cupped the human spirit. Both hemispheres are connected by an intricate collection of nerve fibres called the *corpus callosum*. The left side of the brain deals with practical issues and controls the right-hand side of the body. The right side of the brain deals with creative and symbolic issues as well as controlling the left-hand side of the body.

Marketing researchers have developed these findings into an area of knowledge called 'braintyping':

- A typical left-brain thinking person is very good at organizing things and appreciates order and structure.
- The typical right-brain thinking person is very creative and emotionally led. As advertising relies heavily on images and emotive issues, a great deal of it is processed within the right brain.

Left brain	Right brain
Alert	Intuitive
Unprejudiced	Subjective
Lucid	Hypothetical
Deliberate	Lateral
Focused	Contrary

Strategic marketers often claim that a typical left-brain thinking person is good at understanding order and structure. (This side is particularly apt at language skills.) Ideally, at your most creative, you will make best use of both spheres. When you do that people will be able to appreciate all sides of your argument. Once you understand this dual thinking, you will appreciate why copywriting has to do more than inform; it must address basic human traits. That is why it should be one or more of the following:

intriguing involving charming surprising understanding caring and, above all, rewarding

The human motivation model

Arguably, one of the twentieth century's greatest psychologists was a man called Abraham Maslow. He devised a model of human motivation which many creative marketing experts refer to when assessing the motivation factors that influence a typical buyer.

Maslow's pyramid is constructed from five 'need' levels. Like every construction, its overall strength relies on the integrity of the foundation. Once your creative message satisfies one need level, it should lead on to address the next.

Interestingly, nobody ever reaches the pinnacle. This is great news for copywriters. Just as a market is satisfied that it has the best possible deal, you are able to offer a more attractive option.

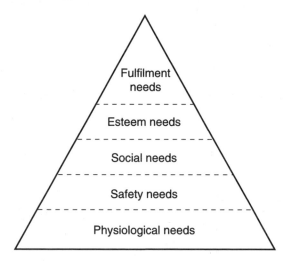

When promoting PenPod, you could develop the model in the following way:

1 Physiological needs.
   Is it portable?
2 Safety needs.
   Will it leak?
3 Social needs.
   Does it match my business or leisure requirements?
4 Esteem needs.
   Will people admire my writing instrument and will it help me to produce well-presented work?

5 Fulfilment needs.
  Can I rely on it to adapt to any future requirements? Will it enable me to write down essential pieces of information at any given time?

In the case of a charity, the model may work like this:

1 Physiological needs.
  Will donating make me feel better about myself?
2 Safety needs.
  Will my donation help save lives?
3 Social needs.
  Will I feel that I have gone some way towards contributing towards a better society?
4 Esteem needs.
  Will I gain satisfaction from knowing that I have been able to help a good cause?
5 Fulfilment needs.
  Does this charity make me feel good?

How brainstorming drives the creative process

You can't sit behind an office desk and just wait to get creative. In the real world of copywriting it often takes team work to really understand a product or service and come up with some original ideas for communicating its benefits. I often encourage writers to do their own thing – even go to the movies. As long as the work gets done to time and budget and is fresh in its concept, I am delighted!

One way to come up with original ideas is to arrange for a meeting of the minds. Brainstorming is so called because it involves a downpouring of spontaneous ideas – however practical or impractical they may be. The ideas can be generated by anyone, irrespective of the person's position within a company. If you are running a very small business, you could even consider asking friends to come over for a brainstorming afternoon. Serve drinks and you could call it a brainstorm in a coffee cup meeting!

Whoever is present and wherever you attend a brainstorm meeting, remove all forms of creative inhibitions. This can be more difficult than it first appears. At almost every brainstorming group that I have attended, at least two types of people have participated:

- The first is 'Eddy the Extrovert', who refuses to believe that a personal idea is unattainable.
- The other is 'Ingrid the Introvert', who at best refuses to believe she is capable of having any good ideas; at worst she is simply too shy to co-operate in the meeting.

A professional facilitator – an independent person controlling the meeting – ensures that everyone gets a fair chance to speak and express their ideas, original or otherwise. A good facilitator will avoid introducing brainstormers to a project too early.

Now let's look at some brainstorming techniques.

Take the mind out for a brisk walk

The more intensive the brainstorming session, the greater your potential for ideas. Any professional dietitian will tell you that the worst way to slim is to stop eating. This deprives the body of essential nutrients which burn to produce energy and which in turn burn the calories. Don't deprive your brainstormers of essential nutrients. Encourage them to exercise their minds and pig-out on a creative feast of ideas.

Virtual brainstorming

Since the first edition of this book was published I have developed a particularly effective mode of brainstorming designed for the twenty-first century. It is called Virtual Brainstorming™.

> Led by a trained market researcher with psychological marketing skills, brainstormers who make up a synectics-led focus group (originally developed at Harvard) are invited to step into a surreal world appropriate to the subject being brainstormed. Then they are led through a highly structured method of rationalizing their thoughts.

Because it is held in a chimerical environment, a Virtual Brainstorming™ session can be conducted anywhere your imagination can conceive – from a jungle to the top of a mountain – provided the location enhances imaginative thought and group-dynamic energy.

Synectics sessions

Synectics sessions were originally developed at Harvard. A research director leads the thinking and a senior member of the team suggests possible directions to pursue. A key feature of a synectics session is that people who are unconnected to the product, service or even company are invited to pitch in their ideas. All ideas are jotted down on a flip chart and made available for everyone to review. Invariably fresh ideas from a mass of off-the-wall thinking emerge at the end of the session.

Getting away from your place of work

In today's mobile society, with palm-top computers buzzing and people interrupting all day, it can be difficult to find a quiet space to be creative. If the creative project is substantial, you should consider holding your brainstorming session away from the office. An away day frees you and your colleagues from possible interruptions and allows you to relax in a different atmosphere, such as a hotel. For this reason, on the whole synectics sessions are held away from a client's or creative person's usual premises.

Ideas can't develop without facts

Let's return to the idea process. If you accept Plato's theories, innovative ideas come about through either the direct or indirect connection of one set of facts with another. ('Mind' and 'body' in unison.) The process is a bit like being detectives looking at all the available clues, examining the facts, drawing conclusions and piecing together a picture of the truth.

You could argue that a great deal of the business of creative copywriting requires pure detective work. Like a detective, you need to identify all the material facts. Then you must consider ways in which you can link these pieces of information in an original and apt way.

From blank page to powerful sales message

Through assimilating all your facts you can move on to styling an innovative copy approach that complements your presentation.

Imagine that individual facts form a kind of Identi-kit generalized description of a product or service. Consider each fact to be a 'suspect'. Any suspect – either individually, or working as part of a team – could be the main culprit who wants to *make the buyer an offer they simply cannot refuse*. This 'offer' is known as the Unique Sales Proposition or USP. Your job is to narrow down the guilty suspect(s).

The way to do this is to set up an identification parade. You shouldn't enter into the exercise with preconceived prejudices about any of your suspects. For example:

> Let's say you are asked to write about nuts and bolts. This doesn't necessarily mean that these particular nuts and bolts have anything new to offer to people who use them. Perhaps they are as unreliable as the ones which you recently used to fix a cupboard at home.

Your initial subjective views about the benefits of a product or service may have little resemblance to the specific facts relating to the product at hand. Besides, your target audience may not share your assumptions. It is they who have the greater appreciation of how a specific product or service can be directly applied. It is you who have to introduce them to the product.

If you are the supplier of a product or service, be prepared to accept that the consumer may base a purchasing decision on reasons other than those first assumed by you. In many cases, those reasons can enhance your sales pitch.

As a copywriter you have to balance each party's indisputable facts with their subjective views – including your own. So keep an open mind and an attentive attitude. Somewhere in the middle of what you assume, the product claims and what the target audience actually needs is the creative Holy Grail.

Go find that big idea!

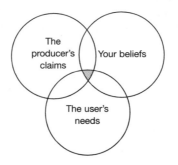

 Actual benefits

The nine-point cross-examination

OK. You are a copywriting detective. Take a good, long, hard look at your apparent facts or suspects. Now it's time to flick on the spotlight and uncover the truth. Pull up a chair and get ready to interrogate.

1 **What are we doing here?**
   It may sound obvious, or even the sort of question to put to a philosopher, but why *exactly* do you or your client want to advertise in the first place? To make money? Is that all? Maybe there is a hidden agenda? It may be to inform, educate, compete, launch, announce ... Once you know what it is that you are really trying to achieve, you can approach the business of fact interrogation appropriately.

2 **Face the facts.**
   What do the facts inform you about the product or service?

3 **Who or what is the missing link?**
   Consider what the facts have told you. Are there any missing bits of information that would help you complete the picture?

4 **Where will you uncover the clues?**
   You need to delve into a lot of carefully planned questions. From where and how will you get your answers?

5 **Do you believe the facts?**
   Do the factual claims make sense to you? Put yourself in the target audience's shoes. Would the product or service instil confidence in you?

6 **Clamp down on any unsubstantiated claims.**
   A fact is not a fact until it is proven. Address this by arguing a good case for why it may be suspicious.

7 **Listen to factual strengths.**
   Try to understand completely the factual strengths for what they are and how your target audience could benefit from them.

8 **Coax out the facts.**
   Encourage the facts to speak out. Allow them metaphorical space to sell themselves.

9 **Get it all down on paper.**
   Now review all your information.

If at any stage you are unsure of the basic facts, return to your nine-point interrogation plan. Remember that the facts are in your custody. You won't release them until and unless you have an idea that can totally convince the outside world of their value and relevance.

Once you have narrowed down your USPs, you can use this nine-point interrogation technique at any level of the brainstorming process.

Research

All forms of research should be undertaken with one clearly defined aim – to understand:

• Why and how a client wants to sell the product.
• Why the buyer wants to buy the product.

Specific ways in which research can help identify a target audience are discussed in full in *Teach Yourself Marketing* and to some extent in Chapter 6, which deals with direct response advertising (mailings). You use research to reinforce facts and give you a basis for a sound strategy, thus enabling you to define clearly a creative and coherent message that stimulates fresh ideas.

So-called *desk research* makes use of a wide variety of sources. These include:

• published work available, such as company reports
• clippings from trade magazines
• information on the Internet
• specialist on-line subscription-based services (available via a computer link).

Of course, your project may be so innovative that there isn't any directly relevant and useful information available. If so, instead look at the closest possible service or product to the one that you intend to promote. Find out if there would be a demand for your product or service and if so why and potentially how great that demand is. The services of a market research specialist may be just what you need in these circumstances.

Market research companies can provide an entire portfolio of research techniques, ranging from group discussions to regional surveys and questionnaires by post or telephone. Bear in mind that – particularly in the case of the small business carrying out its own copywriting – another important reason for conducting research is to check out the competition.

Get a copy research kit

As of tomorrow – or, even better, today – I want you to buy a box file and title it 'My Copy Research Kit'. In it assemble the following:

- examples of previous letters/promotions
- notes on which worked
- a record of who replied (lists)
- samples of competitors' material (How can it be improved? You should try to rewrite an example of your main competitor's material at least once a year. You'll be amazed how it helps you brush up your own copywriting techniques.)
- customers' comments
- sales results.

Creativity's role in the competitive commercial world

It is a common misunderstanding that companies primarily carry out research on competitors to uncover inside trade information. The true main objective for studying competitors is to find out at least as much as your customers do about:

- what is available
- where
- at what cost.

Once you have uncovered these facts, you can begin to compare your (or your client's) products against that of your competitors as regards price, quality and distribution. Most important of all, you can begin to understand what I call the Elvis factor.

The Elvis factor and the G spot

From Kurt Cobain to Ozzy Osbourne

There have been many contenders to the throne left vacant by the last century's King of Rock and Roll – Elvis Aaron Presley. Even during his reign the likes of Cliff Richard, Bill Haley and Jerry Lee Lewis hotly contested the crown worn by Elvis. However, although many talented contenders had personality and show-business appeal, none could match him in the market sector that he had carved uniquely for himself.

Ultimately, you or your client's company have to demonstrate at least one aspect (USP) of a product or service that no other company can either match or beat. I like to refer to that element (or, if you are really fortunate, that list of aspects) as the Elvis factor.

Today, as technology spreads beyond helping one person do their job better towards enabling one person to do two people's jobs equally well, successful distinction between one company and another relies on a variation of the 80–20 rule.

> The greatest proportion of a company's sales and profits may derive from a relatively small proportion of its customers and products. For instance, 20% of the workforce may produce 80% of the product or service.

Given that a growing number of companies are assuming dual roles – for example, many building societies have also become banks – you have to ask yourself to define the 20% Elvis factor.

> ScotsdaleNorth's Elvis factor may be that they are the country's favourite food and grocery retailer.

> PenPod's Elvis factor may be that they are the first to incorporate Mars space technology into an interchangeable pen – everyone else can only imitate, never lead.

Get to know other companies' Elvis factors. They may include:

- heritage
- size
- cost
- age appeal
- fashion
- quantity
- quality
- range
- taste
- scent and so forth.

Then you can identify the most important market segment of them all – what I like to call the G spot.

Did you know?

'G' is short for Ginza – one of the world's most sought-after pieces of commercial land. Ginza is situated at the heart of Tokyo. It is surrounded by other tremendously sought-after areas such as a financial district. Ginza land values can be as much as a hundred times more expensive than, for example, Mayfair in London or Manhattan in New York.

The G spot is the commercially sensual region that lies between two Elvis factor areas that already capture loyal customers. Initially, these customers would take far too much of your time, effort and cash to woo away.

Once you have established a G spot of your own, you can concentrate on enhancing your position. This is far easier than defending it against a bigger competitor as well as simultaneously finding creative ideas to sell the product or service.

Understanding the brand portfolio

Be specific about your G spot. For example, if you or your client's company produces a vast range of products, that's fine. However, if range is one of your main strengths, never fall into the trap of always featuring every product range in the advertisements that you offer. Instead, concentrate on one product at a time. In this way you can start to build individual brands.

A well-positioned portfolio of brands can be likened to a well-trained army. Use the G-spot methodology to address creatively and so add value to every product or service in your range, however great or small each may be. The result is an invincible force that any competitor will find difficult to beat.

Give your troops brand names

Like the Israeli army, the British forces are regarded as one of the most effective armed units in the world. Each of its divisions has a significantly outstanding attribute. Tactically people often think of the British army in terms of regiments rather than an entire force. This diagram shows how it is organized.

Structure of the British army

Ministry of Defence
(controls and directs)

Individual regiments

Special tactical forces
(specialize in modes of
defence – e.g. intelligence)

**High profile
name-led units**

Brands can be likened to such a structure. Each brand (division or regiment) has a core value.

Types of brand

Family brands
Some companies are effectively families or groups with a wide range of products or activities. These include Cadbury, Lever, Heinz and so on.

Product line brands
Some companies have specifically created subsidiary brand names, like Teach Yourself, Homebase and Do It All.

Umbrella brands
Often the main family brand is used to endorse a specific sub-brand. Examples are Cadbury's Snack, Elite Instant Coffee, McVitie's Go Ahead and Heinz Big Soup.

Individual brands
In this group are specific brand names, like Rice Krispies, Cheerios and Persil. Keep in mind that individual products and services may come and go through the natural course of their product life cycle. The master brand, however, goes on and on.

Own label brands
Middlemen or dealers may also put their names to a brand – these are often referred to as private brands or wholesaler's brands. For instance, a major retailer may include its name on labels. These goods are often referred to as 'own label' brands. Examples are Better Buy's Baked Beans, Corner Shop Cola and so on. When groups of retailers market own labels, the brand is sometimes referred to as a distributor's brand.

It's important that you don't associate own label brands exclusively with consumers who simply want to save a few pennies on products. They may have different motives. It is known that dieters, for instance, may purchase own label brands instead of mainstream brands. This is because psychologically they want to feel deprived of enjoying 'the best'.

Own brands shouldn't be confused with discounting. A retailer not directly associated with a major brand sometimes sells it at a discounted price (a supermarket may sell branded jeans cheaply). In such instances, under a ruling by the European Court of Justice, the supermarket is allowed to advertise the branded goods as long as the advertisement doesn't '*seriously* damage the reputation of the trade mark'.

Virtual brands

Sometimes the brand owner doesn't actually handle any part of the production process. Instead, that is conducted by an outside supplier. Richard Branson's Virgin Cola is one example.

Just because consumers go for a lesser-known cola, it doesn't necessarily follow that they will opt for other lesser-known brands as well. As pointed out in the section on research (pp. 32–3), human intellect is far more complicated than that.

Web brands

Web brands are rapidly developed through the Internet. Typically they enjoy short-lived PLCs (product life cycles; see p. 39). Because the Internet is highly scalable, small and international companies compete equally on the Web. Therefore, making your brand distinctive becomes even more important. This requires consistent promotion through all supporting media as well as the Web.

Measuring brand loyalty

Brand loyalty occurs when consumers return to a specific brand time after time. It relies on a core set of values that never change. These may include quality, service and care.

It is possible to measure a brand's popularity. Look at the following table. When you are writing copy, you will need to know how your brand measures up.

Brand extent	Brand magnitude	Brand sway	Brand affinity	Brand sensitivity
Development into new pastures as well as brand stretching into related product/service areas without compromising the core potency of a brand's original set of values.	Supremacy in terms of esteem rather than purely a portion within a market sector.	The relative significance of personal association the brand attracts from various segments of the market, including the internal market (employees and shareholders).	The allegiance and admiration the brand attracts from existing as well as potential customers.	The level of feeling and emotions evoked by the brand.

Over time keen competitors will try to match your brand attributes. The classic reaction to this is to produce advertising known as sales promotions (see pp. 130–5). This is often price or styling led. For example: buy one for the price of two, or buy a limited edition box set.

Sales promotion helps to fight off hostile armies of would-be G-spot owners. However, in the long term consumers tend to return to those brands whose core values remain sound. For example, cola brands may compete on price to such an extent that a price war overtakes the original reason for buying a cola – taste. At the end of the day, one cola may be cheaper than another or both may be equally priced. However, you can be certain that eventually the consumer will return to their favourite cola – one that has endured the test of time, money-off promotions and contenders to its Elvis factor. Ultimately, consumers pay for the quality and reassurance of a 'well-known' brand.

With the emergence of globalization and lots of players all competing to be relevant to as broad a market as possible, many core brands have become mass-market commodity-led products ('cheap and cheerful' clones). Typical product examples include executive pens, sportswear, wrist watches, personal organizers and even certain kinds of hi-fi equipment such as personal stereos and radios.

On the other hand, competition has also made some major brand names enhance their product by constantly adapting to change through restyling, repricing, re-enforcing service and re-creating a healthy and fresh image.

Did you know?

The first-ever gift coupon appeared in 1865. A New Yorker called Benjamin Talbert Babbit overprinted soap wrappers with the word 'coupon'. Ten coupons entitled the customer to claim a 'beautiful lithograph picture'.

When writing copy to reflect your brand remember to consider:
The brand's personality
- how it functions
- what it symbolizes
Its position
- value to market (actual)
- value to community (avidly interested partner) – perceived
Its proposition
- competitive
- credibility

- clarity of message
- consistency of message.

Returning to the British army example, the last century's regional wars such as that in Kosovo are hopefully over, so the troops are now being redeployed to meet new challenges. However, they still maintain their core values and the British army's name is enhanced through its long and proud heritage.

Typical product life cycles

One way to help you plan each stage of your creative message is to consider the typical life cycle of a new product.

1 The *introduction* phase of the cycle usually features low sales. After all, no one has heard of the product as yet. Marketing costs are high and advertising is directed towards the key distributors such as retailers. In this phase, profit margins are low if not non-existent.

2 The next phase is *growth*. Sales slowly start to build. The price of converting enquiries into sales improves. If the product is good, competitors start to move towards your G spot. In terms of advertising and marketing, it is time to look at price, product variations and guarantees. Creatively, the message usually directs itself towards the broader market by building awareness and therefore interest.

3 The next phase is *maturity*. Sales reach their pinnacle. From here on, they either maintain their position or fall, becoming casualties of competition. Your costs are low and profits are high (assuming you have firm control of your G spot). Your first, more adventurous customers may have gone on to try other products. Your mainstream customers will be prime targets for loyalty-type creative messages. Competitors will either operate in parallel against you or drop out of the game. New product ranges are introduced, pricing is aimed against competitors and sales promotion campaigns are introduced to combat brand switching. (Incidentally, consumers who frequently practise brand switching are sometimes called spinners or rate-surfers because they have the tendency to 'spin' or 'surf' between one brand and another.) All of these initiatives require strong creative messages.

4 The final phase is *decline*. Profits fall, sales fall. Even the mainstream consumers begin to move on to fresher ideas. Brand lines are rationalized, distribution is revisited. The bulk of your creative message is directed towards keeping the loyal customers.

How the circle of life could affect PenPod

Introduction
PenPod launches onto the market. There is a big spend on marketing in order to announce the launch.

Growth
People hear about PenPod. They try it out at demonstrations. They like it. They tell their friends. Their friends see the advertising and sales grow. Unfortunately, all this good news about the exciting product also reaches the ears of competitors, who launch their own variations on PenPod.

Price variations and guarantees
With others encroaching into PenPod's G spot, it's time to consider strategic tactics to prevent sales from declining. The company tries offering specially priced pens and even brings out new accessories. Guarantees are made more attractive.

Maturity
It was a long, hard fight, but PenPod made it through – at least for a while. The consumers know that PenPod is first in the market, not just historically speaking but in terms of quality, innovation and reputation. Now all PenPod has to do is maintain their pole position – which requires a new kind of advertising strategy.

Position enforcement
A hard-hitting campaign is launched to reinforce PenPod's values and at the same time keep the competition from matching price and product range.

Decline
PenPod falls into the trap of becoming complacent about its position. It slows down the advertising and marketing process. This opens a gap for the competition. People get bored with PenPod. Spinners start to influence buying habits. The competition is much more fierce and new products are more useful. Farewell PenPod.

The product life cycle phases vary in length and duration according to the individual product or service.

Model of the product life cycle

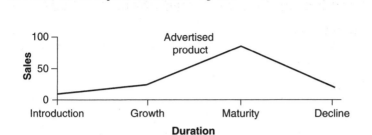

It is possible to configure the strength and exposure of your creative message over a given period. The figure below is an example of this. By extending the message beyond the decline stage, the creative message may help restimulate product interest.

Extension of the product life cycle

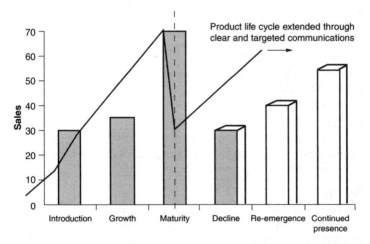

Researching competitors

At this point, the matter of research and competition needs to be considered from a different angle. Now you can be even more selective about competitive research.

- Who is trying to move into you or your client's territory with similar services or products?
- How are they attempting to achieve their goal?
- To whom is their advertising directed?
- How often do they advertise?

- Is their creative tone friendly, professional, casual?
- Which advertising media do they use?
- What kind of creative messages do they use?
- If you are trying to compete, what will your creative message say?

First steps in media selection

I shall discuss specific media later in this book (see Chapter 5). As part of your plan of action it is important to start to consider which media to use.

- Which will be most effective: newspapers, TV, radio or something else?
- Read the relevant papers to determine their style and content.
- Surf websites. What kind of advertiser advertises on them? Are the sizes of the banner ads flexible? Do they look worth clicking?
- If you are thinking of advertising in a specific newspaper, does it have a recruitment section? If so, what kinds of jobs do the readers hold or aspire to have?
- How will an ad reproduce on paper?

Get hold of what is called a media pack – a fact kit that tells you about, for example, a newspaper's readership (the total number of people reached by a specific publication) and circulation (the officially audited number of subscribers to a publication).

Understanding the SWOT analysis technique

A useful way to summarize your findings is to use the SWOT analysis technique. SWOT helps you consider:

Strengths Weaknesses Opportunities Threats
S W O T

- **Strengths** can relate to either your company's or your competitors' enhanced value to a customer. For instance, a supermarket may offer shorter queues at their checkouts. A manufacturer may have a particularly good distribution system, so you can purchase a specific product virtually anywhere in the country.
- **Weaknesses** could refer to a small advertising budget or an inefficient customer service department.
- **Opportunities** could relate to changing consumer habits, or to competitors who have become uncreative in their approach and in what they offer.

- **Threats** may arise from a competitor moving onto your G spot.

The SWOT analysis is also useful for assessing media. (See Chapter 5.)

Now you have an idea of what to write about, pick up a pen or sit down in front of a word processor and start writing!

The big idea quick tips

- Follow the seven steps towards a new idea (p. 19).
- Never settle for an obvious answer.
- Appeal to both sides of the brain.
- Remember the nine rules of effective brainstorming (p. 31).
- Balance your views with those of your client and its customers.
- Research a creative brief as fully as possible.
- Fight for and then defend your G spot.
- Adapt your creative message to suit the life cycle of the product or service.
- Turn a daydream into an idea-generation opportunity.
- Follow the AIDCA formula.
- If you are stuck for inspiration, try brainstorming.
- Never dismiss an idea instantly.
- Interrogate your client's product.
- Know your USPs and those of your competitors.
- Consider the different areas of branding and where your product or service sits in the branding hierarchy.
- Use a SWOT analysis on your company and its competitors.

Over to you

1 Imagine you are the inventor of PenPod. Refer to the seven basic steps towards a new idea. In seven steps, explain how you arrived at the idea of inventing a pen that had an interchangeable nib.

2 You are the marketing director of ScotsdaleNorth.com. Refer to the AIDCA formula. Which of the following statements is the best to apply to an advertising message?

a We sell an extensive range of goods.
b We sell an extensive range of goods that are reduced in price until the end of the month.
c We sell an extensive range of goods that are competitively priced and available, and are all easily accessible via the Web.

d We sell an extensive range of competitively priced goods.

3 Now list the AIDCA points in the statement you selected.

4 You are again in the hot seat at PenPod. This time, you are the managing director. You are meeting a particularly demanding client. She's anticipating a dull introduction to PenPod's product benefits. In two minutes list six 'one-line' ways in which you could praise PenPod's tremendous benefits.

5 Jot down the most attractive idea of the six you have listed.

6 In two minutes, list every secondary idea that your chosen six benefits suggest.

7 First, take a break – have a short nap. Then think about promises that politicians make. In one minute, write down the first thirty things that come to mind.

8 List other ideas that come to mind, thanks to your nap.

9 Now list your choice of the top three ways to promote PenPod.

03
how to structure your copy

In this chapter you will learn
- how to develop a brief
- how to develop your USP
- how to develop perceptions
- how to classify an audience.

I'll keep this section short. Indeed, if I didn't, I would not have time or space to go any further.

Great copywriting is an exercise in conducting an adult conversation. To do so, you have to plan what you are going to say, anticipate objections and then deliver your targeted message. To achieve this, you need a creative brief.

The creative brief

The creative brief is one of the most important documents for the copywriter and for the client who instructs a creative team to produce work. A proper creative brief is a prerequisite for advertiser and copywriter alike. Without it, the facts are vague. This may result in misinformation, misinterpretation and missing the point of why something is being produced in the first place. That is why every brief should be signed off by all the relevant parties.

All too often you may find that clients do not want to take the time to commit an instruction to paper. The easy ways to avoid this are:

- Design a briefing form that is as easy to complete as it is to understand.
- Buy a digital pocket recorder and record the instructions, then write down those instructions as a brief. Make sure they are signed off by all the parties concerned.

Establish a positioning statement

Before you can write a formal brief, you need firm foundations upon which to construct a proposition.

To achieve that you should be able to answer two simple questions:

- Who is your target audience?
- Why should your company only be considered for the job?

In other words, you need to establish positioning:

- for
- only
- because.

My own company's positioning statement is:

For marketing professionals wishing to sustain a top of mind positioning in an already established market. Only Gabay provides value-added, imaginative and innovative through-the-line creative solutions. Because only Gabay's award-winning marketing writing, training, design and strategic implementations are featured by both industry and public institutions alike. This is complemented by a mission to ensure that clients pay for expertise and not overheads. (© www.gabaynet.com)

Every brief – which is, after all, a tactical assignment – can in some way relate to my company's positioning. Apart from securing a clear message for my audience, through basing a brief on my positioning all copy produced has a firm strategic rationale.

Eight steps towards understanding a brand position

1 Pin-point the brand's meaning.
2 Identify the audience's:
  a behaviour
  b attitudes
  c demographics.
3 Establish the problem or need being addressed.
4 How does the competition address this?
5 Target the benefit.
6 How can that benefit be supported?
7 What is the brand personality?
8 Positioning statement.

Types of brief

Now you are ready to write a fuller brief.

The first of the following examples, is the client brief. As a management tool it often doesn't directly affect the creative team, but it helps the client to define who will be responsible for what. Next is an alternative, the informal pre-brief. This may also be an informal document that is preliminary to a full creative brief. This may entail considering research (see pp. 32–3) or ensuring you have enough time available to get the job done.

The quicker an advertiser produces a creative brief, the more time there will be for you to work on the copy. Creative briefs should be submitted before any work gets under way. Indisputably, a creative brief should contain everything a person needs to produce effective creative work. However, bear in mind that your job as a writer is to *communicate* with an audience. Start off by communicating with the person who wrote the brief. Clarify your own understanding of what is required. Now is your chance to question the brief before committing anything to paper. When talking to the person issuing the brief, beware of the LOI syndrome – lack of information. Never be afraid to ask questions. It is better to take the time to get things clear at this stage than to rush ahead and make mistakes when committing yourself to paper.

In my first briefing example, the client brief, I am going to assume you know nothing or very little about the product or service. The second, the informal pre-brief, is an *aide-mémoire* that assumes you know more. The first is meant to educate and inspire. The *aide-mémoire* clarifies and inspires.

The all-embracing client brief and its components

This brief document is self-contained and provides all the information a writer needs.

1 **Who's advertising?**
   Company name only, please. If you feel it is important to include a company report, attach it separately under the heading of 'Background'.

2 **What does this company do?**
   A general heading like 'Publishing', or 'Medical book publishing'. You don't have to talk about the plots of their last five hospital dramas.

3 **What is required?**
   A one-line description such as 'Website commercial' or 'poster'. Don't worry about specific media details at this stage.

4 **What is the format?**
   For example, if you have to write a brochure, how long will it be? Is it to be in colour? Will there be any illustrations? – essential if you want to take advantage of captioning. If it is a direct mail letter, is there a specific length required, and so forth.

5 **What do you specifically expect the creative work to achieve?**
Again, something precise; for example, 750 surfers a day to hit the site.

6 **What are (a) your marketing objectives and (b) your corporate objectives?**
Try to summarize each in one line. For example:
a to increase market share by 15%;
b to be recognized as the leader in the field.

7 **What's the story so far?**
This is the relevant background detail. You could include:
a Where the company stands in its marketplace.
b Where it would like to be.
c Where the creative work will appear.
d What will support the work – for example, other adverts?

8 **Describe the product.**
Include any previous leaflets and adverts. What is it? How is it used? How does it work?

9 **Why would someone want it?**
List the USPs. Why buy this one rather than one offered by a competitor? A classic misunderstanding is that the copywriter is responsible for creating the USPs. This is in fact the role of the marketing department or, in smaller companies, the salesperson or managing director. It is up to the writer to communicate the benefits.

10 **Who wants it?**
a Who would want to buy this product/service? Where do they live? How old are they? Discuss their social economic groupings. What kind of jobs do they have?
b If the audience is a type of business, what sort of business is it? How big is it? Describe its business sector. Who makes the buying decisions? How does the buying process work? (For example, a secretary sees a new kind of pen. She informs her boss and asks the stationery buyer to include it on the next stationery order.) How do they perceive themselves in the market? (For more information, see 'Targeting your message' on p. 13.)

11 **Are there any special offers?**
For example, do you need to write about a special discount or free gift? If so, what is it? What is its value? What do readers have to do to get it and why would anyone want it?

12 How do you see yourself?
Based on the company's image, what style should the copy adopt? Serious? Casual? Caring?

13 Tests.
This is often used in direct marketing briefs. However, it could also refer to tests of advertisements by size, frequency, colour and medium.

14 What media will you use?
For example, national newspapers, the Web, trade press. In all cases, try to include a sample.

15 Why did you choose this medium?
A probing question, this one! However, it is a very useful one if you are to get a firm grip on your target audience and the advertiser's marketing rationale.

16 What is your budget?
No one likes to discuss money. If, for instance, you intend to feature photography, it's less shocking for an advertiser if you announce from the start your intention to shoot your photographs in the Maldives, 'because the sun casts a certain hue in that part of the world'. Wherever possible, it is shrewd to get everyone concerned to agree on available budgets, including, if you work in an agency, the production department. You can base costs on previous projects.

17 What is taboo?
Advertisers are invariably keen to list every USP under the sun. Just as important are the 'unmentionables'. Advertisers may also have to find out about corporate restrictions and trade legislation that may affect copy. These may include financial services rules. For example:

FINANCIAL TOUCH CREDIT LTD

Registered in the United Kingdom No. 12345.

Registered Office: 1st Floor Empire Way London HA9 0PA.

All applicants must be aged 21 or over, resident in the UK and receiving an income of more than £10,000 per annum. Credit is available and subject to status and conditions. If your application is accepted, we will set a credit limit. If you have applied to transfer a balance from another credit card, we will transfer an amount according to this credit limit...

Other restrictions may be dictated by database protection laws and, of course, by specific advertising codes of practice.

18 How will you keep a tab?
All advertisers should monitor response from advertising. This can be achieved simply by featuring a code in a coupon, or a special Website address for a 'click' through dotcom response campaign. Setting up such traffic response measurements may also require you to make arrangements for monitoring services from your friendly Internet Service Provider.

19 Who can tell me more?
However detailed the brief may be, you may have further questions. Who can answer those questions and where can you find that person? Phone numbers, email address and fax numbers are needed.

20 What do you expect to see?
Does the advertiser expect to see a finished creative job, all the way to artwork? Perhaps a rough visual will do? How about the copy – without any visuals or even just some headlines?

21 When do you expect to see it?
When does the advertiser want to see your presentation or finished work? Try to involve everyone connected with the production. In this way you can account for printing times, filming schedules, Website design, publication dates and so on.

Whenever possible, get the advertiser to sign off the creative brief. Other details that may be included are internal project or job numbers.

The informal pre-brief and its components

This type of brief is designed for the copywriter who is already familiar with a particular product or service. It lists the main questions that always need to be addressed.

1	What's the big message?
2	What's needed?
3	What's on sale?
4	What is the USP?
5	What's the TSP (Targeted Sales Proposition)?
6	What's the ESP (Emotional or lifestyle Sales Proposition)?
7	What's the budget?

8 | Who wants it?
9 | What do you want the folks to do?
10 | What do they get out of it?
11 | When and where is the communication going to appear?
12 | What's taboo?
13 | What's the format?
14 | What's the background?
15 | **What's next and when do you want it?**

The next stage is to develop your copy platform. Here, in just a few sentences, you describe the product or service. Then provide a clear statement outlining your objectives. This is followed by a short statement about your target audience and no more than six leading benefits. Finally, you can include two other statements: one that describes your product positioning in the market and one relating to the tone of voice that the advertising should have.

Immaculate concepts

Ask any journalist to list the key attributes of a successful business or compelling news story and the chances are that 'have a good angle' will be in a leading position. The 'angle' in question is the approach to a message that you adopt. This should not be confused with a product or service's USP. By now, thanks to your thorough research and comprehensive creative brief, you should have enough knowledge of the product or service to be able to determine the ideal approach.

The most valuable information to help you decide on the right angle is your understanding of the target audience (see point 9 of the all-embracing client brief, p. 49).

Defining the USP

Already in this book I have discussed various aspects of the USP, the Unique Sales Proposition. I have told you to concentrate on a product or service's main USP as a firm foundation for constructing an advertisement. Few things in life are truly unique and, besides, a unique attribute may be fine for one segment of your target audience but totally inappropriate for another. Also important are the TSP, the Targeted Sales Proposition, or – if you intend to concentrate on a lifestyle value-added statement – the ESP, the Emotional Sales Proposition (concerned with, for example, the emotional value of sending someone flowers). Even when you believe you have found the ideal USP, TSP or ESP, how can you be certain that it is appropriate?

Think of them as seductive Arabian exotic dancers. Let's take a look at the USP/TSP/ESP dance of the seven veils.

Imagine that ScotsdaleNorth.com wants to promote its range of baby foods. You have managed to target the USP as one of several possibilities:

- Convenient, innovative packaging.
- Fresh ingredients (never more than 24 hours old before being canned).
- Tasty – recipes from award-winning chefs.
- Cost effective – usually 10% cheaper than the leading brand.
- Healthy – winner of several healthy eating awards.

Now, start peeling off each seductive veil of promise.

Convenient

- For mum.
- For baby.
- For storage.
- No cooking.
- Self-contained in the package.
- No mess.
- Long shelf life.

Next, go through the same process with each of your other four possibilities. In this example, this process will provide you with up to thirty-five possible USP/TSP/ESPs. (If you really cannot find seven distinct features for each possibility, do not spend a lot of time looking for one just to make up the numbers – USPs should leap out at you.)

You can perform the same exercise in reverse, casting away each choice that is weak or too similar to another. Try to get down to two or fewer features per heading. In the case of the baby food, this leaves you with ten possibilities. Now once again consider, in terms of benefits, which USPs cross over and then discard them.

Your final list can be shown to someone or some group not directly involved with the project. Alternatively, if it's down to you to decide which USP/TSP/ESP wins, think about who or what ultimately benefits from it.

For example, you may cut your baby food USP down to:

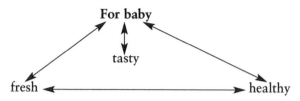

Of these, which is probably the most beneficial to the baby? My suggestion would be *healthy*.

See also 'Targeting your message' (p. 13).

Conceptions and perceptions

There are four key factors that influence a person's positive or negative attitude towards a group or individuals, namely:

1 Cultural issues.
2 Situational (or interpersonal) issues.
3 Historic and economic concerns.
4 Individual experience.

Let us look at these in turn.

1 Cultural issues

Where people live and how people work influence the type of approach they make to everything, from purchasing washing-up powder to investing in the stock market. For instance:

Local area overcrowding affects how people relate to each other.

- On the negative side it may lead to increased crime.
- On the positive side, it may lead to a greater integration of cultural backgrounds and a broader understanding of different cultural values. This in turn affects the street language and interpersonal relationships of the locals. It may lead to greater competition in the job market. It may also result in a wider acceptance of new technology. This results in a heightened need for products such as Webware (Internet software).

2 Situational (or interpersonal) issues

Following the crowd is a basic human instinct. Peer pressure is tremendously powerful throughout our lives (see 'From song writer to copywriter', p. 8). People like to conform. Even nonconformists conform with nonconformists. The reward for conforming is peer group acceptance. For example:

> In the American Deep South, restaurant owners used to display signs that read: I'M NOT PREJUDICED, BUT MY CUSTOMERS WOULDN'T LIKE IT.

This was meant to justify their refusal to allow blacks to eat at their premises.

Many house-cleansing material commercials are typical examples of how the advertisers try to be sympathetic towards a particular social peer group (often a housewife or, to a lesser extent, a house husband). They discuss the possible repercussions in a family unit if the spouse and kids discover that their clothes are not as clean as they should be. Worse still, the possible scandal if poor domestic management by the house-keeper was discovered is hinted at. Be wary; don't overplay the scenario as it could end up as a farce – unless, of course, you want the social group to appear to be making fun of itself. A concept should be angled to cater for cliques without appearing to come across as a cliché.

3 Historical and economic concerns

Often people's attitudes are social inheritances from a bygone age.

> 'We don't trust doctors because our parents didn't.'
> 'We drink it because we've always done so.'
> 'We only trust this brand of wholemeal bread – so we'll leave their white loaves on the shelf.'

Did you know?

Entire national prejudices may be based on historical events. For instance, American Afro-Caribbeans were originally imported to the United States as slaves. A slave had no rights. Now we are in the third millennium yet sadly there are still pockets of prejudiced people who feel that blacks cannot be regarded as 100% American. Some believe that blacks are less intelligent than white Americans.

Historic influences are relatively easy to manipulate. More often than not, people do not question why or for how long their 'tradition' has been practised. If they did, they might upset their peers and be rejected by them.

> Local sign for Hindi-speaking building contractors:
> You've tried the cowboys, now try the Indians.

Is this racist or is it harmless humour?

4 Individual experience

Just as people like to feel they socially fit, they also like to retain their individuality. Doing this may result in their learning some harsh lessons about life. When things go wrong with competitors, advertisers such as banks like to reassure customers that, thanks to the service they offer, the consumer need never be put in an uncomfortable or compromising position again.

These four factors identify the broad character types. The headings themselves contain many subheadings, each a refinement of each broad type. These often link with other traits. For every product there is an ideal advertising target identifiable by analysing character traits. This target would ideally be addressed through traditional one-to-one selling techniques. Alternatively, direct marketing can be used. (This is explained in Chapter 6.) For now, it is important to remember not to misinterpret the categories by stereotyping. If you were to do that, your copy would be one dimensional and have little substance – all sizzle and no steak.

Social categorization

'Socio-economic groups' or 'social grading' were first developed in the early part of the last century, in 1921. Social status is classified according to interests, social backgrounds and occupations. Each piece of data reflects the job of the head of the household. In the past, however, some systems of socio-economic classification graded people by their income.

Social grade	Social status	Occupation of head of household
A	Upper middle class	Higher managerial, professional
B	Middle class	Intermediate managerial
C1	Lower middle class	Clerical
C2	Skilled working class	Skilled manual worker
D	Working class	Unskilled manual worker
E	Lowest level	State pensioner, widow, casual worker, people dependent on social security

Source: JICNARS (Joint Industry Committee for National Readership Surveys)

Armed with this level of information, you can hone your target audience's lifestyle with great accuracy.

Did you know?

In the United States, there is no universal system to grade people socially. Instead, there is reliance on lifestyle data and neighbourhood data such as those used in UK direct marketing (see Chapter 6).

Get a life

Psychographic or psychometric classification of targeted consumers by attitudes and other intellectual characteristics has led to various acronyms for and classifications of typical consumers.

One way of name-tagging groups of people into types is the values and lifestyles approach (VALS). This puts people into categories ranging from being totally unmotivated to having outstandingly balanced perceptions of society and their role in it.

Survivors	Extremely poor and despondent.
Sustainers	Poor but slightly optimistic about the future.
Belongers	Conventional, middle-of-the-road types who like to fit in.

Emulators	Aspiring, upwardly mobile and status conscious.
Achievers	Successful leaders.
'I-am-me's	Young, self-aware and self-driven. Usually acting on the spur of the moment.
Experimentals	Sybarites ready to try a new experience. Very inner directed.
Society conscious	Strive to wipe out social injustice.
Mature integrated	Socially balanced, inwardly confident.

At the beginning of the third millennium the UK government suggested the following customer group classifications. Despite its authorship, marketers rejected the idea outright.

Class 1	The Queen and owners of large companies.
Class 2	Company executives, managers of more than 25 people.
Class 3	Doctors, lawyers, scientists, teachers, librarians, insurance underwriters and computer engineers.
Class 4	Policemen, nurses, fire fighters and prison officers.
Class 5	Sales managers (small companies), farm managers and small hotel managers.
Class 6	Office supervisors, civil servants and lab technicians.
Class 7	Computer operators, professional athletes, nursery nurses, medical technicians, dental nurses, paramedics and secretaries.
Class 8	Businessmen employing under 25 people, newsagents, garage owners and publicans.
Class 9	Self-employed bricklayers, driving instructors, TV engineers.
Class 10	Factory foremen, shop supervisors, senior hairdressers.
Class 11	Craft and related workers, plumbers, motor mechanics, printers.
Class 12	Shop assistants, telephone operators, lorry drivers, traffic wardens and taxi drivers.

Class 13   Assembly line workers, cleaners and waiters.

Class 14   Low skill job-hoppers.

Class 15   Skilled unemployed.

Class 16   Unemployed – previously worked.

Class 17   Unemployed, no skills – never worked.

In order to segment lifestyles, many marketing companies develop acronyms even further. Here are a few popular psychographic terms, including acronyms, that may help you define your target audience.

Very young	Young/dynamic	Married	Established	Retired
Baby Boomer Originally people who grew up after the 1960s baby boom. Also refers to people born at historical periods of population increase.	*Skotey* Spoiled kid of the 1980s. *Millennium Junkie* Early adopter who wants to change society. *Buppies* Black upwardly mobile professionals.	*Dinkies* Dual income, no kids, married couple. *Empty nesters* Couple, no kids. *Managing mums* Guilt-ridden mothers.	*Woopies* Well-off (over 55). Pre-retirement. (AKA Grey Panthers) *Glams* Greying, leisured, affluent middle-aged.	*Wrinklies* People in their 20s during World War II. *Crinklies* Same as Wrinklies. *Silver market* People aged 60+.
Baby Busters Born just after original Baby Boomers generation so, in the 1990s, had less need of housing and goods.	*Road Warriors* Well-travelled executives – usually salespersons. *Crusty* Lifestyle: rough clothes, matted hair.	*Minks* Multiple income, no kids. *Puppies* Previous young upwardly mobile professionals.	*Markas* Middle-aged re-nester, kids away. *Jolies* Jet-setting 49–59, free of financial worries.	*Internots* Anti-Webs – cyberphobes. *Dippies* Dual income pensioners.
Current Boomers – 45–55 Baby Boomers resist 'growing old'. They offer the imaginative marketer a great opportunity to produce youth oriented campaigns far longer than the traditional young/dynamic. Hence Baby Boomers will often be open to accept youth culture language and concepts.	*Yuppies* Young upwardly mobile professionals. *Y-people* Y-person, Yuppie. *NETizen* Member of Net Heads community. *Cybernaut* Surfer. *Bimboy* Male bimbo. *Cyberkids* *NetGen*	*Islington Person* Social left winger. *Foodie* Hobby is food. *Tik* Two incomes with kids. *Muppie* Middle-aged urban professional. *Tins* Two incomes, no sex.	*Whannies* We have a nanny. *Holiday Junkies* 'Hooked' on holidays. *Methuselah market* Rich – 5 years pre-retirement. *Power Bimbo, Killer Bimbo* Careerist, previous airhead. *Lombard* Lots of money but a real fool.	*Farte* Fearful of ageing or retiring too early. *Guppies* Breed guppy fish. *Grey Panthers* *Cocoons* *Golden Oldies* *Coffin Dodgers* *Wrinklies with Attitude* *Grannies with Readies*

Very young	Young/dynamic	Married	Established
Sandwich generation Cares for ageing parents and children.	*Grumpies* Grim ruthless upwardly mobile professionals.		*Fluffy* Feminine, loving, understanding, faithfully yours – typified anti-feminist wives of the late 1990s.
The Millennials	*Nummpie* New upwardly mobile media person fascinated with New Media marketing (pronounced Nu Me Yah).		
The Millennium Generation			
Generation 2000			
Echo Boomers	*Hoho* Happy, optimistic, home owner.		
The Baby Boomlet			
The Baby Clickers Brought up in an era of clicks rather than actual writing pen.	*Inbetweeners* They don't fit neatly in pigeon holes.		
	Generation P The Pokémon Generation.		
	Generation Why Why not?		
	Generation Next The next generation that social researchers can't understand.		
	Bridger Generation Bridging the gap between Xers and Boomers.		
	Net Generation		
	The Dreamcast Generation		
	Generation Wired		

04
getting to grips
with your copy

In this chapter you will learn
- how to understand grammar
- how to use copy techniques
  such as clichés
- how to use colloquialisms
- how to use punctuation
- how to develop headlines
- how to build bodycopy
- how to construct subheads
- how to develop slogans
- how to measure readability.

Grammar and copy

Hopefully, my English teacher will be happy that I ended up as a copywriter. However, knowing how much of a stickler he was for precise grammar, I think that he would give up on my sentence construction.

Often, copywritten sentences are a complete grammatical nightmare. For example:

An advertisement headline for a competitively priced laptop disk drive

Drive. A Hard bargain.

There is not a complete sentence here because the verb is separated from the rest. The advertisement's text (commonly referred to as bodycopy) explains that the company is offering a laptop drive at a competitive price. In this context, the headline seems appropriate. As it stands, the headline is intriguing enough to make you take a second glance and so, hopefully, lead you into the bodycopy. I shall discuss bodycopy at greater length a little later.

Copywriting is very different from formal business writing, journalism or novel writing. For example, the responsibilities of most national tabloid journalists are confined to the details of the story. In great journalism, called *reportage*, only the facts are told, so that the story is untainted by bias. The job of writing an eye-catching headline or caption rests with the sub-editor. The picture editor deals with photographs. The page layout is managed by a page make-up person. Typography may be the job of a typographer (although with the advent of desk-top publishing this is currently much less likely than it used to be).

The copywriter, on the other hand, has to consider the advertisement from every creative angle:

- Headlines
- Bodycopy
- Illustration
- Frequency of appearance
- Sub-headlines
- Design
- Size

You can liken a copywriter to a musical composer who is also a conductor. The advertising message (the copy) is the musical score. It is up to the copywriter to ensure that every note in it is harmonious and keeps tempo.

Using clichés

Unlike other forms of writing, copywriting tends to rely on one of the all-time big 'no-nos' of correct grammar – the use of clichés.

Providing they are not overused, clichés help to make advertisements immediate. They provide impact and can stimulate action. Copywriters like them because they help to convey a message quickly. Flick through most mainstream magazines or newspapers. Before long, you should come across one of the following advertising clichés:

Buy now	Act now
Exclusive offer	Yours free
Limited offer	Open now
Order now	At last

Of these 'Yours free' is probably the best. Wherever possible, try to get 'you', 'you'll' or 'yours' in the first paragraph of your copy. Obviously, if you haven't got a free offer, you can't use 'yours free'. However, you should always be able to offer the reader at least two relevant benefits from your product within your opening copy.

In addition to literal clichés, you should consider graphical clichés – but remember the old proverb, *Everything in moderation and nothing in excess.*

Here are some graphical clichés:

Car on the open road. Stream of 'freshness'. World in hand. Spark from finger. People around a board-room table. Light bulb (for idea).

Comparison copy

You can tell a lot about a society by the way it personifies objects and compares subjects. In the Victorian age, people were petrified of being drowned in sewage; hence the expression, 'I'm in it up to here.' Here are some more comparison copy lines. Try adding to them.

- Copy comparing health
  - Our relationship is dead.
  - This book makes me sick.

- Copy comparing food
  - That's a half-baked idea.
  - She looks very tasty.

– I can't swallow your argument.
– It leaves a bad taste in my mouth.

Figurative language

There are lots of useful literary devices for the copywriter to use.

Similes

These liken one thing with another, usually something quite different. They are introduced by 'as' or 'like'.

- Business without advertising is like winking at a girl in the dark; you know what you're doing, but nobody else does.
- Does your head feel like a bucket of wet sand?
- Are you as busy as ants at a picnic?
- Is your copywriting as dull as cold tea?

Metonymy

In metonymy the name of one thing is applied to something with which it is closely associated. For example, 'the turf' stands for horse racing and 'the crown' stands for a monarch.

Metaphors

In a metaphor a word that signifies one kind of thing, quality or action is applied to another without expressing a relationship between them; for example, 'She drank in every word.'

Homophones

Homophones are words that sound the same (or similar) but are spelled differently. For example:

- The finest Scottish whisky is kept under *loch and quay*.
- Hire cars at lower prices.
- Spend £10 at Virgin and get a Young Person's Rail Card for a *tenor*.

Homonyms

Homonyms are two words with the same meaning. They first appeared within English language in the seventeenth century. For example:

- Have you seen the light? (new brand of torch)
- Enjoy the lighter side of life. (diet plan)

Oxymorons and chiasmus

These rank as some of my favourite copywriting techniques. Oxymorons are contradictory terms used to emphasize something. They are useful for copy in speeches. Examples are 'plainly magnificent', 'horribly wonderful', 'simply ingenious', 'clearly confusing'.

A chiasmus is the reversal in the order of words in two otherwise parallel phrases. For example:

> Never let a fool kiss you or a kiss fool you.

> A statesman is a politician who places himself at the service of the nation. A politician is a statesman who places the nation at his service.

Synecdoche
Synecdoche derives from a Greek expression meaning 'to receive jointly'. It relates to when the name of a part of something is used to refer to the whole thing. For example:

- She's all hands.
- You're all heart.
- She's got ten mouths to feed.

Introducing idioms

Copywriting also uses a lot of idioms, especially in slogans. They help a copywriter to capture within a single sentence a product's key consumer benefit. Often an idiom is used completely out of context. This helps to add intrigue.

Idioms can be used in a corporate context. For example:

You're producing an advert for ScotsdaleNorth.com. Your idiom could be used as a strapline (or sign-off line) that appears at the foot of every ScotsdaleNorth.com advertisement.

You could choose something like:
- ScotsdaleNorth.com – for goodness sake.
- ScotsdaleNorth.com – the Net catch of the day.
- You're WWWelcome, any day of the week.

Perhaps you want to advertise the ScotsdaleNorth.com's cyber-café division:
- Where you, coffee and the Web clicks.

Alternatively, you could extend the idiom:
- Where you click with coffee, the Web, friends ... an entire network of good times and great surfing ... at a price you can afford.

I shall tell you more about the specific use of straplines later in this chapter.

Colloquialisms

Another thorn in the side of grammarians is the use of colloquialisms. Generally, mass-media advertising that directs itself towards the ordinary person in the street adopts a lot of colloquial language. It enables the copywriter to communicate to people at an informal one-to-one level. Colloquial use of language subtly tones down the advertising sales pressure. See for yourself:

> The company would like to invite you to participate in viewing our new website.
> Or:
> Surf our site.

Telly tottie talk

Did you know?

Youth has always enjoyed a rich colloquial dialect. In the 1950s, the Cappuccino Kids (named after the growth of cappuccino bars at that time) were 'cool for cats'. In the 1960s, flower-power generations were 'feeling groovy'. In the 1990s, Generation Ys were 'chilled out'. Millennials (born after Y2K) were 'phat'.

Telly tottie talk highlights

Raid – Road	Pih as in Brad Pih
Ream – Changing reams	Yessss! – Definitely
He goes – He says	I'm like – I said
Phat – Great	Rude-attitude – good
Lo-yoods of – A lot	No-yoo – No
Brilliah – Brilliant	Orsum – OK
A resulh – Good	Sor'id – Very good
Rilly gid – Best compliment you can give	Quality – Sarcastic approval

---

A word of warning about the use of colloquialisms. Usually there is little to gain from poor sentence construction 'just coz you reckon your audience is downmarket'. Plus, just because your words are correct, without substance and credibility your message becomes laughable. As T.S. Eliot so aptly put it, 'If we spoke as we write, we should find no one to read.'

Proverbs

These should be used only if they are relevant to a product or service. They are one of the tools for you to use to create word pictures. The best way to use them is to add a different angle to their meaning. If ScotsdaleNorth.com wanted to advertise two chickens for the price of one, they could adapt a proverb, like this:

> A bird in the shopping basket is worth two at the checkout.

Creative persuasion

Copywriters walk a very fine line between overtly pushing a product or service and gently persuading a person to buy it. The art of persuasion is far more subtle than ram-raiding the sales message. On occasion, you will have to think of various indirect ways of making sure a product name is seen, or a message is heard, time and time again. Here are some ways of doing that:

- Use direct or indirect repetition in the headline.
- Repeat your point in the picture caption.
- Repeat it in the bodycopy.
- Repeat it in the coupon.
- Repeat it in the strapline.
- Repeat it in a jingle.
- Let them hear what you have to say, first time.

Your aim is to lead them to a buying conclusion every time.

A classic way to slip in repetition is to turn a product name into a noun. For example:

> ADD STYLE TO LETTERS. PENPOD THEM.

This cutting of a word into a sentence is sometimes called a 'diacope' or 'tmesis'.

Punctuation

The Victorian rules of punctuation

Sentences start with a Capital letter,
So as to make your writing better.
Use a full stop to mark the end.
It closes every sentence penned.
Insert a comma for short pauses and breaks,
And also for lists the writer makes.
Dashes – like these – are for thoughts.
They provide additional information (so do brackets, of course).
These two dots are colons: they pause to compare.
They also do this: list, explain and prepare.
The semicolon makes a break; followed by a clause.
It does the job of words that link; it's also a short pause.
An apostrophe shows the owner of anyone's things,
It's quite useful for shortenings.
I'm glad! He's mad! Don't walk on the grass!
To show strong feelings use an exclamation mark!
A question mark follows Where? When? Why?
What? and How?
Can I? Do you? Shall we? Tell us now!
"Quotation marks" enclose what is said.
Which is why they are often called 'speech marks' instead.

(Based on *A Victorian Schoolmistress's Rules of Punctuation*)

According to the Campaign for Plain English:

- You may start a sentence with 'and', 'but', 'because', 'so' or 'however'.
- You may split infinitives (the most famous TV example of the last century came from *Star Trek* – To boldly go where no man has gone before).
- You may repeat the same word twice in a sentence *if you can't find a better word.*

Advertising copy needs to be arresting and beguiling. At the heart of copy construction is punctuation. Long sentences are rare. Yet in certain circumstances, length can contribute to a sales proposition, especially when it is important to squeeze in a lot of relevant detail that enhances the product sale, leaving the prospect gasping for breath. This is ideal if, for example, you are promoting a medical charity and wish to demonstrate what it feels like to be an asthma sufferer.

> OFTEN, SENTENCES ARE SHORT.
> TAKEN OUT OF CONTEXT.
> LIKE BUILDING BLOCKS.
> INDIVIDUALLY INTRIGUING.
> COLLECTIVELY INSPIRING.

The use of ellipsis can reinforce the tempo. For example:

> NOW ... FOREVER ... FLOWERS SAY IT ALL.

Short, sharp headlines with an emphatic full stop can make a proposition particularly arresting. Here are some:

> CHEAT ON YOUR WIFE.
> (DON'T LET HER KNOW THAT THE MEAL CAME OUT OF A PACKET.)
> GET AHEAD. CHANGE YOUR HEAD.
> (COULD BE USED FOR THE PENPOD PRODUCT.)
> GET STUFFED.
> (SCOTSDALENORTH'S RANGE OF CHICKEN STUFFING?)

Refer also to page 80. This type of headline could work as a complete advert without any supporting bodycopy.

Using punctuation should be like using an artist's brush. At a stroke, you can create a highly complex picture or a simple one. You can surprise people.

Sentences could start with a lower case letter for particular effect.

They could incorporate a dropped initial capital letter or even an entire dropped word. (This particular technique is at least as old as Magna Carta.)

Check you're spelling

Always check your spelling by reading through your copy. Don't rely on your word processor's internal spell-checking program. This is particularly important when you design copy for websites.

I have a spell cite programme
Its part of my win doze
It plainly marks for my revue
Ear ors I did knot no
I've run this poem on it
Its letter purr fact you sea
Sew I don't have too worry
My pee see looks after me.

The tills are alive with the sound of copy

Browse around your local High Street. Read the slogans on the posters and the leaflets, take a look at the product packaging, and you will find musical advertising alliteration:

> BEANS MEANZ HEINZ
> YOU CAN'T FIT BETTER THAN A KWIK-FIT FITTER.
> SAVE A BUCK. RENT A DUCK.
> (SLOGAN FOR US CAR RENTAL COMPANY)
> ANYTIME, ANYPLACE, ANYWHERE.

The possibilities of creative alliteration are enormous. A theatre group could use the technique like this:

> CENTRE STAGE, CENTRE ATTRACTION.
> LIFE. WHATEVER YOUR STAGE WE STAGE IT ON OURS.
> LOCAL THEATRE. ONCE YOU'VE BOOKED, YOU'LL BE HOOKED.

A charity could use the technique like this:

> HELPING THE HANDICAPPED HELP THEMSELVES.
> EVERY PENNY MEANS EVER SO MUCH.
> SHOW YOU CARE ABOUT THE AIR. (ENVIRONMENTAL CHARITY)
> MAKING IT BETTER BY GETTING TOGETHER.
> (CHARITY TO FIND PARENTS FOR CHILDREN)

Alliteration – through the repetition of letters, words or syllables – has the same kind of effect as one of those odd tunes you can't seem to get off your mind. Eventually the message becomes deeply embedded within a prospect's mind. Every time they think of a particular type of product or service, the slogan comes to their mind and they select that brand. This technique is even more effective if the slogan is written as a musical jingle.

Grammar quick tips

- Never use two words if one is enough.
- Never opt for a long word if a short word will do.
- Be specific – *talk*, not *communicate*.
- Check your words – *computer program*, not *computer programme*.
- Don't use bureaucratic banality – not *in due course, the management board will inform you of its decision*; instead, *we'll let you know.*
- Always veer towards the positive thought rather than the negative – *You've won second prize in our contest*, not *You have not come first in our contest.*
- Heu, modo itera omnia quae mihi nunc narravisti, sed nunc, Anglice. (Oy! Repeat everything you just told me, but this time in plain English.) We speak English, not Latin. In case you haven't heard, Caesar est mortuus.
- Above all, don't get obsessed with grammatical correctness. Make your message interesting, easy to read and straightforward. If you offend grammar puritans in order to achieve a winning creative response, go forth and offend!

In order to communicate a message powerfully you should aim to ensure your copy is straightforward and understandable. This said, not all words from people in power are instantly understandable:

> I mean a child that doesn't have a parent to read to that child or that doesn't see that when the child is hurting to have a parent and help neither parent's there enough to pick up the kid and dust him off and send him back into the game at school or whatever, that kid has a disadvantage.
>
> President George W Bush

Let's get down to the nitty-gritty

Your job is to carry a message to the Attention of your audience, stimulate Interest, solicit Desire, Convince the audience that it's worth listening to you, then encourage Action – that's AIDCA.

The first thing that a person sees when looking at your creative advertisement is its shape. Your message has to compete against the many other messages that the consumer will see during the course of an average day. These messages are not just those on posters and TV, in the mail, on the Web or in the press. There are also messages on pieces of sales promotion like drinks coasters in pubs and on T-shirts. Messages are heard on the radio, seen on hot-air balloons and hidden within public relations announcements passed on by word of mouth.

So think of an original way to present your piece of communication visually. Often this is the job of an art director.

An art director is responsible for the visual appearance and concept of a piece of advertising. As a copywriter you will be working either independently or as part of a copywriter/art director team. Whether that team is a permanent feature or you drift in and out of working with various art directors, it is important to bear certain musts in mind when considering the look of a piece of communication:

1 **People look at pictures before they read words.**
As children we grow up to recognize pictures before words. Pictures are worth a thousand words but the 1001st word – your final word – completes the story.

2 **Never clutter the look – or layout – of your piece of communication.**
However trendy you wish to make it look, always make it flow logically.

3 **Don't use two pictures when one will do.**

4 **Don't use one general picture when one relevant detailed picture is available.**

5 **The logo is sacred.**
Never mess with it and always include it in the piece of communication. It acts as corporate seal of approval.

6 **Develop a distinctive 'look' for all your pieces of communication.**
This too acts as a subtle corporate seal of approval. Each time your creative work is seen, even if people don't read it, they know from its style that you are active in the marketplace. A 'look' includes consistent use of typeface, consistent use of borders and, wherever possible, consistent shape of layout.

7 **Balance your copy with pictures.**
Depending on the power of the image, adjust your copy to complement rather than undermine the image. Conversely, never allow the image to undermine your copy.

8 Adapt the look of your creative work.
Your work should blend into the media in which it will
appear. (See Chapter 5.)

9 Always stick to one theme.
Too many ideas in one piece of creative work dilute your key
message (USP).

10 Make room for impact.
Include a sensible amount of 'white' or empty space that
tones down the overtly hard sell in the layout.

11 Make a citizen's arrest in three-quarters of a second.
It is thought that on average a person spends about one-and-
a-half seconds looking at a printed advert. Your piece has
only half of that time to make an impact.

Making the headlines

If your prospective buyer reads only one part, it's going to be
your headline – the key proposition. So it's not surprising that
copywriters devote so much time getting it right. If your
headline is dull, your bodycopy will never attract anyone's
attention.

There are two kinds of proposition:
1 based on experience
2 based on logic
Of these, the easiest to feature is (1) the experience of your
audience looking for (2) the logic of your solution.

As explained in point 7 above, it is important to balance your
copy with your visual elements. Curiously, you may be able to
write an advert without the support of a graphic such as a
photograph. However, you will rarely create an advert without
a headline. (The exception would be if you were trying to 'tease'
your audience.)

That is not to suggest that all pictures need a headline to explain
their relevance. In fact, none does. Headlines and pictures are
equal partners in the communication business. One (either one)
brings one of the following elements to the venture and the
other brings the other!

Intrigue <> Impact

Headline propositions are just the beginning of your copy story.
It is vital that every consequential part of the communication
follows on.

All-embracing copy structure

The ideal all-embracing copy structure is:

- Your headline (proposition).
- Your lead-in paragraph (relating to your proposition).
- Your main argument (which can incorporate bullet points to hammer specific issues home – provided those points are substantiated).
- Your lead-out paragraph (relating in some way back to the main proposition).

In brochure writing, this structure is adapted to become one of plots within a plot. Each plot has a similar make-up: proposition lead-in, main argument, lead-out, but this time the proposition can be a sub-headline.

One other thought on photography and headlines.

Did you know?

During a political advertising campaign for the British Conservative party in the late 1950s, the plan was to run a series of advertisements featuring a photograph of a bright-eyed, ready-for-anything person waking up. The headline read: *Get up and go with the Conservatives.* Everyone thought it was a good advert. However, just as it was about to run in the papers, someone noticed the bedside alarm clock in the photograph – the time on it was 09.45. Not exactly very get up and go! The entire advert had to be scrapped.

The moral:

It's true, photography may offer detail that can never be matched by illustration. However, unless you pay attention to everything during the shoot, those details could be your downfall.

Headlines as picture captions

Headlines should never be literal explanations of what is in pictures. A way in which they can enhance a message is to use them to refer indirectly to a picture, drawing attention to certain of its elements.

The headline could answer questions such as these:

- Who's in the picture?
- What is the person doing?
- What is the product?
- In a word or two, what makes it all relevant?

Returning to the limit of one-and-a-half seconds to make a citizen's arrest, it is vital that you use that time effectively. Tests have shown that virtually everyone reads the first two or three words in a headline. Only 70% of people will read six or seven words. Thereafter attention begins to go astray. The only exception to this rule is direct marketing copy, where the figures are sometimes different.

As you will learn in Chapter 6, response advertising often makes use of time and space to convey a story involving the reader. You will find lots of examples of long copy headlines in direct response material. They offer two advantages over the shorter pithy lines:

1 There are millions of short, pithy headlines. A longer one helps to make an advertisement outstanding.

> **355,024 PEOPLE AGED OVER 50 DIDN'T PLAN TO CHECK THEIR PENSION VALUES ON OUR SITE. SOMETIMES LIFE DOESN'T ALWAYS GO TO PLAN ...**

2 A longer headline can be viewed as an expanded lead to the bodycopy, luring the reader deeper into the text.

For example, I once wrote the following headline:

This approach enabled me to stir sufficient curiosity to stimulate the reader's interest and to complete the story in the text.

Even if your message is refined to only two or three words, there's no point in writing an arresting headline if it isn't relevant to your message. The headline is worse still if it doesn't encourage the reader to find out more by reading the bodycopy. So, eight out of ten times, create a headline which delivers an immediate and relevant benefit to the consumer. Anything else is just icing on the cake. (And nine-and-a-half out of ten times make sure you get to the point in your opening paragraph.)

Grabbing the market share

Your copy must hold the reader's attention. Let's take a look at what stories appeal to people.

Universal film plots

According to popular belief in the film industry, there are only eleven Hollywood scenarios.

1 **Love** Boy meets girl, loses girl, wins her back.
2 **Success** The lead character has to succeed at all costs.
3 **Cinderella** An ugly duckling is transformed into a perfect human being.
4 **Triangle** Three characters in a romantic entanglement.
5 **Return** An absent lover, father or spouse returns after wandering off for years.
6 **Vengeance** A lead character seeks revenge.
7 **Conversion** Bad guy turns into a good guy.
8 **Sacrifice** The lead character gives everything up for their or someone else's good.
9 **Family** The interrelationship of characters in a single place or situation (e.g. a hotel, prison, office).
10 **Jeopardy** A life-and-death situation exploiting adeptness and survival instincts of the lead characters.
11 **Forbidden liaison** Gay relationships, incest and other social taboos.

Universal news stories

In journalism, the news list is longer, including:

1 Natural disasters.
2 Man-made disasters.
3 Sex.
4 Commercial gains.
5 Commercial losses.
6 Political gains.
7 Political losses.
8 Murders.
9 Suicides.
10 Law and disorder.
11 War.
12 Political rebellion.
13 Scandal.
14 Mr or Mrs Good/Bad.
15 Social struggles.
16 Royalty.

Universal copy themes

Advertising's key list of attention motivators is shorter in length but infinitely greater in substance.

There are eleven underlying headline themes:

1 Question	5 Invitation	9 Representation
2 Directive	6 Promise	10 Demonstration
3 Comparison	7 Anticipation	11 News-making
4 Challenge	8 Location	

Using headlines

Question headlines

Who?

There are two ways to use the Who? approach in headlines.

1 Simply include 'Who' in the headline:

> **WHO KNOWS WHAT CHIPS KIDS LOVE BEST?**

A ScotsdaleNorth.com advert for frozen chips

> **WHO CAN YOU TURN TO FOR IMPARTIAL ADVICE?**

A financial services advertisement

2 The other route to consider in using the Who? approach is the testimonial type of advert. Testimonials add credence to a benefit by featuring a celebrity, character (fictional or historical) or person who is typical of the audience that you are trying to attract. Testimonial headlines must be believable or else they fall flat. If you are going to quote a person or have permission to construct a quote for a person, always ensure that it is written in the style in which that person would say it.

> **'PENPOD IS THE ONLY PEN I EVER NEED'**

As opposed to:

> **'OF ALL THE PENS I USE, MORE OFTEN THAN NOT I FIND MYSELF USING THIS MOST EXCELLENT INSTRUMENT CALLED PENPOD.'**

Can I quote you on that?

Copywriters often use quotations as an emergency exit out of a difficult project when they cannot find anything original to say.

Sometimes *Who?* headlines refer to historical or fictitious characters. Use this technique only if it is relevant. There wouldn't be much point in a headline that incorporated a picture of Winston Churchill and read:

> 'GIVE US THE TOOLS AND WE WILL FINISH THE JOB.'

(Mind you, as an advert for PenPod...) Remember to let the product – not the models or personalities – take the sales lead.

Why? Which? and How?

Questions should act as a kind of mental tickling-stick, to tease your audience:

> WOULD YOU LIKE TO GET **20,000** EUROS
>
> A WEEK FOR NOTHING?

The headline achieves three things:

1 It poses a question.
2 Taking account of human instinct, you, the copywriter, can make an intuitive stab at the likely response: 'Yes, but what's the catch?'
3 Based on the question you have put and the response you expect, you can proceed with the bodycopy.

One of the danger signs to watch for when writing question-led answers is the question that answers itself. If you use one of those, nobody will bother to read any further. For example:

> WOULD YOU LIKE SOME LIFE INSURANCE?
>
> ARE YOU OVERWEIGHT?

'Yes' or 'No' answers choke the interest factor at birth. One way to avoid this is to answer the question in a subhead:

> ARE YOU OVERWEIGHT?
>
> CALL US ON **08700 123 124**
>
> WE'LL SAVE YOU POUNDS THE MOMENT YOU DIAL.

This example shows how the manipulation of words can help you avoid a 'Yes' or 'No' answer to a question.

By the way, whenever possible try to edit out superfluous words creatively:

> **OVERWEIGHT?**
>
> CALL **08700 123 124** – SAVE POUNDS
>
> HOW DO YOU THINK PENPOD'S INK-SAVING FEATURES SAVE YOU MONEY?

When questions make answers

You can turn many a bland statement into a powerful sales message, just by adding a simple 'Why' or 'Where' or 'How'. For example:

> WE SELL THE GREATEST RANGE OF PALM HELD COMPUTERS

This is a strong statement. Add the word 'Why' and it lifts off the page:

> WHY WE SELL THE GREATEST RANGE OF PALM HELD COMPUTERS
>
> [LEAD-IN COPY:]
>
> YOU'VE GOT TO HAND IT TO US ...

You can use a leading question to demonstrate a product's simplicity. The following would adapt well:

> BUILD A **950 MHz PC**

The same method could be applied to:

> THIS INSURANCE POLICY WILL COVER ALL YOUR
> COMPANY'S BAD DEBTS.

Here's how to make both examples more rewarding for the reader:

> WANT TO BUILD A **950 MHz PC?** HERE'S HOW ...
>
> HERE'S HOW THIS INSURANCE POLICY WILL COVER
>
> ALL YOUR COMPANY'S BAD DEBTS.

Directive headlines

Don't walk on the grass!   **Eat your greens!**
Clean your teeth!   **Stop biting your nails!**

Advertising headlines are stuffed from first letter to last with orders to follow. With so many to be seen and heard through the media, it's a wonder that anyone has time to get on with their life! What makes people listen to one instruction and ignore another? Simply, it's the way you phrase your instruction. If you aggressively order people about simply to shock them into doing something, often all you achieve is their doing the opposite – just to spite you.

Plan to use verbs as persuasive tools. Wherever possible, consider the use of verbs in a headline. Not every headline features a verb. You may prefer to imply one.

Here is a headline referring to PenPod's durability and reliability. The text could appear as though it has been written on a piece of paper that stretches for miles:

Yours, PenPod.

Verbs add impact to a headline. Without them you can still conjure up provocative images. With them you drive your message home. For example, ScotsdaleNorth.com announce a new phase of anniversary celebrations. The press release (for more information, see Chapter 13) is headed:

ScotsdaleNorth.com News.

This could be spruced up considerably:

ScotsdaleNorth.com always makes news.

Comparison headlines

When a comparison headline is used, often a striking visual that shows clear differences is incorporated. Historically, comparison headlines work particularly well for diet plans, when the advertiser wishes to demonstrate differences in appearance before and after participating in the plan.

One trick to highlight how the 'after' result has had a dramatic effect for the user of your product or service is to show the 'before' appearance in its worst possible light. If you are promoting a dieting programme, the person in the 'before' shot would be wearing something dull and unattractive. In the 'after' shot, the same person wears something fetching and eye-catching.

Comparison ads work well with inanimate objects too. For example:

> ScotsdaleNorth.com want to show how they include more biscuits in their packets than their competitors. The ad could feature a substantial pile on a plate alongside a plate with a few of the competitor's biscuits on it.

Here is another example. A DVD manufacturer wishes to demonstrate the durability and quality of its product compared to other manufacturers' DVDs.

> There are two pictures (a) and (b):
>
> a shows a clear TV picture clip of the *Titanic*;
>
> b has a fuzzy TV picture clip of the *Titanic*.
>
> The headline reads:
>
> Should watching *Titanic* leave you feeling all washed up?

A drawback of comparison-type headlines is that they can be construed as 'knocking the competition'. In the United States this is more acceptable than in the UK. In the UK, such tactics can lead to lawsuits. Of course, you may wish to create a stir in the marketplace and invite public relations coverage (so-called PRadvertising). The best way to avoid this is to have evidence ready to support your claim in case you are challenged.

Challenge headlines

> I BET YOU THAT AFTER TWO WEEKS OF SWITCHING TO BRAND X YOU WILL PERMANENTLY USE IT IN PREFERENCE TO YOUR USUAL BRAND.

The only way a customer can dispute the claim is to pick up the gauntlet and accept your challenge. There are several methods to help you enliven challenge headlines. One is the blindfold test approach in which the identities of the product and that of your competitors are concealed until the results are presented. Often blindfold testing produces surprising results. For example:

	Open	Blind
Prefer Pepsi	23%	51%
Prefer Coke	65%	44%
Equal/Can't say	12%	5%

(Source: *Relationship Marketing*, by Christopher, Payne and Ballantyne)

Apart from highlighting people's perceptions about the drinks, this table also demonstrates the power of brand loyalty. (See 'Give your troops brand names', p. 35.)

A variation of the blindfold test is to blindfold the prospective buyer. You could include an offer to refund the cost of the product. It works like this:

> If the prospect still believes after an acceptable period of time of testing out your product that it is better than that of your competitors, the purchase price is refunded. Of course, refunds are made only upon proof of purchase. After, say, a two-week challenge period for a relatively low-priced item, how many people will be bothered to claim back their money?

Invitation headlines

Everyone likes to be invited to something special. Invitation headlines work particularly well for launches or in conjunction with demonstration headlines.

> **TEST DRIVE OUR LATEST CAR.**
>
> **BE ONE OF THE FIRST TO VISIT OUR NEW CYBER CAFÉ.**

Invitation headlines work well when they incorporate a reward for accepting the invitation.

> **TEST DRIVE OUR LATEST CAR AND YOU COULD WIN IT IN A PRIZE DRAW.**
>
> **BE ONE OF THE FIRST TO VISIT OUR NEW CYBER CAFÉ.**
>
> **NEXT TIME, YOUR SURF'N'TURF IS ON US.**

In order to clarify these examples, I have made the offers quite implicit. However, in practice you should try to allow your headline to withhold an element of your offer – either for further explanation within the bodycopy or to be completely realized when the invitation is accepted. So:

> TAKE IT FOR A SPIN AROUND THE BLOCK AND KEEP THE KEYS.
> A GREAT DEAL, A PERFECT MEAL, COMPLIMENTS OF THE CHEF.

Promise headlines

A promise headline obliges the advertiser to offer guarantees on the product or service. A guarantee is a legal commitment that must be honoured. So, if you decide to make a guarantee, you have to be specific about its duration, value and restrictions. You also have to ensure that any promise doesn't affect standard consumer rights.

Some may say cynically that guarantees create more loopholes than sales. The answer is, it depends on how you phrase your guarantee. You don't want to end up with a headline that is two pages long and includes numerous clauses. Nor do you want to design an advert with more small print than bodycopy. Keep your guarantees simple, like:

> AND YOU CAN TAKE MY WORD ON THAT – OR YOUR MONEY BACK.

Anticipation headlines

An old vaudeville magician once said, 'To grab an audience, keep them waiting and they'll come back for more.' You can imagine the scenario:

> The magician would claim that he could escape from a locked tea chest immersed under water. He climbed in. Someone sealed the chest with heavy chains and complicated locking devices. The chest was lowered into a huge glass container. Water spilt everywhere. After about thirty seconds, the audience began to grow concerned about the poor performer locked in the chest. Sixty seconds passed. No sign of the chains being removed. Two minutes lapsed. A distraught woman appeared from backstage and screamed for the stage hands to retrieve the chest. After that exchange, five minutes had passed. The bandmaster stopped playing. He tried to console a member of the orchestra who broke down into tears.
>
> The chest was finally hauled out, dripping water onto the stage. Someone approached with a huge chain cutter. Out spilt tons of water, but the magician had vanished. At that precise moment, he appeared in perfect shape at the back of the auditorium. The audience applauded.

Keeping your advertising audience waiting almost contradicts the 'get the message quick' approach of headlines. But it works! Try placing your product in an impossible situation. For example:

> You want to demonstrate PenPod's amazing strength. So why not drive over it with a Jumbo jet?
>
> You want to demonstrate the creamy thickness of one of ScotsdaleNorth's yoghurts. Why not 'load' the product with lots of fruit that defies gravity by nestling on the yoghurt's surface?
>
> You want to demonstrate the strength of a piece of string. Why not suspend a 26-stone woman in a bikini from it?

The next technique is to feature a headline that can be appreciated by very few – no one else will understand the proposition. Usually these types of headlines have the niggling itch effect. They work well with youth brands or drinks. The consumer sees the advertisement and, not wishing to appear stupid, makes every effort for it to appear to their peers that they understand the message. So the puzzled consumer starts to scratch away at the obscure message.

That's why you may get a beer advert wrapped up in riddles. Then when you go to the pub to order a beer, you will find a certain group of people adopting the beer not just as a refreshing drink, but as a statement that reflects a social attitude.

A third anticipation headline technique is the 'taste of the things to come' approach:

> **THE CHOCOLATE BAR THAT LOOKS SO GOOD**
> **YOU COULD EAT IT OFF THE PAGE.**

> **THE HOLIDAY THAT LOOKS SO RELAXING**
> **YOU CAN'T WAIT TO GET ONTO THE BEACH.**

Finally, you could try the leading …

… **teaser headline.**

However, I have found that this seems to work only if you reserve it for mailing pieces where the headline may start on the outer envelope …

... and conclude as you open the envelope.

I sometimes refer to this technique as the greetings card device –
many greetings cards rely on leading headlines:

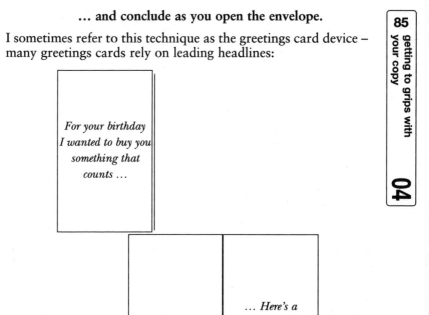

*For your birthday
I wanted to buy you
something that
counts ...*

*... Here's a
calculator*

Location headlines

A short cut to a consumer is to create unique locations where
your brand has the freedom to really excel. Location headlines
can be useful when you want individual brands to be perceived
as being part of a bigger family of products and services.

As you have already learnt (see 'The Elvis factor and the G spot',
pp. 33–5), brands should be able to stand alone as well as when
looked at as part of a whole.

Did you know?

The ultimate brand location must surely be Disneyworld or
Disneyland. Here, individual brand items, such as specific film
titles with unique characters, club together with carnival rides and
attractions to produce a global parent brand with a cultural
following all its own.

You may not have the odd couple of billion pounds to build a themed location. In advertising terms, it doesn't matter. Many world leading brands have used advertising to create artificial locations that are just as evocative as the real thing. Alcoholic beverage brands often conjure up a paradise island where their drinks are served all day.

Representation headlines

Now you have invented your magical land of Oz you will need a guide to show your prospective buyer around. You can either maintain the momentum of imaginary places by inventing a character or feature yourself or your client in the advertising.

In general, you should avoid the latter. You and your client may not have appearance or delivery that comes over well, especially on screen. There are exceptions to the rule. For example, a fashion buyer's explanation of why a certain line of suits caught her eye can be effective.

Occasionally, you will come across a client who really does have what it takes to appear sincere in every medium. However, I advise you to remain cautious. Instead, feature professionals who can stimulate a prospective consumer's imagination. An imaginary land gives you the opportunity to paint a vivid picture of a type of utopia; it makes sense to use an imaginary escort to guide consumers through it.

Catering companies often use this approach, inventing everything from a person made of dough to one formed from liquorice. Animated characters can be manipulated precisely to show perfect facial characteristics. The combined detachment from reality and precision use of facial expressions may enhance the impression that you want your brand to leave on a prospect.

Did you know?

Highly successful animated characters have included giants, walking milk bottles, dancing credit cards, singing raisins, marching toothbrushes, flying sprays of polish and a variety of others.

Imaginary characters need not be animated. Some of the world's longest-running advertising campaigns have been built around fictitious characters played by actors. For example:

Advertisements featuring the 'ideal' couple who try to build a sustaining relationship over a cup of coffee.

Did you know?

One of the most famous of all classic advertising characters, the man in the Hathaway shirt. (The eye-patched man has a sophisticated lifestyle that meant he always had to be suitably attired – in a Hathaway branded shirt.)

Fictional and non-fictional brand characters

Captain Birds Eye
Yes, he existed! His name was Clarence 'Bob' Birds Eye and he was a New York furrier.

John West
Yes again! He was Scottish and set up a canning factory in Oregon in 1873.

Uncle Ben
No such person – sorry. The face is that of the maître d' at a Houston hotel.

Captain Morgan
Yes, he existed. He was Governor of Jamaica, was knighted by Charles II and renowned for piracy.

Mr Kipling
He never existed, but he does make exceedingly good cakes.

Demonstration headlines

Ask vacuum cleaner salespeople how to impress a prospective buyer and they'll tell you to throw a binful of rubbish on your lounge carpet. The real shock for the prospect is that the vacuum cleaner tidies up the mess in minutes, leaving not even a speck of dust behind. Demonstration headlines are closely related to anticipation headlines in that they feature the product in an unusual setting – a brand of glue may be shown as sticking a man to a flying plane.

One of the best media for demonstration headlines is TV. Here you can play out an entire scenario in front of an audience. There is more about TV in Chapter 8.

News-making headlines

Did you interpret the heading immediately above as saying that advertising makes the headlines? If so, you read it correctly. If not, you are still correct. A lot of people believe that advertising sets trends. For 99.9% of the time, this is nonsense. Advertising panders to society's needs by using an understanding of how people see their roles in society. To do this those in advertising have to listen and watch trends, then follow those trends alongside the consumer. Topical headlines can either be directly or indirectly connected to a company. Directly topical headlines could refer to specific use of the product in a news-making context. For example:

> You produce the oil in a Grand Prix winning vehicle, so you write a headline that refers to the great race.

Alternatively a topical headline could be indirectly associated with the current news:

> A national football team wins the World Cup. ScotsdaleNorth.com could refer to it in the following headline:

Congratulations England
from one league leader to another.

Topical headlines help make a company appear as part of a living community. They provide scope for humour, compassion and responsibility.

I mentioned a 99.9% chance that advertising does not set trends – what about the 0.1% chance that it does? Sometimes advertisers create risky advertising that is meant to be banned and make headlines (so-called PRadvertising). At other times advertisers use themes that suddenly become fashionable, such as a particular piece of music. However, even in these cases you generally find that the advert is based on a variation of a published or known theme. When ads are just plainly shocking for their own sake, that is called 'adsterbation'.

Heads you win

I can't leave the world of headline propositions without discussing one of its most fascinating aspects: word pictures.

Once you have decided which of the eleven headline themes you wish to take – or which combination suits your needs – consider the possibilities of word pictures. These impress a product personality on the reader. In addition to highlighting a benefit, they set the agenda for the advertisement's tone of voice.

Here are examples:

> **DOES YOUR MOBILE LEAVE YOUR EARS RINGING?**

> **IS YOUR WALLET BURNING A HOLE IN YOUR POCKET?**

Word pictures match elements of a product's name or use with the situation or location that you place it within.

So, for example, you may wish to present a relaxing ferry journey:

Headline:

The not so cross ferry.
(Picture of contented passenger alongside frustrated passenger.)

A variation is a combination of two separate words into one message. Here are some possible examples:

> **Smoke Ring:**
> Message: Give up smoking, dial this number.
>
> **Action Replay:**
> Message: Action-packed computer game that you'll want to play time after time.
>
> **Air Lift:**
> Message: New kind of hydraulic elevator system.
>
> **Weather Eye:**
> Message: All-weather eyewear protection.
>
> **Ironing Board:**
> Message: Company's own management tests a new iron.
>
> **Vampire Bat:**
> Message: High-impact cricket bat.
>
> **Help Line:**
> Picture: Hook and line picking up a phone.
> Message: Fisherman's help line.

Never confuse word pictures with puns. Puns are overused and often poor substitutes for clear messages. Don't toy with sentences for no other purpose than to make something sound funny when it is clearly not. One of the crudest puns I have ever seen was for a scaffolding company whose trade advertisement's headline read:

SATISFACTION GUARANTEED WITH EVERY ERECTION.

Unlike puns, word pictures open doors to creative writing. Once you enter into a proposition, bodycopy completes the story.

Nitty-gritty quick tips

- Design your advertisement to gain the maximum impact on the page.
- Invest time in creating a powerful headline.
- People read or reject a headline within one-and-a-half seconds.
- There are eleven basic film plots.
- There are about seventeen journalistic plots.
- There are eleven underlining headline themes.
- Testimonials must sound realistic.
- Quotations can be an excuse to avoid writing something original that's quotable.
- Wouldn't you use a leading question to direct a prospect to a sale?
- Persuading a prospect is different from pushing a prospect.
- Consider writing 'before and after' creative copy.
- If a product is difficult to sell consider throwing down the gauntlet by setting a challenge.
- Invite your prospect to view the product before buying it.
- All prospects are VIPs – Very Important Prospects.
- Guarantee your proposition.
- Make your product or service something that's worth waiting for.
- Position your product or service in a special unique location.
- Add product personality by inventing a unique character.
- Demonstrate your product or service.
- Advertising doesn't invent, it innovates.
- Link words to create pictures.

Over to you

1 List three standard film plots.
2 List four standard journalistic plots.
3 Using six headline themes, write headlines for the previously listed plots.
4 Write fifty words to persuade a person not to jump off a mountain.
5 Apart from slimming products, list six other products or services which could use a 'before and after' technique.
6 Write a list of ten word pictures.
7 Write a headline that captures the spirit of:
   a the *Mona Lisa*
   b a traffic light.

8 Write a headline that incorporates a witticism.

Understanding bodycopy

Without bodycopy a firm sales proposition has no substance.

One of the most common questions asked about bodycopy is 'How long should it be?' There are three interlinked replies:

• As long as it takes to convey all the information.
• The greater the commitment that is sought, the longer the copy.
• Finally, as long as it takes until you lose enthusiasm for the project.

Let's look at the implications of these answers in more detail.

Your headline, accompanied by a suitable visual, provides the carrot that entices the reader into your message. The bodycopy supplies the detailed reasons why a buyer needs to make a purchase or take appropriate action.

Depending on your requirements, you need either *to identify* a product or service or *to provide information* about a product or service. Your bodycopy should be adapted accordingly.

1 In the case of identifying products or services, strong headlines and visuals usually suffice. Examples of this are posters and bodycopy for impulse purchases such as sweets or household detergents. In-store posters are specific examples.
2 In the case of providing information about a product or service, bodycopy takes the lead from headlines.

Informative advertising needs to convey the benefits of a product or service. Good examples of this are dot.com and financial products. Often business-to-business advertising also relies on longer copy.

Copy with conviction

Believe me, your mood can always be 'read' in the copy you write. Too often copywriters let themselves and the communication down by writing over-long copy just to fill the space. If you are sincere, the copy will sound sincere. If you are blasé, the copy will appear crass.

Another cause of unbelievable bodycopy is unbelievable claims. Very few people will suppose that a particular item will change their lives, especially if your bodycopy oversells the product. There is an exception to this rule: you can adopt the technique of overtly overselling in order to draw attention to your product. This is often used by American-style car salespeople who may make claims such as:

> **OUR DEALS ARE SO GOOD THAT IF YOU DON'T BUY WE'LL EAT THE CAR.**

Remember that direct claims from a product supplier or manufacturer can also sound feeble when compared to endorsements from users of the product or service. (See p. 77.)

Here is an extreme example of a manufacturer overselling a product:

> **One sip of our health drink will make you feel pukka**
> **One sip of our competitor's drink will make you puke**

Sure, someone somewhere will buy your drink. However, it may well be a one-off purchase. And a lot of people won't touch it. If you want to keep a customer for life, not for just a moment, keep your claims credible and people will come back again and again. By the way, you should not make such a direct competitor-knocking claim as it infringes the rules of the Advertising Code of Practice.

Bodycopy structure

Once you are familiar with the brief, you'll feel more confident about writing bodycopy. Generally, your headline sets the tone of voice for the copy. Light-hearted headlines lead into light-hearted copy. Technical headlines demand technical explanations.

The first sentence of your bodycopy (also known as the lead-in sentence) is the second most important part of your main text. (The most important is the call to action.) The lead-in sentence links your headline with the rest of your piece. It's as if your headline is a shop window and the bodycopy is the showroom that has all the gadgets ready to be discussed by a salesperson. (If you want to go into a lot of further detail, you'll need a brochure.)

As the lead-in sentence links two complementary lines of thought, you should never use it to repeat the headline or to fill in gaps that your headline and/or visual failed to achieve. That is a waste of words. You need to make a link that is secure enough to keep a prospect hooked on to your message. Get to the point, lead your prospect to all your benefit points. For example:

SCOTSDALENORTH.COM ARE OPENING A NEW CHAIN OF CYBER CAFÉS

Headline:

Wild West grub?
Far Eastern chow?
Southern fried chicken?
Northern hospitality?

Subhead:

IT ALL POINTS TO US ...

Lead-in sentence:

WHEN YOU'RE PECKISH AND JUST CAN'T DECIDE WHICH FOOD MATCHES YOUR MOOD, HEAD TO THE ONE PLACE THAT HAS IT ALL – DIRECTIONS.

Here is how not to write your lead-in sentence:

> FRESH FOOD AND GREAT SURFING CAN BE FOUND IN OUR
> NEW CAFÉ CALLED DIRECTIONS.

Copy progression

So-called copy tracking provides a catalyst for ideas to flow in a logical sequence. The test of good copy tracking is to remove one of the sentences from a paragraph. If the rest of the sentences still add up to a reasonably plausible message, your copy tracking hasn't gone off the rails.

Now, prioritize product benefits in the order you want them read. For example:

> Here are some of the benefits of ScotsdaleNorth's Directions chain of cyber cafés:

1 Locations throughout the country.
2 Cheap surfing.
3 Terminals at every table.
4 Tables can email each other.
5 Delicious food from all four corners of the world.
6 Reasonable prices.
7 Special pre-measured portions.
8 Excellent service.
9 Tempting dishes for young and not so young.
10 Different speciality menu every day.
11 Cyber-cool decor.

Depending on where your advertisement appears, your bodycopy should concentrate on a suitable feature. If your advertisement appears in a family-style publication, benefit 9 (Tempting dishes for young and not so young) may take priority. Remember, every benefit has one feature or more – never vice-versa.

Address arguments before the questions start

Once you have prioritized your benefits, state them as well as addressing questions that may arise. To do this, as you write each sentence think of how it will affect any of the subsequent ones and, more importantly, how each proposition or benefit feature creates a possible response that is against it.

For example, you want to address families using their cars for long journeys:

Headline:

If you're feeling peckish pull off at junction 21 and fill the Watford Gap.

(Picture of a family in a car. One of the kids is acting wild. Another looks glum. The front passenger is trying to placate everyone and the driver is looking desperate.)

Bodycopy:

When you're stuck in a five mile tail-back and the kids are screaming for lunch, you need a new direction – pronto.

What are you going to do about it?

Look out for the special Direction Compass sign and you'll be just a junction away from a satisfying meal that all the family will relish.

What's so satisfying about it?

Directions is the cyber café up your street. It features scrumptious dishes from all four corners of the world, including Wild West feasts, Far Eastern specialities and the coolest surfing that all the family will enjoy.

Is there anything else that's special?

You can choose from three types of order. The Hearty Filler – ideal for a wholesome snack. The Big Deal – big on portions, small on price. Or The Giant Slayer – a massive portion that will knock your eyes out and fill even the biggest appetite.

Sounds expensive. What does it cost?

Just because we serve the best choice of food from around the world, it doesn't mean that our prices are out of this earth. The Hearty Filler costs as little as £6.99. Even our Giant Slayer starts from only £12.99.

I want some of that. What do I do next?

The next time you're feeling peckish, pull in and fill up at Directions.

Where can I find it?

(Include a map or list of restaurant locations, website address and telephone number.)

Writing for a specific audience

All professional copywriters are also copy readers. Whenever possible, study previous examples of corporate copy style. There are hundreds of ways in which you can blend styles of copywriting. To simplify matters, I have narrowed them down to half a dozen main types.

Six elements of style

1 Get on with it

This picks up where the headline and visual left off. It prioritizes USP/TSP/ESPs and then explains each, one at a time.

- A great panacea for all styles of bodycopy.
- Essential if you have a lot of benefits to convey.
- Maintains momentum.

2 View from the top

This takes a corporate view of a product or service. It concentrates on the ideology behind an advertised item rather than its immediate specifics.

- Often used by large corporate organizations.
- Helps boost confidence in a company.
- Waves the corporate flag.
- Useful to promote umbrella brands.
- Can be used in conjunction with public relations activities.
- Commonly used to imbue confidence in shareholders or financiers.
- Facts must be totally accurate.
- Exaggerations must be avoided.

3 Story line

This tells a narrative that develops into a discussion of your salient benefits.

- Ideal for lifestyle copy where feelings associated with a product or services are equal to, if not stronger than, features. For example, gold credit-card advertising often uses a story line (narrative copy) to describe a rich lifestyle.
- Pigeon-holes readers.
- Reinforces a company's corporate image.
- Can be written from the user's viewpoint or can be the writer's description of the user's viewpoint.
- A good story takes longer to express than a short description.

- Adds human interest to products or services.
- Helps you use emotive copy when there are not many benefits.

4 Character led

This method empowers the characters in your advertisement to introduce your message. Characters may include celebrities, end-users or even characters from comic strips.

- Covers all kinds of testimonial bodycopy.
- Testimonials must be clear, plain and – above all – sincere.
- Only use relevant celebrity testimonials. (Don't get a magician to sell a cure for cancer.)
- If you are going to write a testimonial on behalf of a celebrity, write it as they would say it.
- Never write a testimonial that forces the celebrity or end-user to state something that they would not normally know. (e.g. 'I always write with a PenPod. The 30% oil in the ink means that it clings even to non-porous paper.' *Yuk!* It would sound more credible if you wrote 'This PenPod is great. It works anywhere.' Please refer to p. 77.)
- Testimonials can be implied through bodycopy style; you do not have to include a named person.

5 Different strokes

This method relies on unusual language such as poetry, humour and foreign words.

- It is rarely used, but particularly potent for bodycopy aimed at the youth sector of the market or when something quirky is required.

There was a young writer from Kirk,
Whose copy never quite worked.
When someone asked why?
He curtly replied,
It's the brief,
Not me, that's the berk.

6 Caption captured

This method uses visuals such as photographs or illustrations, together with appropriate captions.

Subheads and captions

You may have wondered why I did not include subheads and captions in the previous section about headlines. Well, they act as direction indicators within a bodycopy context rather than as conspicuous 'headline' signposts. Subheads allow you to segment your copy into specific areas of interest. By using them a reader can concentrate on bodycopy from anywhere within the piece of communication without disrupting the copy tracking or flow.

Subheads highlight key points of interest to be explained by the bodycopy. Captions for visuals either encapsulate the spirit of what is being shown or hint at something that is unseen (and usually brought to light through the bodycopy). Subheads and captions should be short.

- People read less nowadays than they used to and often rely on subheads or captions to complete the picture.
- If subheads or captions are not brief, they become chunks of bodycopy in their own right.

As with lead-in copy, it is important that picture captions do not repeat what the visual shows.

Too many subheads can slow down a message, especially when space is at a premium and ideas can be expressed in very simple terms. Therefore, before you decide to include subheads, think about how they will affect your flow of copy. Subheads can be compared to refreshment breaks beside a motorway. The longer your journey, the greater the need for a refreshment break and direction check. The shorter your journey, the lesser the need.

Many copywriters use headlines and captions as guides to lead themselves through the process of writing bodycopy. Often, subheads are padded out with one or two lines of copy that suggest the style and content of the bodycopy for each heading.

Keep your copy chatty

Understandably, many novice writers are over-sensitive about high-profile big-business copy, to such an extent that their copy may seem stilted or distant. This is particularly likely to happen in view-from-the-top, corporate-style bodycopy. Some writers believe that big corporations deserve aloof, first-person-type language. On the contrary; the bigger the organization, the more intimate you should make your copy.

> **JUST BECAUSE WE'RE BIG THAT DOESN'T MEAN
> THAT WE'RE NOT PERSONAL.**

Actually, that line could be improved – particularly if the context is corporate-style advertising.

> **YOU ARE NUMBER ONE. THAT MAKES US COUNT.**

In other words, whenever possible try to avoid using 'we'. Instead, use 'you'. If you have to use 'we', complement it with 'you'. As you will see later, this technique is particularly effective when incorporated in direct mail letters.

How to close your bodycopy

Closing your bodycopy requires more than a final full stop. You need to tie up any loose ends and feel confident that your reader will know how to proceed further. If you are after a response, choose options such as website addresses, telephone numbers or coupons (see Off-the-page advertising, p. 138). On the other hand, you may want to stimulate awareness or want the reader to have a good feeling about the company. Either way, you still have to close your proposition and leave the reader wanting to do something.

One of the best techniques for closing copy is to refer to the headline and lead-in copy. Turn the proposition into a full circle where the beginning leads to a middle, the middle leads to an end, and the end refers to the beginning. By this I do not mean that you should just keep your reader going endlessly around in circles. Instead use a subtle reminder of where the proposition kicked off. For example:

> Headline:
>
> ### WE ARE 1
>
> (Picture of an 11-stone birthday cake for the Directions cyber café chain, with a person about to blow out the candles.)
>
> Lead-in copy:
>
> **365 days, 45,000 meals, 2,000,000 clicks and we're still only one year old.**
>
> Bodycopy:
>
> (Then, central explanation copy.)
>
> Close:
>
> **So now you *really* can have your cake and eat it.**

Straplines, slogans and other pay-offs

A slogan, also sometimes known as a strapline, is the last thing people see but the first thing they remember about a company. This makes them a powerful form of communication that has to be designed to leave a warm and lasting impression on your target audience.

More often than not, slogans are inherited, so you don't need to become involved with their conception. However, copywriting – like all forms of business life – is unpredictable and you may have to devise a slogan sooner than you think. How do you do that?

Well, firstly you have to consider the purpose of slogans:

- They add continuity to a campaign.
- They instil public confidence in a company.
- Finally, they act as a surrogate logo (a company's trademark) when logos are impractical (such as on radio commercials).

Slogans should be short. If possible, a message should be conveyed in under seven words, preferably in three to five. Slogans are conversational. They need to be memory joggers so that when a consumer considers making a purchase the slogan will remind them to consider a specific supplier.

Often slogans evolve from headlines or particularly succinct pieces of bodycopy. Over the years, I have noted a dozen different slogan observations.

The twelve slogans of constructive persuasion

1 **Slogans are about *you***
Successful slogans tend to use the word 'you' somewhere in the copy. Occasionally they may feature 'we', but if they do the overall benefit is still aimed at 'you', the consumer.
Directions
Your friendly cyber café.
ScotsdaleNorth.com
We always sell lower.

2 **Slogans make promises**
PenPod
Reliability on paper.
PenPod
Quality you can sign your name by.

3 Slogans call for action
ScotsdaleNorth.com
Click and enjoy.
Directions
.com and get it.

4 Slogans create ideals
PenPod
The little pen that does it all.

ScotsdaleNorth ice-cream
Don't you wish every day was a Sundae?

PenPod
If only life were this simple.

5 Slogans may rhyme
ScotsdaleNorth.com
Top for shops.
Directions
Meals that appeal

6 Slogans are 'it'
Go for it.	Buy it.
It's here.	It's now.
It's more.	It's less.
It's forever.	It's together.
Stick it.	You can't lick it.
You can't beat it.	You can't touch it.
It's hot.	Click it.
Believe it.	It's tasty.
It's cool.	It's the best.
It's yours.	It's everything.
Try it, you'll like it.	Be part of it.
Live it.	Help it help you.

7 Slogans are in a world of their own
PenPod
Step into a new writing dimension.
Enter a new world of writing.

8 Slogans can be full of alliterations
ScotsdaleNorth.com
Supremely Scottish Salmon.
Buy better. Buy bigger, by far.

9 In order to sell, slogans don't have to be clever
PenPod
The best pen you can buy.
The writer's choice.

10 Slogans conveniently package everything in one sentence
PenPod
Affordable reliability in your pocket.

ScotsdaleNorth.com
A world of shopping from your PC.

11 Slogans repeat key word patterns

ScotsdaleNorth.com
The right price. The best quality.

PenPod
The writing choice for the right occasion.

12 'The' slogan is king

The Best.	The greatest.
The One.	The Shape.
The Answer.	The experience.
The genuine article.	The One you need.
The industry's choice.	The Professional's choice.

Used subtly, slogans reinforce brand values. However, many adverts appear without slogans and are highly successful. (There is an argument that applying a slogan to a one-person business may be considered a little self-indulgent!) If you do have to work on a slogan, remember to keep it short and keep it sweet.

Measuring copy effectiveness

Bodycopy can be an uphill struggle to read. Over the years, various people have come up with methods or formulae to measure the readability of copy.

1 Academics who have contributed to this field include C.R. Haas, who produced two significant formulae: one to highlight the readability differences between literary texts and advertising copy, and another to evaluate the effectiveness of advertising copy based on the relative number of verbs and nouns.

2 Then there was R. Gunning. He devised the so-called Fog Index. This was based on the average length of sentences and the percentage of words with three or more syllables.

3 The Dale-Chall Index was a formula based on a list of 3000 words most easily understood by at least 80% of pupils in the 4th grade of post-World War II American schools. It took into account the average length of sentences. Like similar tests, the Dale-Chall Index and the Fog Index are sometimes used by copywriters who are particularly concerned about the readability of copy, although their use is becoming rarer.

The Flesch formula

One of the most commonly used readability tests is the Flesch formula, devised by Rudolph Flesch – an Austrian born in the USA (1911–86). Flesch is a good example to look at in greater detail.

Flesch provides a Reading Ease score based on four elements:

1 The average number of words per sentence.
2 The average word length (number of syllables per 100 words).
3 Percentage of personal words.
4 Percentage of personal sentences.

The Reading Ease (RE) score can vary between 0 and 100. It is inversely proportionate to the difficulty of the text that is being judged. The relationship between RE and difficulty is shown like this:

Level of difficulty	RE
Very difficult	Below 30
Difficult	30–49
Quite difficult	50–59
Average	60–69
Quite easy	70–79
Easy	80–89
Very easy	90 and above

Flesch's formula, which is adopted by most word processing grammar checkers, takes into account what many writers have always surmised: short sentences with short words are easy to read.

Flesch stressed the use of personal words and sentences to gain added reader interest. Personal words include words like 'guys', 'OK' and 'cheers' as well as personal pronouns and names. Personal sentences include spoken sentences with quotation marks as well as sentences addressed directly to the reader.

There are several drawbacks to Flesch's formula.

- First, it only works if your bodycopy is fairly long.
- Next, it assumes that every target audience wants to read colloquial copy or that the copy fits within a mass-market category. Just because your copy achieves a high readability score, it doesn't necessarily follow that it is suitable for your target audience. If it did, every writer would produce pithy sentences with short words.
- Also, the formula doesn't work in broadcast media, where the spoken word reigns supreme.
- Finally, it fails to judge the sales effectiveness of copy. It may read well, but does it provoke the reader to buy?

To its credit, however, you can use the formula as a fair indicator that the bodycopy is either quite readable or too stuffy for most people. It also warns you about imprecise writing – you should use 'The company' rather than 'The team'. Finally, it helps you to keep an eye on the lengths of your sentences.

Copy fitting

There are several ways to ensure that your copy will fit snugly into a specified space. Most designers and typographers rely on copy-fitting tables. These are mathematical mazes. First, you have to measure character lengths. Next you find the right pica (a unit of measurement used in typesetting) for the selected character. Finally, you multiply the number of characters to each pica by the length of line to be typeset. Believe me, if you think that sounds complicated, it is. Thankfully, there are other methods available.

You could count the average number of words per line, then multiply them by the number of lines per page to arrive at a final total. However, this system is unreliable when your sentences include long words (an extreme case would be 'pneumonoultramicroscopicsilicovolcanoconiosis' – the longest word in the *Oxford English Dictionary*, meaning a lung disease occasionally contracted by miners). And a humble, short word like 'a' can confuse matters.

The quick-fix copy fit

There is a way around all of this. Below are examples of type sizes ranging from 9-point type to 24-point type. Newspaper copy often uses 10–11-point type. Most business letters feature 12-point type. Of course, different type styles affect the space available on the paper. However, you can use the following as a good copy-fitting guide. Here's how it works:

> Firstly, decide what type size you wish to use – say, 12 point. This, including spaces, allows for 14 characters per 30 mm, so 135 mm will allow for 63 characters. Program your word processor to take 63 characters per line and you're off and running.

All you have to do from this stage is type until you have reached the permissible number of lines per page. If you are asked to write to a specified number of characters to a page, simply multiply 63 by the number of lines on the page. You can then see how close or how far off you are from your target figure.

Here are two examples to show you the difference type size makes:

9 point (Times)

Advertising has been described as the science of arresting the human intelligence long enough to get money from it. Mind you, few people at the beginning of the nineteenth century needed an adman to tell them what they wanted. At the end of the day, you can tell the ideals of a nation by its advertisements.

12 point (Times)

Advertising has been described as the science of arresting the human intelligence long enough to get money from it. Mind you, few people at the beginning of the nineteenth century needed an adman to tell them what they wanted. At the end of the day, you can tell the ideals of a nation by its advertisements.

Body-building quick tips

- Bodycopy should be either as long as the space that you have to write in, or as long as it takes to write a convincing and reasonable argument.
- A writer must put conviction into their own copy.
- Never oversell in your bodycopy.
- The first sentence of bodycopy is called the 'lead-in sentence'.
- Get quickly to the crux of your bodycopy message.
- Keep your line of thought on track.

- Address arguments before they arise.
- Write for your audience – not yourself.
- Remember the six elements of style (pp. 96–7).
- Use captions as directions within the bodycopy.
- Keep your copy user friendly.
- Present your bodycopy in a logical sequence that relates to the rest of the text.
- Use one of the twelve slogans for constructive persuasion (pp. 100–2).
- One way to measure copy readability is to use the Flesch formula (p. 103).

Over to you

1 Write six slogans which describe a friend.
2 Rewrite the first two paragraphs of the copy detailing the conditions of use of a credit card to make them sound chatty.
3 Rewrite a newspaper headline as if the subject were a product.
4 List twelve features of your left thumb.
5 Write a linked headline, lead-in sentence and closing sentence about a paper clip.
6 List the six elements of style.
7 Write an advertisement that never actually hints at any form of direct sale for an encyclopaedia.
8 Write six captions which could be read in sequence – without the support of bodycopy.

05

media and understanding its creative language

In this chapter you will learn
- how to gauge the effectiveness of media
- how to plan a media campaign
- how to write a classified ad
- how to write a recruitment ad
- how to write b2b copy
- how to use incentives
- how to write 'off the page' sales copy.

The table below outlines the features of different sections of the press.

Medium	Creative pros	Creative cons
Trade magazines	Relevant readership. Long shelf-life. Readers are searching for new ideas and announcements. Opportunity to be endorsed by a market's own official journal. Opportunity to address decision makers in a market sector. If the magazine is published monthly, you can take advantage of extra time to submit your final advertisement. Often the chance to include loose leaflets. (Ideal when you want your copy to stand away from the crowd or when you have a longer story to tell.)	Danger of too many magazines in each sector, which dilutes your creative impact. Some magazines lose editorial credibility by featuring too many adverts – this adversely affects circulation figures. Danger of advertising perceived to be supporting favourable editorial write-ups. In comparison to some mainstream consumer magazines, some trade magazines may be hindered by inferior reproduction qualities. In markets which are represented by one title alone, advertising costs can be relatively high and creative use of space restricted.
Consumer magazines	Ideal for attracting consumer enthusiasts such as car buyers, the health conscious, the fashion conscious, and so on. At the same time as attracting enthusiasts, you have a chance to broaden your readership. A chance to blend innovative copy with the latest trend-setting fads and styles.	Popular magazines may impose long-term copy dates (the copy day is when advertisements must be submitted by). Compared to newspapers, can be a costly way to reach an audience.

	Often good reproduction for photography. The opportunity to include loose or bound material inside the magazine.	
National press	Your message is reinforced by the credibility and urgency of news items. Excellent national coverage. High believability factor. A better chance of securing an innovative use of creative space on the page.	You're up against lots of other ads. You need to feature in more than one paper to gain blanket national coverage. Depending on your design, creative impact can be enhanced or reduced by predominantly black-and-white advertisements. Poor colour reproduction in the main newspaper. Messages are flicked through rather than studied (except in week-end newspapers, as the reader has more time to enjoy them).
Local press	Good for targeting locals. Loyal readership. Copy is often quite friendly in its approach. Adverts can be big on a page while economical in cost.	Reproduction can be poor. Too many free-circulation local papers hindering your message. Limited or non-existent use of colour. Editorial is often light in substance. (This has an adverse effect on the general creative quality of advertising.)

The Web	Fastest growing medium of all time. High personalization. Immediacy. Interactivity. Ideal for combining text with audio and video. Enlivens a brand message. The world's biggest direct marketing tool.	Intrusive. Can be difficult to navigate. Needs a PC or GPRS technology. Pages can be relatively slow to download (unless you can be sure your audience has 3G or broadband technology). Hyped up. Banner ads are often totally ignored.
Television	Reaches people directly in their homes. Viewers are usually relaxed and therefore open minded to creative propositions. Excellent national coverage. Thanks to satellite, excellent for international markets. Immediate short-term results. Flexibility to target a commercial to appear at a set time and within a specific type of programme schedule (e.g. breakfast cereal commercials can be highly effective when shown during morning television programmes). A commercial can be shown regionally. The greatest possible opportunity for 'all singing, all dancing' and for especially entertaining creative communications.	Production can be incredibly expensive. Transmission air time can be equally expensive (although the growth in cable and satellite channels is making it a more financially viable option – see Web TV below). Can take several months to make a sustained long-term creative impact. Creative messages have to be sensitive to the greater viewing public who may tune in (e.g. children who may watch before the so-called watershed at 9 p.m.). Open to wide creative criticism. Too gimmicky.

	Excellent for extending a creative theme into another medium. Can refer to offers in other media (e.g. watch the commercial and clip the coupon in the press). Web TV is highly interactive – combines best of broadcasting with best of narrowcasting, direct to the home.	
Radio	Very loyal listeners. Local and national coverage. Marvellous creative possibilities using sound to stimulate the imagination. Far cheaper than television. Immediate impact. Digital broadcasting – opens up further opportunities for interactive advertising. Quick production times.	A danger of too many radio stations diluting the initial creative impact. Short creative life. Relies solely on one sense – sound. The listener can't actually see what you are offering.
Posters	Big, dramatic, colourful images. Excellent for building awareness. Copy can be reduced to one powerful headline.	You may have to book space several months in advance. Except regular local traffic, you can never be 100% sure about who sees your creative message. Image is often more important than copy.

	Mobile billboards ensure precise targeting.	You generally do not have the time to provide detailed copy.
	Special billboards can include anything from 3D objects to Web links.	
Cinema	Ideal for targeting the youth and younger adult market.	Audience attendance is variable.
	Good for attracting locals. Big screen excitement.	You have to rely on a 'big' movie to pull in substantial audiences.
	Ideal for reinforcing awareness to an audience in relaxed frame of mind.	Production costs can be as high as advertising costs.
	Unique audience ambience.	

The advertising industry map can be divided into three territories.

1 The first is ruled by the advertiser. The servants are the agencies and media.
2 The second territory is governed by the agencies. Here, associated suppliers like TV commercial producers and printers group together with media owners to sell their wares to the advertising agencies.
3 The final territory is dominated by media owners who take decisions according to the needs of their audience – readers, surfers, viewers and listeners. They rely on advertisers' budgets to serve those needs and extend their territory to accommodate an even larger audience.

Together, all three make up a thriving community whose members depend on each other for survival. The advertisers want to reach the maximum number of appropriate people. So a medium has to be editorially as well as commercially attractive to a specific audience. This requires investment, which calls for more advertising.

Advertising feeds the media with the financial support to attract a bigger readership. The media feed the audience with editorial that attracts greater interest.

The audience feeds the advertiser with sales leads which attract a bigger percentage of an advertising budget.

The media are split into two categories: above-the-line media and below-the-line media. The 'line' originally referred to the commission paid to advertising agencies for booking advertisements in mainstream media like the press, television, cinema, posters and radio.

- All above-the-line media paid commission directly to the agencies.
- Below-the-line suppliers – such as direct mailing companies, design agencies, incentive brokers and sales promotion specialists – did not pay commission, so the agencies invoiced a service charge to clients.

Today, most suppliers are willing to pay commissions to agencies, and areas such as direct marketing use above-the-line media such as television and radio. So the term 'through-the-line' has been created. It covers *any* aspect of communication media. (See Chapter 6.)

Did you know?
Your choice of above-the-line media is staggering. To take websites alone, there are in excess of one billion pages on the Web, with more being added as you read this sentence.

Deciding which media to select for an advertising campaign can be daunting. Each working day, thousands of media salespeople contact companies aiming to sell the virtues of a particular medium. Countless deals are struck, offering everything from full-page discounts to discounts for multiple Webvert impressions.

So how do you draw up a short list of media?

- First, look at your bank account. How much money can you invest in communicating your message?
- Next, return to your targeting parameters. Which media offer the greatest number of appropriate readers, viewers or listeners for the project? You should remember that mass-market media like TV and the national press may offer lots of readers or viewers. However, you have to ask how many of

those people will actually be interested in your product or service. (The Web offers both a mass market and a direct market – particular care is needed when deciding where you advertise.) It boils down to quality as well as quantity. Which media offer the greatest value for money, dollar for prospect?

- The tighter your budget, the narrower you or your client's media choice. Small budgets tend to direct advertisers towards concentrating all their buying power (often termed 'media spend') into one specific media title. The broader your budget, the wider your media potential. Often larger-scale advertisers with substantial budgets target media in an upside-down funnel-like formation: the high-cost items (TV, cinema) at the wide opening of the funnel, the lower-cost items at the neck.

- Broad awareness is needed to launch a product or to speak to the mass population. The more a budget is concentrated into one narrow target area, the greater the chance of making that area profitable.

ScotsdaleNorth's traditional retailing may promote its range of coffees in a broad awareness campaign. However, it may also promote its special Italian super-strength coffee to targeted coffee drinkers.

Each level in the funnel complements the next. The copy in a TV commercial may refer a consumer to a press advertisement, a press advertisement may refer the consumer to a sales promotion and so on. In order to re-enforce the strength of the message, creative elements used in one medium are often shared with another. For example:

A poster may feature a specific scene from a TV commercial. Through doing this, the power of the commercial is reinforced by the strength of the poster and vice versa. One reminds the consumer of the other.

Getting the right mix of media is as essential as pruning the creative solution to its core benefit. After all, it would be fruitless to produce a stunning piece of creativity if it were communicated via an unsuitable medium. (Refer to *Teach Yourself Marketing* for more information.)

Arguably, media planning is beyond the realm of the responsibility held by a copywriter. However, given the fact that poor media selection can ruin a great piece of creative work, it is important to understand the basic process of media planning. That way you can avoid pitfalls before they appear.

The eight steps to effective media planning

115
media and understanding
its creative language
05

1 Will it enhance the creative work?
   Can you answer 'Yes' to the following?

   • Is it targeted at the group that is addressed by the copy and visual?
   • Does the medium allow for elements like colour or coupons?
   • Will the general editorial style be in keeping with the copy's tone of voice?

2 Media penetration
   Does the medium deliver *fewer* people who are *unlikely* to become customers?

3 Prove it
   Consider the medium's track record. Have other advertisers who produce similar products used it? If so, and most importantly if they used it consistently, the chances are strong that it is a good vehicle. You can track the type of advertiser who has appeared in a medium through contacting an organization called the Media Register. They can supply relevant data showing who has advertised in which media, including TV and radio as well as some overseas media.

4 What's the 'hit' rate like?
   How often can your target audience see your advertisement? Opportunity to see (known as OTS) isn't a quality-led judgement. It doesn't consider whether an audience pays particular attention to the contents of a magazine and style of copy, for example. It is more concerned with the number of times the audience is able to see the advertisement. Specific interest would be governed by the type of reader and whether that person identifies with the content and style of the magazine.

   If you plan to write an advertisement to appear in a specific magazine, how do you choose the publication? Is it the kind of magazine that is published only every now and again but is constantly referred to by the readership? A good example of this kind is the type of magazine you find in a dentist's surgery – great for longer bodycopy. Do you want your product to be repeatedly seen by an audience or is your message more suitable for a one-off appearance, perhaps in a national newspaper?

The share of the Web targeted audience is sometimes called MindShare or Eyeball Share. You can learn more about this in Chapter 12. It would also be worth your while to read *Successful Cybermarketing in a Week.*

5 Does it whisper or does it shout?

How targeted is the medium? For instance, if you are writing about vegetarian restaurant dining, would it be appropriate to place an advertisement in a regional paper which covers the restaurant's locale? Or would it be better to place the advertisement in a magazine?

6 Back to back, who comes out front?

Comparing it to another kind of medium, list the proposed medium's advantages. Don't get confused into comparing one title against another – for example two magazines.

7 Describe the audience

Precisely whom is the medium targeted towards? List their ages, sex, income, job type and social grading. (Refer to 'Social categorization' on p. 57.) You could take the media owner's word about the audience profile or you could refer to figures supplied by an organization such as JICNARS (the Joint Industry Committee for National Readership Surveys).

There is more advice about this in the section below, 'Further sources of media statistics'.

8 Add more ingredients for success

You may wish to use more than one medium. Although your product is aimed at a particular person (user), the potential buyer may be someone else. For example, if ScotsdaleNorth wants to promote its own brand of healthy foods, it could place the advertisement in a woman's magazine, yet your copy could discuss the health benefits for men with high cholesterol.

Additional media also enhance the funnel effect discussed at the start of this section. In the example of the ScotsdaleNorth healthy-eating campaign, during the course of a typical day the housewife may be exposed to a message several times via several media.

Wakes up
Hears a radio commercial
Sees a TV commercial
Reads a press advertisement
Receives a direct mail promotion

Takes the kids to school
Hears another radio commercial
Drives past a roadside poster

Mid-morning
Sees a TV commercial
Hears a radio commercial

Lunch
Reads a magazine advertisement
Surfs the Web – spots a banner ad

Afternoon
Goes shopping
Sees an in-store promotion

Picks the kids up from school
Hears a radio commercial
Passes a poster

Evening
Sees a TV commercial
Participates in Web TV contest
Serves the healthy meal

Further sources of media statistics

If you need to find out more about your choice of media, you can refer to several key organizations.

BARB

The Broadcasters' Audience Research Board calculates terrestrial as well as satellite TV audience figures. It is based on a combination of special TV-set monitoring equipment and diaries completed by members of households who make up the sample audience. BARB takes into account video recording, sex and age, even including the age of any guest who visits the home of a member of the sample audience.

TGI

The Target Group Index is operated by the British Market Research Bureau. It draws upon the questionnaire that is completed annually by many thousands of adults. It details demographic and media exposure information. The results highlight key data on hundreds of product fields, ranging from washing-up liquid to beers.

ABC

The Audit Bureau of Circulation carries out an audit on UK press circulation figures. It can work on a daily, weekly, monthly or bi-annual basis. It finds an average audited net sale by calculating the final figure after complimentary copies and copies sold for less than the cover price are deducted from a print run.

VFD

Verified Free Distribution figures are produced by the ABC. The data show the circulation of free newspapers which are either delivered door-to-door to households or handed out in the street. The figures can be segmented regionally.

MEAL

Media Expenditure Analysis Ltd publish quarterly reports showing the estimated media spending on TV as well as in the press. They estimate company advertising budgets and show where advertising appears.

Other types of media analysis data include:
• JICPAR – Joint Industry Committee for Poster Audience Research.
• OSCAR – Outdoor Site Classification and Research, outdoor advertising association.
• PETA – Pan-European TV Audience Research.
• CAVIAR – Cinema and Video Industry Audience Research, deals with cinema audience figures.

The press up close

This section deals with different aspects of specialized press advertising.

Recruitment advertising

Recruitment advertising is often much maligned by copywriters as not being creative enough for their needs. However, it is surprising just how many great copywriters started their craft in the recruitment advertising industry. Person-wanted ads are more than simple employment announcements. They reflect a company's expansion plans. Every new job is an example of how the organization is helping the community through providing job opportunities and how it is investing for the future.

Recruitment advertising falls into four categories:

1 The first is the standard line advertisement which you often find towards the back of publications.
2 The second is the box or classified ad which literally boxes in the copy, thereby giving the advertisement a much greater page presence.
3 The third is the display advertisement. This provides the greatest creative opportunities – but at the greatest advertising placement cost.
4 The fourth is the multi-media approach. This often utilizes radio in addition to press advertising.

1 Line ads

Line ads usually accommodate two to three lines (up to thirty words) of copy which describe the job opportunity. With such tight restrictions you have to make sure that your requirements are clear and to the point.

First, assuming that you have thirty words to work with, deduct the copy that provides response details (like your email address). Never feature a lengthy address as this is a waste of words; instead always feature a telephone number and URL (uniform resource locator). Allowing for telephone codes, that reduces the words to twenty-seven. Is it essential that you include a name to contact? If it is, you have to deduct a further one or two words. Now you are left with only twenty-five words to convey your message.

Let's assume that ScotsdaleNorth.com is looking for a Web warehouse manager. Before you write any bodycopy, consider the main requirements that you are looking for in a candidate. For example:

1 Aged 25 to 50 years.	4 Fit.
2 Experienced.	5 Good manager.
3 Qualified.	6 Available for shift duties.

Out of these six attributes, how many are *essential* for the job? Perhaps you are able to narrow the list down to:

- Good manager
- Aged 25 to 50 years
- Available for shift duties

Next, think about three key adjectives that describe the kind of person you want. For example:

> CONSCIENTIOUS. THOROUGH. CHEERFUL.

Finally, think of three key adjectives that describe the kind of work lifestyle that the warehouse manager would experience. For example:

1 Hectic
2 Rewarding
3 Enjoyable

Combine the two:

> CONSCIENTIOUS, EXPERIENCED SHIFT WAREHOUSE MANAGER
> AGED 25 TO 50 REQUIRED TO WORK IN A BUSY YET REWARDING
> SCOTSDALENORTH.COM WEB DEPOT. CALL 123 4567.

The finishing touch is to embolden the job title and perhaps the contact number.

> CONSCIENTIOUS, EXPERIENCED SHIFT **WAREHOUSE MANAGER**
> AGED 25 TO 50 REQUIRED TO WORK IN A BUSY YET REWARDING
> SCOTSDALENORTH.COM WEB DEPOT. **CALL 123 4567.**

Often, publishers suggest that the first few words are emboldened. You could allow for this. However, featuring the emboldened job title a few words within the copy helps make the entire advertisement more effective.

If you simply cannot accommodate all your message in such a small space, you can either move up to a classified box advertisement or opt for an alternative solution that is becoming popular. I call it the Read 'n' Ring recruitment advertisement. Explained simply, your advertisement includes the most basic details and then invites the reader to phone a special number for a complete job specification. For example:

> FOR A REWARDING **WEB WAREHOUSE MANAGEMENT** OPPORTUNITY
> WITH ONE OF THE COUNTRY'S LEADING RETAIL CHAINS,
> **CALL 123 4567** FOR A PROFITABLE WORD IN YOUR EAR.

2 The box or classified advertisement

Box advertisements provide even greater impact on the page. Although they allow more words, they are best managed by using their extra space through incorporating fewer words.

Remember, be clear about the job title and precise about the candidate profile.

> **Warehouse Manager** Conscientious, experienced, aged 25 to 50, required to work in a busy yet rewarding ScotsdaleNorth.com Web depot. *Call 123 4567.*

Notice how using fewer words makes greater use of the box's available space.

> **Warehouse Manager**
> Aged 25 to 50 for a busy yet rewarding ScotsdaleNorth.com Web depot. *Call 123 4567.*

3 The display advertisement

Display recruitment advertisements provide the space, scope and positioning to make the maximum impact on a recruitment page. This gives candidates – as well as any competitive organization seeing the advertisement – a favourable impression.

The display advertisement has three features essential for success:

- Consistent and dynamic borders
- Relevant graphics
- Succinct copy

Borders

In the section 'Let's get down to the nitty-gritty' (p. 71), I mentioned the importance of consistency in borders. This is particularly relevant in recruitment advertising, which has to make each display-format recruitment advertisement do several tasks:

- Advertise the job vacancy.
- Reinforce presence in the marketplace.
- In some cases, demonstrate to shareholders and the public that the organization is prospering.

Borders can incorporate logos, twisted perimeter lines – in fact, as long as they operate within the space available on the page, borders can be stretched to the limits of your imagination and the frontiers of style dictated by those concerned. In order to make a recruitment advertisement as distinctive as possible, always try to use typography creatively.

Relevant graphics
Poor use of graphics can spoil an otherwise well-planned display advertisement. A common mistake is to show people at work. It is obvious that people work at the organization. Instead, why not show fringe benefits of their job? An air stewardess could be shown using her free time to live it up in the big city.

Succinct copy
Copy needs to be succinct. Traditionally, display recruitment advertising follows a formal order of contents. These are set out below.

Display recruitment advertising's order of contents

1 Headline featuring job title, geographical location of office and, depending on the salary, the salary level. Usually the bigger the financial reward, the greater the need to include it in the headline.
2 Introduction paragraph of about forty to fifty words about the company and its caring attitude towards employees, as well as its success story to date.
3 Whom the candidate reports to and who in the company reports to the candidate. This provides an idea of seniority of the role.
4 What the key tasks involve.
5 What key attributes are needed to perform the tasks.
6 How the job will help the candidate achieve something personally as well as contribute something corporately.
7 A summary of the educational qualifications, work experience and personal qualities required.

8 Instructions on whom to contact and where to send a CV.
9 The contact address details.

123
media and understanding
its creative language 05

4 The multi-media approach

Traditionally this approach combines press advertising and radio commercials. Depending on the general state of the economy, this kind of recruitment advertising falls in and out of fashion. Currently, the mode is to list various jobs in press adverts and provide complete details, including the option to send a CV, via the Web.

Chapter 9 provides details about producing an effective radio commercial. The main point to bear in mind when creating a recruitment radio commercial is that it should work in tandem with press advertising. The close of the commercial should refer the listener to the appropriate advertisements in the press. Also, the copy technique of including

- who is wanted ...
- where ...
- for what reward ...

should be applied on the radio as well as within the press advertisement.

On the Web, never write more than an 80-word three-paragraph description of the job. This is because surfers naturally want copy to be succinct. If you are asking the surfer to submit a CV, make sure your server and browser technology can read NT, Windows and Mac formats. (If a surfer may be submitting in Mac, always include a line of copy which instructs them to name the CV as .doc file.)

Recruitment advertising quick tips

- State the job title clearly in the headline.
- Make sure your copy is not discriminatory by sex, religion or race.
- Check which media produce the best response. You can achieve this through incorporating a code in the advertisement.
- Highlight the company's achievements and goals.
- Refer to salary, experience and qualifications.
- Consider testing your advertisement in several media.
- Make your copy appealing and enthusiastic.

• Set out the potential employee's long-term career and additional financial benefits.

Over to you

1 Write a recruitment advertisement for a prime minister.
2 Explain what MEAL stands for.
3 Name an advantage and a disadvantage of television advertising.
4 What are the three media territories of the advertising industry?

Business-to-business press advertising

Business-to-business advertising is a vast subject area. There are hundreds upon hundreds of specialist trade publications dealing with everything from accountancy to zoo management. Advertisers who use trade publications fall into three broad categories:

1 **Sellers of materials and products or of the equipment to process those materials**
The first category uses business- and industry-specific magazines either to highlight a new product or endorse the credibility of an existing one. This kind of advertising tactically influences a specific professional sector. Once you can prove that those within an industry choose your product or service above another, you can influence others such as distributors and retailers as well as the end consumer.

2 **Sellers of services to help run a company's operations**
These include software, accountancy and office equipment. This category employs business magazines to inform one industry sector about another industry's products or services. For example, a financial software company advertises an accountancy computer program for accountants in the relevant business press.

3 **Resellers (the sales channel, i.e. the resellers and retailers of goods and services)**
The third category is aimed at the person who resells the product to make a direct profit. This audience is the front-line interface between you or your client and the ultimate consumer. Your creative message to them has to incorporate

product enhancements as well as to encourage loyalty through ongoing promotions.

Highly targeted business-to-business campaigns often feature direct mail. This is because direct mail is a precise form of targeting and has the added bonus of being something that can be filed away by a potential customer, for future reference.

Trade magazines have an equally important role. Through them, you are able to:
- create awareness
- invite a response for further information by using some kind of response device.

Keep an 'I' on business copy

To solicit an appropriate response your copy has to:
- Influence the decision makers.
- Inform those people about your product or service benefits.
- Instruct those people on how to contact you.

Trade advertising encourages distributors and retailers to specify your brand. It requires copy that pushes one of the following:
- The commodity or product.
- The promotional offer.
- The bottom-line profit margin.

Job specification categories

Typically, business-to-business advertising copy addresses:
1 *Users*, like secretaries or mechanical operators who want to try out a product.
2 *Choosers*, like purchasing managers who have the power to place an order.
3 *Proprietors*, like directors who have the authority to sign the cheques.

A fourth category, *Investors*, like shareholders, are addressed in corporate advertising.

THE USER WANTS TO READ COPY THAT SHOWS HOW
A PRODUCT WORKS.

THE CHOOSER WANTS TO READ COPY THAT DEMONSTRATES
AFFORDABILITY.

THE PROPRIETOR WANTS TO READ COPY THAT HIGHLIGHTS TRUST
AND INTEGRITY.

THE INVESTOR WANTS REASSURANCE THAT THE COMPANY IS MAKING
THE RIGHT PROFIT-DRIVEN DECISIONS.

Job title	Target group	'I' want	Your copy offers
Secretary/ administrator	User	Efficiency Supply Reliability	Competence Willingness Trust
Sales person	User	Support Results Credibility	Encouragement Reassurance Qualification
Technician	User	Performance Adaptability Maintenance	Demonstration Tailor-made for you Guarantees
Manager	Chooser	Service Speed Economy	Dependability Proficiency Competitiveness
Director	Proprietor	Trust Stability Control	Integrity Certainty Character
(Corporate advertising) Shareholder	Investor	Experience Direction Profit	Knowledge Objectivity Optimism

The smaller your business, the greater the chance that Users are also Choosers.

The overwhelming difference between trade and business advertising on the one hand and consumer advertising on the other is that your copy has to answer the question 'What's in it for me?' Your creative challenge is to combine the hard corporate commercial messages with softer mass-market appeal.

The headline:

> **PENPOD MEANS BUSINESS**

offers a promise of further business for the industry but it lacks direct association with a specific promotion.

> **PICK UP A PENPOD**

may be a neat message for the ultimate user, but it isn't really all that relevant to the retailer. However

> **BUSINESS PICKS UP WITH PENPOD**

offers one route by which you can combine the two messages and at the same time stimulate the retailer.

Even if you write copy that complements the consumer campaign, don't leave it at that. There's no real reason why a trade advertisement should have less time and effort spent on its production than a consumer advertisement. Show the industry that you mean business.

One of the important things to watch for when writing a trade-press advertisement is to avoid falling into an open trap. Just because you or your client may spend a great sum of money directing your advertising towards the consumer by using, for example, TV, the Web or the press, you can't ignore trade advertising. The trade is your support. The people behind the counter ultimately sway the people in front.

Every sentence you write will be studied in detail. Each fact will be checked for accuracy. Of course, if as a copywriter you knew everything there was to know about every single subject you ever wrote about, you would be in line to pick up a special sort of Nobel Prize. Instead, simply carry out as much research as reasonably possible and never be afraid to seek further information. Nine times out of ten, people will respect you for asking and dismiss you for not. The worst thing you can do is to try to fob off the trade reader with clever prose when commercial facts will suffice.

Conducting research for trade-style copywriting

There is an old joke concerning a man who went into a shop and asked, 'Do you take anything off for cash?'

The shop-keeper replied, 'Sir, I think you have the wrong shop – you want the striptease joint next door.'

The point of this (let's face it, not so very rib-ticklingly funny) story is that, as with all forms of copywriting, you have to understand the language of the business sector you are writing for. More importantly, you have to be sure that the sector will understand the jargon.

Each business sector has its own vocabulary. Professionals within a specific area prefer their particular industry language. Nevertheless, however much jargon you use, you should always balance it with user-friendly copy, within the sector's acceptable creative bounds.

Pictures and illustrations should also be industry friendly. Only show what is relevant to your message. If, for example, you want to demonstrate a printing machine to a printer, feature graphics that highlight the mechanics rather than the gleaming body work. (Sparkling machines don't necessarily add up to sparkling results.)

Keep your business copy human

You may recollect that earlier in this book I told you about the virtues of using 'you' in your bodycopy – especially for bigger companies requiring corporate-type advertising. Remember too that you should tone down the use of informal language. Indeed, make a point of writing in a formal style. Often corporate-type business-to-business advertising is directed to a person who, if they are at all interested in what you are saying, will pass it on to a colleague whose job is to delve further. They want facts, not chat, so avoid humour in business-to-business advertising. Anyway, if you can't take your own product or service seriously, how can you expect anyone else to view you as a professional copywriter earnestly? Balance a friendly tone of voice with a powerful and convincing fact-led commercial proposition.

Examples of specialized industries that have specific vocabulary include:

- the financial sector
- the medical sector
- the legal profession
- chemical and mechanical engineering
- Information Technology.

The key to writing for each of these sectors is to allow your creative language to enhance rather than engulf a factual message. For example:

An advertisement directed towards doctors treating asthma

Headline *(creative approach)*:

Asilaz.
A breath of fresh air for doctors.

Bodycopy *(factual)*:

The combined active ingredients of silbutalmol, bricanontl and sodium cromoglycate in Asilaz deliver immediate relief for asthma sufferers. Recent tests carried out by the British Pharmacy Association show that when compared to traditional asthmatic treatments containing compounds such as droxy 7 or betamac, Asilaz delivers a relieving 20% improvement in bronchial congestion. As with all similar products, it is recommended that patients follow dosage and treatment instructions as specified on the label.

Logo

Asilaz

Recommended dosage – one spray twice a day.

Strapline *(creative)*:

Delivering relief.

Retaining your trade reader's interest

Business people are out to make money. That requires an investment in time and effort. Time the immediacy of your message to match a business person's busy lifestyle. Don't waste people's time by requiring them to grapple with clever headlines or subheads which are clever for the sake of it. If your proposition is relevant, then, and only then, will the reader consider investing time in studying your copy. Once such a commitment has been made by the trade reader, you will discover that they are much more willing to extend that investment by reading longer copy than the average consumer will.

How to handle falling sales

Trade advertising can combat declining sales. For example:

> Toothpaste manufacturers are constantly improving their products. It is not uncommon for one brand of toothpaste to be found less effective than a newer brand. Sales decline. Market share begins to decay.

In terms of copy, what should the manufacturer do to address this? One way is to challenge the findings of the newer brand indirectly through organizing an independent research project. The manufacturer could inform the trade that latest tests prove the effectiveness of brushing with the original brand as opposed to the newer brand. Of course, the research has to be conclusive and indisputable.

If you can't beat 'em, another way to combat falling sales is to announce a modified toothpaste.

> Headline: **WITH AN EVEN BIGGER BITE OF THE MARKET MORE CUSTOMERS THAN EVER ARE SAYING AAH!**

The bodycopy for this advert explains how the company has improved the toothpaste's ingredients as well as offering greater trade offers.

Once you have relaunched the toothpaste, adapt the new USP (in this case, unbeatable cleaning power, better trade discounts) into an entire trade campaign. You could include point-of-sale material such as cardboard cut-outs, price-reduction coupons for distribution to the public and so on. (For more details see p. 38.)

When a product is not sufficiently differentiated from other similar competitive products, sales promotion can concentrate on incentives and display material available to the reseller.

> LEAFLET TO TRADE ABOUT TOOTHPASTE BRAND
> **10% MORE IN EVERY TUBE FOR YOU AND YOUR CUSTOMERS**
> POINT-OF-SALE FOR THE COUNTER
> **10% MORE IN EVERY TUBE**

Of course, the toothpaste may be just one of literally scores of products produced by a company. Advertising each brand separately in the trade press would be costly and frankly a waste of three invaluable business commodities: time, effort and money.

Why not consider advertising the umbrella brand within which the toothpaste is a successful product in its own right? Try to position the product as part of a bigger picture.

> TINGLE TOOTHPASTE – FROM SCOTSDALENORTH.COM
> – THE PEOPLE'S CHOICE.

What if your own product is neither part of a multi-national company's portfolio of brands nor fits neatly into the category of 'me too' types of product? An example of this is PenPod. In this case, the trade needs to be reassured that apart from being innovative, the product has distribution and marketing support that makes it a viable product to stock. Above all, you need to produce trade advertising that anticipates genuine potential profit.

> Headline:
> PENPOD. WE'RE INVESTING £700,000 WORTH OF MEDIA
> SPENDING TO GET YOUR CUSTOMERS WRITING OFF FOR MORE.

In Chapter 4 (see p. 94) I discussed keeping one step ahead of your reader by tackling difficult questions before they arise. This is particularly helpful when you want to placate the business user. Your ultimate customer may be concerned with everything from security to durability. You can address these concerns effectively by highlighting a possible problem up front. For example:

> Headline:
> INFERIOR COMPUTER BACK-UP DISKS CAN CAUSE YOU TO
> LOSE MORE THAN A GOOD NIGHT'S SLEEP.
> Subhead:
> XYZ DISKS ARE GUARANTEED NEVER TO LET YOU DOWN.
> Bodycopy:
> Losing data is a nightmare. Now you can sleep easy. XYZ
> have produced the most effective back-up disks ever. They
> are certified 100% error free under our 10-year warranty …

Corporate-style press advertising

Corporate advertising has to achieve much more than just announcing products or educating a market about product use.

It may need to do one or more of five things:

1 Explain a company's policy direction

It may be important to demonstrate a company's open culture of discussing its exciting plans for ever-expanding market penetration with the people who will be responsible for helping the organization implement those schemes (retailers, wholesalers, distributors and so on).

New directions may involve new markets. They may entail announcing joint ventures with companies that make products complementary to the ones that you or your client already produce. (An example would be a digital camera manufacturer who links up with an ISP.) You may plan to expand into new markets by enhancing the features of an existing product or service. For example:

Teach Yourself Books (professional division); Teach Yourself Tapes; Teach Yourself Kits; Teach Yourself Away Days; Teach Yourself DVDs.

2 Endorse sub-brands

Creative corporate endorsement copy comes into its own when you promote umbrella brands. Such advertisements need not be directed solely at the trade. For example:

Headline:

**Since first opening up shop 100 years ago,
we've put a few extra products onto our shelves.**

(Picture of original interior of small ScotsdaleNorth corner shop with proud shop-keeper in front of shelves, stocking a couple of dozen products.)

Lead-in bodycopy:

To be exact, 37,481 own brand products ...

3 Instil confidence

There are numerous creative messages that can instil confidence. One is to discuss outstanding levels of service, as in this PenPod advertisement:

Headline:

> **After 9 days, 2 cartridge refills and 2.7 miles of ink,
> Bob decided to exchange his PenPod for another model.
> (No questions asked.)**

Lead-in copy:

> Bob loved using his PenPod. Yet, even when he bought it, he was never sure which model he liked best – the 'Sleeker', the 'Styler' or the 'Gripper'. Thanks to our no-nonsense 10 days' money-back guarantee promise, Bob swapped his PenPod without any problem.

Another method is to discuss a company's excellent track record:

> *An advertisement for ScotsdaleNorth.com*
>
> Headline:
>
> **1959
> Mrs Jones insists on doing all her shopping at
> Scotsdale Northside**
>
> (Picture of Mrs Jones shopping at her local ScotsdaleNorth corner shop.)
>
> **2009
> Her granddaughter Mrs Smith can't find any reason to
> change a family tradition.**
>
> (Picture of her granddaughter in 2009, surfing website.)
>
> Lead-in copy:
>
> Just like her mother and her grandmother before, Mrs Jean Smith does her weekly shopping at her local ScotsdaleNorth.
>
> True – over the years, our product range has improved radically. However, some things remain the same today as they have always been: great food, discount prices, terrific service …

4 Show ability

Copy can demonstrate how a company professionally fulfilled the tallest of orders:

> *An advertisement for PenPod*
>
> Headline:
>
> **When the British Antarctic Team order PenPods**
> **They don't want to be left on ice**
>
> Lead-in copy:
>
> On 9th February 2008 we received an email for 50 PenPods to be dispatched post haste to the South Pole.
>
> It was from the British Antarctic Team. They chose PenPod because of its proven reliability even at −60°F. Captain Johnson, the team leader, needed supplies within 48 hours. He didn't want excuses.
>
> We met the demand ...

> *An advertisement for ScotsdaleNorth – traditional*
>
> Headline:
>
> **Everything checks out perfectly – just ask Sandra.**
>
> (Picture of housewife at check-out with Sandra, the check-out girl.)
>
> Lead-in copy:
>
> It's Sandra's job to ensure that our customers' groceries are speedily and efficiently packed and priced, saving them time and hassle.

5 **Empathize with a businessperson's own goals and concerns**
Business people are beset by daily challenges. Ideally, each problem should be turned into an opportunity. On behalf of your client, your copy has to demonstrate how a product or service can help turn those opportunities into profits:

> **Give business people a break.**
>
> | *Most business people want to be ...* | *Creatively, your message should demonstrate ...* |
> | --- | --- |
> | Rich | Financial credibility |
> | Efficient | Business support |
> | Confident | The ability to meet deadlines |
> | Respected | A tried and tested heritage |
> | Innovative | Investment in the future |

Competitive	Market understanding
A leader	The choice of the professional
Successful	A sound track record
Popular	The preferred choice
Technically competent	Leading-edge products or services

Typical key creative corporate feel-good phrases often sound a little cheesy. They may include:

- We're on your side.
- We react to your needs.
- Helping you to help your customers.
- The right choice.
- Just call, we'll answer.
- We want you to win.
- Your partner in (the industry *not* crime!).
- By your side.
- Committed to your success.
- We help you make it happen.

Addressing managers

Managers have a strictly defined agenda, to meet deadlines and make deals. In order to satisfy commercial demands they need to be worldly wise. They have to keep in touch with industrial news as well as international news. They read leading newspapers, surf the Web, browse through trade journals. They are influenced by trends. They set standards.

Accordingly, your copy has to be sharp, appreciative of their needs and modern in context. Visuals should be dynamic and people-centric. Bodycopy content frequently incorporates a promise of achievement: to become the all-round, totally professional person (thanks to whatever the product or service may be).

Management- and executive-targeted copy needs to demonstrate that you are on 'their' side without sounding grovelling or insincere. It has to present a goal and provide the facts by way of the product or service. For example:

(Picture of luxurious executive car cruising along a motorway at sunrise.)

Headline:

The meeting is 7.30 a.m.
For the discerning few, the ride ahead will be
exceptionally smooth.

However turbulent the meeting ahead, thanks to your new turbo-powered Pastiche 2001 you can face the music in considerable style.

Car Choice magazine described the new Pastiche 2001 series as 'the ultimate Executive car'.

Everything about it is special. Beneath the bonnet sits a razor-sharp 2.3 litre multi-valve engine. It purrs a panther-like performance, which if the law permitted could pounce at exhilarating speeds of up to 130 mph within a cat's whisker of 0–60 in 8 seconds. Yet unruffled acceleration is never compromised by ambient noise. Fuel is sipped, never guzzled – providing an astounding 61.2 mpg at a steady 56 mph – even with its catalytic converter.

Step inside and relax in one of the luxurious leather-upholstered colour co-ordinated seats. Each features computer-controlled air-sprung cushioned support as well as side impact air cushions – tested to standards which easily exceed the legal minimum requirement. So you can enjoy comforting peace of mind.

The driver's console is clearly defined, combining hi-specification features like air conditioning, multi-play all-round speakers CD drive, central door locking and electric window power – all at finger-tip reach.

Your passengers will feel equally at home with on-board integrated seat-mounted television. There is even a fold-away courtesy work desk for any last-minute paperwork.

Other captivating features include alloy wheels, heat-sensitive electronic sunroof and ABS braking, all fitted as standard.

Why not arrange for a test drive today? Just call 0800 00 200. It could be one of the smoothest management decisions you've ever made.

137
media and understanding
its creative language

05

> **Did you know?**
> This type of tough management creative approach was particularly popular in the 1990s.

During the so-called 'Caring Nineties', as well as the 'Noughties' (the first decade of this century), management attitudes changed radically. Expressions like 'hands-on management' (meaning a manager who gets physically involved with the business at all levels) were replaced with terms like 'hands-off management' (meaning everything is delegated to someone else). Advertising reacted by addressing issues in a different way. Of course copywriters never took this too far; if they had, their copy would have sounded 'suboptimal' (lousy). The serious point to all this is that the Caring Nineties was a period in which creative advertising typically followed, rather than set, trends.

Returning to the advertisement aimed at the busy manager on his way to a hectic meeting, during the early 1990s the headline may have appeared rather like this:

> Headline:
>
> **7.30 A.M.**
>
> **THERE'S A TWO MILE TAIL-BACK.**
>
> **THE FORECAST IS RAIN.**
>
> **THE REPORT NEEDS TO BE FINISHED BY 11 A.M.**
>
> ***ISN'T IT JUST A BEAUTIFUL MORNING?***

The copy describes the relaxed state of mind enjoyed by the manager. After all, she (most likely) or he drives a Pastiche 200 series executive car.

Business-to-business quick tips

- Trade magazines can help create awareness and provide an educational platform.
- Copy needs to push your product, push your offer and push your client's own profits.
- Always ask yourself, 'What's in this offer for my clients?'
- Never assume that consumer advertising alone will satisfy the business market.

- Try to get out and actually meet the people who sell your client's product or service to the consumer.
- Make time to understand the business language and jargon of a specific business sector.
- Remember, you are dealing with business *people*. Keep your copy professional but 'human'.
- Never allow your creative message to dilute your product or service facts.
- Get to the point.
- Use research to substantiate claims – especially when you want to re-establish a product's or service's credibility.
- Always stay one step ahead of your buyer's questions.
- Reward managers with the tools to save time and earn respect.
- Address declining sales positively.

Off-the-page advertising

As you enter the world of off-the-page advertising, you leave that of general informative or announcement copy dealing purely with issues such as branding and image. You enter a completely different dimension. Your words need to leap out and pull customers all the way to your doorstep.

You are about to become involved in direct marketing. In this distinctive area, customers react immediately by contacting a company through a response device. Here, advertising can be likened to a sign outside a kitchen which reads, 'Come and Get It'. All the customer has to do is open the door, step in and enjoy it.

Off-the-page advertising enables you to sell something off the printed page. It is highly popular with small businesses wanting to produce advertising that pays for itself.

One thing to bear in mind when measuring advertising that pays for itself is that you must take into account the cost of placing the advertisement, the cost of producing it and the cost of you or your client fulfilling an order, *before* assessing its value. Then you have to consider the longer-term enhanced value that one off-the-page advertisement has for a future advertisement:

> The would-be buyer sees the first advertisement but doesn't make a purchase. When the second new advertisement makes an appearance, its copy and contents, along with the credibility of seeing the advertiser is an ongoing enterprise, enhances the chances of an eventual buying decision.

Protecting off-the-page interests

In the past, some shady advertisers have used off-the-page advertising to sell dubious products and services. Trade-imposed legislation helps protect publishers as well as readers from disreputable traders. Copy that is approved by The Mail Order Protection Scheme reassures readers that if the company were unable to meet the orders generated by a campaign, there would be some financial compensation.

Completing the off-the-page sales cycle

Off-the-page selling offers you a choice of two creative copy steps towards securing a sale:

1 The first is when you make an offer, ask for payment and then dispatch the product.
2 The second is when you make an offer, provide some outline details about the product or service and then offer to mail back further information. The final purchase is made through either mail order or another avenue of distribution.

Examples include:

- *Selling property off the page* – read the ad, ask for a brochure, see the property, sign the contract.
- *Selling insurance off the page* – read the ad, call for advice, request more details (a standard legal requirement). See your financial adviser if appropriate, sign the contract.

Even if your copy generates a sale from your advertisement, it doesn't necessarily follow that you have created the ideal self-financing advertisement. And never be fooled into believing that all that is needed in order to produce a powerful off-the-page advertisement is the inclusion of a response device.

The acid test to measure the effectiveness of an off-the-page advertisement is whether it generates a sale *and* encourages continued future purchases from the same buyer. Here is one way to encourage that:

> BUY THIS PRODUCT AND START A COLLECTION

Describe everything

In all direct marketing copy, always provide as much descriptive detail as possible. If you are advertising a record collection, somewhere in the copy leave space to list every single track.

139
media and understanding
its creative language
05

Believe me, someone somewhere will want to buy the collection just because of one special track. If you are writing about a dress, discuss its texture, how it flows, how it feels, its colours and so on:

> ITS PRETTY PASTEL IS AS DELICATE AS THE SILK THAT WOVE IT.

If you are selling something that is big, explain in an original way just how big that really is:

> THE TRAVEL BAG CAN CARRY TWO SUITS, THREE DRESSES, SIX
> PAIRS OF SHOES, TWENTY SHIRTS, THREE SCARVES ...

And if the product is small, describe just how small it is:

> IT'S SO TINY – YOU'LL NEVER KNOW IT'S THERE.

That's a good copy line for a hearing aid.

If you are selling an artistic collection, like bone china plates, provide details of actual size, the work that went into crafting the piece and so on:

> THIS BEAUTIFUL COLLECTOR'S PIECE HAS BEEN SPECIALLY
> COMMISSIONED BY LEADING ARTIST BOB JONES.
> EVERY VASE IS HAND MADE. EACH FLOWER IS HAND PAINTED.
> SO EACH PIECE IS PEERLESS.

If you are selling electronic home entertainment products, provide details of things like power and MHz:

> A SCORCHING **1000 MHz** OF RAM.

Does the product come complete with everything you need to switch on and go? Yes? Then say so – even the plug can be a selling aid.

For greater urgency, consider the limited edition technique:

> ONLY **1000** EVER MADE.
>
> YOUR PIECE IS INDIVIDUALLY NUMBERED.
>
> ONCE WE'VE SOLD THE **999**TH PIECE, WE'LL BREAK THE MOULD.

The role of incentives

Having read about the many product benefits and features of your client's product, the potential buyers may still need one final creative push before taking the plunge and responding. This could call for the incorporation of some kind of reward for prompt action.

Your copy can accommodate this by combining the reward with the instruction to respond. For example:

> ANSWER IN **10** DAYS AND CLAIM A FREE GIFT.
>
> REPLY TODAY AND SAVE **10%** OFF YOUR BILL.
>
> RESPOND NOW AND YOU COULD WIN A HOLIDAY FOR TWO.
>
> REPLY SOON AND *WE'LL* PAY YOUR FIRST MONTH'S
>
> INSURANCE PREMIUM.

Another plunge-making technique is to feature a time limit:

> HURRY. THIS OFFER ONLY LASTS **5** DAYS.
>
> HURRY. STOCKS ARE LIMITED.
>
> HURRY. FIRST COME, FIRST SERVED.
>
> HURRY. AVOID DISAPPOINTMENT BY REPLYING TODAY.
>
> HURRY. THERE ARE ONLY **20** SHOPPING DAYS TILL XMAS.

These plunge-makers can be further enhanced by making them flashes:

> ONLY **12** REMAINING
>
> BUY ONE GET A **2**ND **FREE!**
>
> **OFFER ENDS FRIDAY**

Generally speaking, there are two popular response options available to you, apart from the Web: coupons and telephone. Whichever you decide to take, always make it as simple as possible for a prospect to get in touch.

Coupons

Strategically, your copy should refer to how easy it is to use a featured coupon. The closer the prospect gets to the coupon, the greater the creative emphasis given to simplicity.

Coupons often have specific captions that reinforce the easy buying process as well as urge fast action. Over the years, designers have tried various ways to balance urgency with style. Coupon captions have been reversed out of boxes, run along the coupon's edge, 'splashed' with colour, enlarged, reduced ... the list is endless. As in many aspects of creative copy and design, as long as you try to tone down the trite and keep everything sounding as well as looking credible and in keeping with the overall creative tone, your coupon should get clipped.

Here are some typical coupon captions:

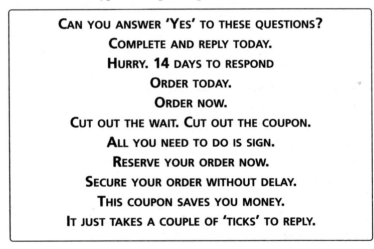

CAN YOU ANSWER 'YES' TO THESE QUESTIONS?

COMPLETE AND REPLY TODAY.

HURRY. 14 DAYS TO RESPOND

ORDER TODAY.

ORDER NOW.

CUT OUT THE WAIT. CUT OUT THE COUPON.

ALL YOU NEED TO DO IS SIGN.

RESERVE YOUR ORDER NOW.

SECURE YOUR ORDER WITHOUT DELAY.

THIS COUPON SAVES YOU MONEY.

IT JUST TAKES A COUPLE OF 'TICKS' TO REPLY.

Making coupons user friendly

Some people actually enjoy completing coupons. However, many find them offputting. Try to make them as easy to fill in as you can.

A good coupon is simple – not just for the benefit of the person who has to complete it, but also for the benefit of the person who has to process all the information on it. Wherever possible, guide the prospect to completing things in legible CAPITAL LETTERS. Think about how one question should logically be followed by the next. Consider the person in the back room who has to process all of the coupons.

Hopefully, sacks full of coupons will arrive. Someone should gauge the effectiveness of the various media in which the coupons appeared. Here's how:

- Incorporate a discreet publication code that indicates a publication's title and date.
- Create an artificial order department. One publication features coupons addressed to a certain department, whilst another features a different department. This is useful for very large-scale, even international campaigns.

Coupons should be positive pieces of communication:

YES! I AM INTERESTED IN WHAT YOU HAVE TO OFFER.

They should minimize laborious writing:

Ordering is as easy as 1.2.3.

1. WHAT IS YOUR NAME**? ....**

2. WHAT IS YOUR POSTCODE**? ....**

3. WHAT IS YOUR HOUSE NUMBER OR NAME**? ....**

4. HOW MUCH WOULD YOU LIKE TO SPEND**? ....**

Please send me a:

RED   ☐

PINK ☐

BLUE ☐

dress (just tick the relevant box).

Please charge my

VISA   ☐

ACCESS ☐

credit card

My account number is _____

The expiry date is _____

Explain what happens after the person sends in the coupon. How long will it take to process the order? Say when the offer expires.

One completed coupon shouldn't just mean one completed sale. The information can be used again and again for selling other products or services in the future. This technique is called cross-selling.

It is illegal to pass on the information contained within a coupon to another company without permission. If you think that you may want to do this, always inform the prospect. Use copy on the lines of:

> MAY WE PASS YOUR DETAILS ON TO OTHER SUPPLIERS WHO
> COULD BE OF INTEREST TO YOU?
> YES/NO

or:

> WOULD YOU LIKE TO BE KEPT IN TOUCH WITH OTHER
> FUTURE OFFERS?
> IF NOT, PLEASE TICK THE BOX. ☐

Notice that the copy reads: 'If not'. This is a tried and proven technique to secure more YES answers. It is easier to ignore a box than tick it.

Finally, think about the confidentiality of the information contained within the coupon. People don't like to send their address details openly, ready for anyone to read. To get around this, offer a FREEPOST address in which you pick up the postage costs. All the prospect has to do is pop the coupon in an envelope and then post it.

Call now!

Telephone response advertising adds greater urgency to a creative message than coupons. A strong telephone graphic accompanied by copy, such as:

> CALL NOW
>
> ACT NOW
>
> DIAL FREE
>
> CALL OUR HOTLINE
>
> DIAL ANYTIME
>
> WE'RE WAITING FOR YOUR CALL

tells your prospect that you mean business and are ready and waiting for their call. This may be essential for organizations such as charities that need to raise money quickly.

> ONE PHONE CALL CAN SAVE THIS BOY'S LIFE.
>
> TO SAVE HER THE TWENTY-MILE TREK FOR A CUP OF WATER
>
> JUST WALK TO THE PHONE.
>
> YOUR PHONE IS HER LIFE LINE.

You'll notice that one of the copy lines above the charity examples includes the word 'Hotline'. Hotlines are nothing particularly new. However, their implied exclusivity makes them a valuable tool to include in telephone response-led copy. You could drop the first syllable, 'hot', in 'hotline' and replace it with the product name or company name. This makes your phone response number even more memorable.

In the case of PenPod variations could include:

> THE PENPOD HOTLINE LINE
>
> THE PENPOD LINE
>
> THE CARTRIDGE LINE

If Scotsdale (traditional) wanted to promote a particular own-brand service (say, nappies) and sales line they could call it:

> SCOTSDALENORTH NAPPY LINE
>
> THE NAPPY ADVICE LINE
>
> NAPPIES DIRECT LINE

Fax Back is an interesting form of response. On dialling a special number on a fax machine, a respondent is redialled with a printed fax sheet(s) giving relevant information. This is useful for companies wishing to send extra details of a product or service. Restaurants, for example, could use this facility to send menus. Holiday companies could use it to send details of last-minute bookings and so on. A variation on the Fax Back device is a multiple Fax Back that can send multiples of pages selected from a large database. This is ideal if, for example, you wish to fax travel information concerning various destinations. A traveller could request travel details about Rwanda, Brazil and Portugal on one fax. Another variation of Fax Back is simply to ask the respondent to fax back a coupon – or even a letter with a coupon printed on its reverse side.

A further creative way of including a telephone response number is to use an existing enquiry line that caters for lots of companies, all on one externally promoted number.

Finally there is the option to promote a telephone number that is a prime-rate telephone number which pays the advertiser each time the number is dialled:

• The downside of this approach is that people know that the call is costly; by law you have to include a line of copy that details the cost. It can also be seen as irresponsible – especially if the product encourages the young or vulnerable to call.
• The upside of using prime rate numbers is that they can be great money-earning devices.

All UK premium rate numbers are regulated by ICSTIS (the Independent Committee for the Supervision of Standards of Telephone Information Services).

Telephone response devices can be extended to cover Order by Fax techniques as well as ordering via the Web (this is discussed in Chapter 12).

Assuming you are not using the Web and still cannot decide between featuring a telephone or coupon response, you could always feature both:

> **CLIP THE COUPON**
>
> **OR FOR AN EVEN FASTER SERVICE**
>
> **CALL NOW ON 0800 00 123**
>
> **EVEN BETTER ...**
>
> **HIT WWW.GABAYNET.COM**

Whichever route you choose, ensure that you or your client can handle the anticipated response. There's not much point in producing a great advertisement if the consequent enquiries are ignored.

As mentioned above, not all off-the-page advertisements complete sales transactions immediately off the page. For example, medical or financial services may require further information. High-priced items may call for further creative reassurance that can only be provided by a next step: either a salesperson or a brochure.

Getting your prospect to make the next step often relies on the only form of advertising which offers the creative opportunity to be as intimate as the law allows with your target audience. This is covered in Chapter 6.

Off-the-page quick tips

- Decide whether you want to sell directly or indirectly off the page.
- Encourage future as well as immediate sales. (Buy today and start a collection.)
- Describe everything about your product, from its size to its material – even down to the plug, if applicable.
- Reward response (e.g. discounts).
- Feature a time limit for responses.
- Endorse the simplicity of responding.
- Keep coupons concise and easy to complete.
- Track the effectiveness of a publication by incorporating a special coupon code.
- Encourage action with directive headlines.
- Add urgency by offering hotlines.
- Test response by telephone or coupons or both.

Over to you

1 Design and write a coupon to be used in an off-the-page advertisement for PenPod.

2 List twelve different directive headlines.

3 List six business benefits offered by a photocopier machine.

4 Write an advertisement that highlights the business benefits of an old second-hand car.

5 Write four versions of a headline that announces a business merger:

   a to Users
   b to Choosers
   c to Proprietors
   d to Investors.

6 PenPod has a big competitor with a better product. Write an advertisement which supports PenPod's position.

06

**selling through
the letterbox**

In this chapter you will learn
- how to understand the role
  of direct marketing
- how to construct the perfect
  direct mail letter and when
  to use direct mail gadgets
- how to draw inspiration for
  classic direct mail ideas
- how to write catalogue copy.

Above-the-line advertising helps you get a strong hold on a market (i.e. increase your market share). Direct marketing helps you increase your share of the individual's buying decisions. To achieve this, you need to know as much as possible about your client – more than just why a buying decision is made. This requires extensive data – which is why direct marketing is sometimes referred to as 'database marketing'. It has many other names too:

- Relationship marketing
- One-to-one marketing
- Response marketing
- Through-the-line marketing
- Quantitative marketing
- NSM marketing (Non-Specific Media marketing)

Whatever you call it, direct marketing builds sustainable relationships between a company and their audience. Direct marketing using direct mail reaches a client through the letterbox and leads them to your point of sale. Reaching the appropriate letterboxes calls for accurate lists. These can be purchased from list brokers (see p. 153) or generated from completed sales promotion coupons, press advertising coupons and telephone research – or even questionnaire mailings.

Direct marketing increases the chances that a person will choose your product or service. It also encourages a sustainable relationship between you and your customer – that is why direct marketing is sometimes referred to as 'relationship marketing' or 'one-to-one marketing'. This relationship can become so strong that eventually, by the company keeping in touch at appropriate times with relevant information and incentives, the customer will remain loyal and recommend it to others. The person's value to your company is doubled with every new customer they introduce.

This is demonstrated in a classic sales model originally conceived by Ray Consada, an American salesperson, and then developed by authors Ray Considine and Murray Raphael in their book *The Great Brain Robbery. Business Tips*, published by The Marketer's Bookshelf, Philadelphia, 1986. The model is still commonly used throughout the marketing industry.

The loyalty ladder

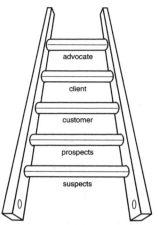

Direct marketing is not confined to direct mail. It includes virtually any marketing activity where your prospect responds to you directly – especially the Web. It establishes a direct connection between you and your customers as individuals so that they remain loyal and prove a lasting valuable asset, distinct from a casual one-off sale.

Many names – one aim

Direct mail's position in the following list of people's pet hates speaks for itself.

Junk mail	65%
Drivers who hog the middle lane of the motorway	34%
Companies where the phone is answered by a recorded message	33%
People who use mobile phones in public places	29%
Car/house alarms going off	29%
Too few checkouts at the supermarket	24%
Piped music	17%
Plastic shopping bags that split	13%
Traffic lights that turn red at pedestrian-free crossings	13%
Opening Tetrapack cartons	11%
Programming video recorders	4%
Hand dryers in public toilets	4%

(Source: *Sunday Times/NOP*; respondents answered at least three questions from a list of 12)

Direct mail in more detail

What exactly is direct mail? It is simply postal advertising.
When correctly implemented, direct mail can:

1 Target a message in a controlled campaign.
2 Personalize a message to a specific audience.
3 Prioritize a message by delivering it directly into the hands of
a specific audience.
4 Time a message to arrive at a specified time – day, week,
month or occasion.
5 Explain a message in detail by including enclosures such as
brochures and leaflets.
6 Offer confidentiality when a message is sensitive.
7 Hasten a message through using first-class postage.
8 Stimulate sales leads by following up messages by phone or
post.
9 Offer outstanding value in terms of cost for each reply when
compared to other media such as pure awareness
advertising.
10 Test the effectiveness of a message by segmentation of your
mailing's distribution.
11 Update your message by content or distribution.
12 Allow for unusual formats such as pop-ups, video mailers
and large or small size envelopes.
13 Keep customers in touch with company developments and
stimulate interest in future offers.
14 Ask customers for views and opinions.
15 Stimulate sales by offering special vouchers against new or
ageing products.
16 Fight competition quickly by promoting revised prices.
17 Increase store traffic by inviting consumers to special retailer
or distributor events.
18 Tie-in with other media such as the press who
may feature an awareness/information-type advertisement.
19 Cross-sell with other direct mail users. (For example, the
ScotsdaleNorth.com's cyber café, Directions, could share a
mailing list with a restaurant guide publisher.)
20 Cover sales areas not readily accessible by sales staff.

Is there anybody out there?

In a word, YES. Lists – either business lists or consumer lists –
can help you pin-point target areas with amazing accuracy. The
importance of an accurate, or 'clean', list in direct marketing

can never be overstressed. Good copy without a suitable clean list isn't even worth the cost of the postage.

In the UK, many consumer and business lists offered by professional list brokers are 'cleaned' by checking against people who have registered an opt in or opt out request to either the mail preference service, or the telephone preference service.

The best source of lists is a client's own customer database. Every coupon returned – even one with a 'no' reply – is worth its weight in gold. Every list generated by distributors or agents should be used. Every lead followed up by sales teams is vital. From a creative copy view, you must always design your direct mail to sell a product or service *and* provide an opportunity to capture data – including data about other potential future clients (see 'Member-get-member mailers' on p. 172).

Once a suspected customer has become a prospective customer and then an actual customer, you can spend less time crafting your copy to sell a proposition and more time crafting it to encourage your customer to become a regular client. Regular clients will help promote your product or service further by recommending your company to others.

Where's the list?

There are the following distinct ways of obtaining a list:
• You can use lists belonging to other companies whose product or service complements your own product or service (this makes so-called affinity mailings possible).
• You can ask a list broker to build a new list from scratch.
• You can purchase an existing list that targets people by geographical area, type of household, zip or postcode, size of business, types of interest, purchases patterns, financial status, information based on national censuses and much more besides.

In all these cases the key questions to ask a list broker are:
1 When was this list last updated?
2 How was it compiled?
3 How many other companies use the list?
4 Of those companies, how many offer the same or similar creative message?

Instead of all these, you can build your own new list through carrying out research of your own.

Direct mail contents

Envelopes

Once your mailing hits the doormat, it has to compete with many other enveloped items ranging from utility bills to letters from friends or relatives. Your envelope should indicate, at a glance, that its contents are:
- interesting
- relevant
- worth the effort of opening the envelope.

Above all, your mailing has to be *involving*. The more you can involve a reader with your creative proposition, the higher the likelihood that they will follow your copy all the way to a sales conclusion (if you are selling).

The envelope's copy and design need to reflect the mailing's contents. Never be afraid to use colour – even photography – on the envelope, but use it only if it is relevant to the enclosure.

Envelope copy needs to entice the reader. One of the strongest words you can incorporate is *free*:

> OPEN NOW FOR DETAILS OF A **FREE** GIFT.

An implied variation:

> OPEN NOW AND SAVE **25%** OFF YOUR NEXT GROCERY BILL.

Another technique is to give the recipient a peek at what's inside the envelope. This is achieved through having one or more transparent windows on the envelope. One may show part of a picture from the brochure inside, whilst another shows part of the message on a sales letter – such as details of a cash prize.

Why not use a 'zipper' envelope? The recipient is asked to pull a tab on the envelope which zips it open. As the tag is pulled, a message is revealed on its reverse side. Here are possibilities:

> PULL OPEN FOR GREAT NEWS
> EXERCISE FOR A HEALTHIER LIFESTYLE:
> START BY PULLING OPEN HERE.

A further idea is to announce that there is a secret message inside:

> **ARE YOU A MILLIONAIRE?**
>
> **INSIDE THIS ENVELOPE IS YOUR KEY TO SUCCESS.**
>
> **CAN YOU FIND THE HIDDEN MESSAGE WORTH £500,000?**

You can personalize an envelope with the recipient's name:

> **YOUR TABLE IS WAITING, MR JONES, AT DIRECTIONS ...**

> **SOMEONE SHOULD GIVE MR JONES A MILLION POUNDS ...**
> (The recipient pulls a zipper tag.)
> Copy on reverse of tag:
> **... LIKE US.**

Envelopes are ideal vehicles for short teaser copy lines. Such copy lines are particularly effective when you do not want to plaster your envelope with brash illustrations or use unusually large envelopes, which may give the appearance of tacky junk mail.

Teaser envelope copy lines are invariably unanswered questions. To find the answer, the recipient is obliged to open the envelope:

> ***DIRECTIONS***
>
> **WOULD YOU PREFER A CREAMY PRAWN COCKTAIL OR**
>
> **A FILLING MINESTRONE SOUP?**
>
> **DOES $9.99 SOUND APPETIZING FOR A THREE COURSE MEAL?**

> *PenPod*
> Business-to-business mailing:
> ***Isn't it annoying when your pen runs out just a***

People often open envelopes from the back rather than the front, so use the reverse side as well. The minimum you can do is feature a return address for use if the mailing is undelivered. The maximum is to strengthen the offer by featuring further details about the product or service inside. Alternatively you could highlight a free incentive – such as a holiday weekend or complimentary travel bag.

Gabay's tips to guarantee your envelope gets opened

Follow at least three of the ideas in the following list and I guarantee that your direct mail envelope will be opened:
- Feature a hand-written address – this is up to twenty times more powerful than using a confidential or urgent stamp.
- Feature a thick package.
- Don't use a clear envelope.
- Consider using a real stamp on a reply-paid envelope.

> **Did you know?**
> The world's first pre-paid envelope was issued on 1 November 1838 by the New South Wales Post Office.

- Make sure your copy approach matches your audience's mind-set and the setting in which they will open your envelope.
- Be warned that bar codes and other forms of electronic postal tagging make it clear that a piece of direct mail is just that.

Your letter

There are scores of copywriting techniques that can help improve the effectiveness of letters. To sum up all these methods:

> Write to a person as you would write to a friend or colleague – formally enough to be credible yet informally enough to be sincere.

Letters should be as long as it takes you to write them – by this, I mean either until you run out of permissible space (e.g. one side of A4 paper) or until you have nothing else to discuss.

Long copy letters take time to read but short copy letters may not be adequate. The ideal compromise is to structure your letter copy with several entry points. Whether your copy is long or short, that means that the reader can dip in at key points. If your message is interesting, the reader will read on or return to the letter at a later stage. (Just because you sent a direct mail piece by first-class mail, it doesn't necessarily follow that it will receive prompt attention.)

Letter entry points

Possible entry points include:

- headlines
- captions
- illustrations
- diagrams
- underlined words

- hand-written sections
- arrows

- postscripts
- boxed or shaded-in copy (originally termed a 'Johnson Box')

- subheads
- panels
- photographs
- bullet points
- words highlighted or in CAPITAL LETTERS
- ticks
- reversed-out printing (white out of black)
- marginal notes
- tables

A step-by-step guide to letters

Letter structure

S alutation
T opic (headline)
R eason
I nformation
P rompt to action
E nd

Overall appearance

Your letter should be clearly laid out on good-quality paper. (However, remember that the heavier your paper, the more costly your postage.) A company logo adds to the overall credibility as well as increasing recognition.

It is not necessary to force all your text onto one side of paper. Readers tend to skip the reverse side of a letter, so if your letter is particularly long you may have to spread it over two or more sheets.

> Wherever possible, give your copy the space
> to breathe. Crammed sentences look messy and are
> very difficult to read.

Type styles should also be easy to read – save the creative flourishes for your message *not the typeface.*

Letters that are set in a typeface such as the one used in this book, with a serif (the small stroke at the end of a stroke of a letter) ...

T ... are easier to read than sans-serif type like this: T

Think about how the eye tracks your letter. You may have chosen a serif typeface to aid reading, but if your layout is generally messy the whole mailing could be a fruitless exercise.

Eye-tracking is an easy technique to pick up. Unless you are writing for the Middle-East market, which reads from right to left, or the Far-East market, which reads from top to bottom, structure your letter with its headline and any leading subheads or illustrations at top left. Then flow the copy neatly left to right, with your final push at the bottom right-hand side of the page. Remember this is only a basis for your letter layout, not the template for *every* letter.

Never staple or clip your sheets of paper together. This can tear the letter and staples and clips may get caught on finger-nails. Even paperless staples make a letter seem bulky.

Your letter is a person-to-person affair. Make it appear as personal as possible. Photocopied letters look and feel tacky. Printer type-set letters look like printer type-set letters. It is wasteful to spend much time and effort preparing a letter to a named person, and then wipe out all the elements of individuality by inappropriate production.

Dear ...

Address your reader by their name. (Remember that direct mail is also called 'one-to-one' marketing.) Check that you have spelled the recipient's name correctly and included the correct address details. If you don't know the person's name, address them by job title. If this isn't possible, address them by category (e.g. Dear Diner, Dear Shop-keeper, Dear Fellow Director).

Headline

Wherever possible, try to encapsulate your main proposition in a headline. When you write such a headline, try to include copy words that stimulate involvement or action. For example:

> <u>At last</u> here's a restaurant that caters for all the family

> <u>Announcing</u> ScotsdaleNorth.com's brand new site

> <u>12 Reasons</u> to pick up a PenPod.

> <u>Don't buy anything</u> until you have read this.

> <u>Yours free ...</u>

> <u>Everything you ever wanted to know about ...</u>

Opening paragraph

If you haven't included it yet, now is a good time to use the word 'you'. (Remember, direct mail is a personalized, targeted form of communication.) For example:

> You are clearly a person who appreciates the finer things in life ...
>
> Your continued support for the local action group is really appreciated ...
>
> Our records show that you are a keen reader of Teach Yourself books. You already know how the series features fascinating insights into everything from marketing to writing for children. Each title is written by a respected expert in his or her field.
>
> Now you can extend your library knowledge by taking advantage of our exclusive reader's Teach Yourself book club.

> Each month you can select another Teach Yourself title that will be sent <u>direct to your home</u> at a price that is guaranteed to be at least 25% off our recommended retail price.
>
> Just think. All that invaluable information available when you want it.
>
> School projects are made even more fascinating. Hobbies come to life ...

Your opening paragraph needs to grab the reader's attention quickly. It should be succinct. Opening paragraphs should contain no more than six lines of provocative copy.

In general, try to keep all your paragraphs reasonably short (no more than about eight lines). Always vary the length of paragraphs so that the copy looks lively on the page. Overloaded copy can lead to overloaded readers. In terms of a creative message, one paragraph should lead to the next. Use the techniques of asking a question and then following on with a reply within the bodycopy of the next paragraph. And why not get your reader really involved with something in the last paragraph on a page ...

... and then complete the message on the next page? Alternatively, introduce a fresh idea into the end of each paragraph.

Benefits

Hammer home your benefits. Tease your reader with further details of benefits (e.g. a free mystery gift) which will be revealed later within the copy. Highlight your benefits with bullet points. Stress the benefits:

> Believe me when I say …
> When they told me, I couldn't believe it.
> What do you think?

Incorporate benefits in captions:

> (Picture of PenPod)
>
> ```
> Stainless steel casing, tungsten tip and
>     tested to write for miles and miles.
> ```

Explain why the reader needs the product or service. Show examples of how the product or service can enhance their lives:

> ```
> Compared to many other credit cards, the
> ScotsdaleNorth credit card can save you up to
> 25% off purchases and an additional 5% off
> every bill totalling over $50 each and every
> time you shop at ScotsdaleNorth.
> ```

Get involved from the start

Your letters need to involve the readers. Make them feel:

- intrigued
- charmed
- surprised
- rewarded.

To do all this, your letters should be:

- relevant
- tactful
- clear
- interesting
- personal
- courteous
- conversational
- right length.

Above all, put yourself in your reader's shoes:

- People are procrastinators – give them a reason to respond.
- People are sceptical – offer a believable message.
- People are lazy – make it easy to reply.
- People worry about making the wrong decision – use case histories to offer assurance.
- People avoid risk. Give them a guarantee.
- People say 'I can't read all this.' Give them all they need to make a decision and not a word more.

Another way of highlighting benefits is the Grim Reaper approach. Rather than stating the positive benefits of buying your product or service, discuss the consequences of *not* making a commitment. Life assurance companies use this technique:

Should the worst happen, your dependants
could be left to cope with financial burdens
such as funeral expenses and mortgage
repayments.

The Protection Plan helps to ensure that
even if your existing life policies from
work have matured or been cashed in, you can
still leave a significant cash sum to the
ones you love.

It pays to reply today

Offer an incentive for a quick response. This can be anything
ranging from a money-off coupon to a service incentive.
Whichever incentive you use, as with the rest of the copy,
describe it in full.

Reply today because ...
- ✓ We can't hold this price for ever.
- ✓ Stocks are low.
- ✓ We'll give you a 'cashback' for your old product.
- ✓ The bigger your order, the more you save.
- ✓ We'll refund the cost of your entire purchase when you place your next order.
- ✓ We want to demonstrate it in the comfort of your own home.
- ✓ This offer is exclusive to you.
- ✓ We want you to try it before you buy it.
- ✓ We want to offer you a personalized quotation.
- ✓ This is only a small sample of something even better.
- ✓ If you buy it we'll give you a second one free.
- ✓ If you buy the bread, we'll give you the butter.
- ✓ We want to explain it to you in person at a convenient time and date.
- ✓ If you don't like it, you can exchange it for something else.
- ✓ It's delivered free.
- ✓ We don't want your money until next year.
- ✓ We're always here to service it.
- ✓ You can sample the entire range for a special price.
- ✓ You have our guarantee on it.
- ✓ Buy it today and we'll extend our guarantee.
- ✓ We'll also send one to your friend.

✓ We'll enter your name in our prize draw.
✓ Every applicant wins a prize.
✓ We'll match every penny with a donation to charity.
✓ We'll pay the extra costs.
✓ We'll eat our hat if you don't like it.

Guarantee your guarantee

Don't just make an ordinary guarantee. Offer an extraordinary level of assurance – after all, an amazing product or service such as yours is perfect:

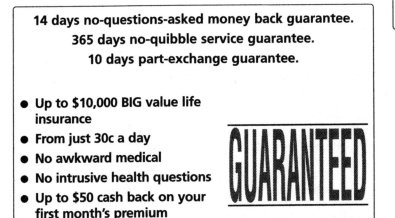

14 days no-questions-asked money back guarantee.

365 days no-quibble service guarantee.

10 days part-exchange guarantee.

- **Up to $10,000 BIG value life insurance**
- **From just 30c a day**
- **No awkward medical**
- **No intrusive health questions**
- **Up to $50 cash back on your first month's premium**

Save the best till last

Just as the reader thinks that you couldn't possibly offer more – Bang! You fire off your dynamic closing shot. Urge the reader to 'act now'. Quick! Before it's too late!

It's so easy to order

Nothing could be easier than saying 'Yes' to your terrific offer. All they have to do is complete the simple reply device that either is attached or can be found in the mailing package.

Yours sincerely

Every letter should be signed – if not in person, at least the signature should be printed in blue ink so it looks as if it was individually signed.

Don't forget the PS

The PS is your last opportunity in your letter to reinforce your sales argument. You can use it in a number of ways, including:

- Adding a last-minute benefit.
- Reminding the reader about a special free gift.
- Drawing the reader's attention to one of the key points made within your copy.

PPS – just in case you didn't hear the first time

The postscript is one of the most powerful creative elements in a letter. Keep your postscript short. Response may be further increased if you enclose your postscript in a box or simulate a hand-written typeface.

The optional gizmo

Gadgets help give a mailing an extra creative dimension. For example, you could include a a pair of 3-D glasses to view a specially printed leaflet, or a pen to sign the order form. One interesting idea is to attach a dime or a 50 pence piece to your sales letter, then ask the reader to use it to scratch out a panel revealing whether or not a prize has been won. (This technique is sometimes called 'Coin rub'.)

The OK guidelines for including gadgets

It's not OK to:
- include anything that can be squashed or melts in the post
- include anything that's perishable
- include a gadget that may offend (e.g. a key ring holding a condom)
- include a particularly bulky or heavy gadget
- treat a live animal as a gadget – *never* include anything that's live.

It's OK to:
- attach your gadget to one secure spot
- try and tie your gadget in with the copy
- strengthen your envelope so that the gadget doesn't rip it to bits.

Let's see how some of the above techniques can be incorporated into the text of a typical direct mail letter:

Relevant gadget
(Packet of seeds stuck to the letter)

```
Cultivate these seeds for a beautiful
         display of flowers.
```

Strong headline:

**BUY THIS BOOK AND CULTIVATE YOUR GARDENING KNOWLEDGE
AT A NEVER TO BE REPEATED PRICE**

Personalized salutation:

```
Dear Mr Jones
```

Intriguing opening paragraph:

John Willis once said that the 'essence of caring
for and understanding a garden starts with appreciating the
simple botanical make up of a seed'.

(Now show how all of this is directly relevant to the reader.)

In fact, you will probably agree the longer you
spend caring for and nurturing a garden, the greater
your horticultural knowledge becomes.

Now, you can develop your understanding and so gain even
greater satisfaction from gardening.

Note the use of the words 'you' and 'yours' in the example above.

Now introduce the three Ws.

What is it?

> The Gardening Almanac is the most
> authoritative work of its kind
> ever published.

What does it offer?

> It draws on the highly respected experience
> of over 100 world-leading botanists and
> horticulturists. Their combined knowledge means
> that this book sets the plant classification
> standards which are practised internationally.
> The almanac classifies and describes practically every
> plant species available to gardeners the world over.
>
> Everything you'll ever need in one volume.
>
> ■ Over 10,000 ornamental and economical plants.
> ■ 350 specially commissioned, beautifully accurate
> line drawings.
> ■ In-depth facts that help you accurately identify
> and name even the rarest plants.
> ■ Practical guidelines that will help you achieve
> spectacular results with your own plants.
> ■ The 'inside secrets' of creating spectacular
> urban landscapes such as rock gardens, water
> gardens or even coastal gardens.
> ■ Revealing explanations of the world's great
> gardening traditions.
>
> This is just a small example of how the
> extraordinary Gardening Almanac deals with
> all your gardening questions.

Wow! – save the best until last

> You can own this outstanding work at an
> exclusive price. Just $99.99 for over 2000 pages.
> That's a saving of $60 off the recommended
> retail price.

It pays to reply today.

> However, you must place your order before 31st May.
> Please do so – as a token of thanks, we will
> send you a complimentary copy of 'Gardening
> Secrets'. This is an essential reference that is
> packed with tips on how to make your garden bloom.

It's easy to order.

> Ordering your Almanac is easy. Simply complete the
> enclosed order form and return it to me with payment
> in the pre-paid envelope provided. Alternatively you
> can order with your credit card. Just call our 24-
> hour customer Hotline on 1234 5678, quoting reference
> number 'one'.
>
> I look forward to sending your almanac and hope you
> enjoy the complimentary packet of seeds.
>
> Yours sincerely
>
> Name
>
> Title
>
> PS Remember, this offer will never be repeated. You
> must respond before 31st May.

Other elements

Although the sales letter plays a key role in communicating your message, it is rarely the only content. Leaflets, for example, explain the benefits in greater detail. Leaflets don't restrict your creativity as a letter does. You can use illustrations to show how a product is used or a service operates. As long as the leaflet fits into the outer envelope, size can be made to work for you.

A common leaflet format is 'roll fold'. This type of leaflet is folded up to six times. As the reader unfolds each page, the creative message is explained in greater detail.

IF YOU THOUGHT THAT WAS A GREAT IDEA ...

(Unfold the page to the next 'reveal'.)

... THEN LOOK AT THIS:

As with advertisements, allow subheads to direct the reader through your leaflet copy. If the product is particularly technical, you may like to consider including a question-and-answer panel towards the end. These help you to address legal requirements:

- How long will this service operate?
- Who is eligible to apply?

and so on.

The one-page leaflet encapsulates your benefits on a double-sided (often A5) sheet of paper. One-page leaflets are ideal for recapping the benefits of an early reply – for example:

Headline:

REPLY EARLY AND YOU WILL RECEIVE A
FREE TRAVEL HOLDALL

YOURS **FREE** IF YOU APPLY IN **10** DAYS.

(The tighter your deadline, the better the response will be, so 10 days is better than 14 days and 24 hours is better than a week.)

THIS HANDY TRAVEL HOLDALL DOESN'T ONLY LOOK GREAT
BUT WILL HELP LIGHTEN THE LOAD WHEN OUT ON YOUR TRAVELS ...

One-page leaflets detailing incentives should always feature a picture of the incentive and, if practicable, close-up pictures of certain special details. In the case of the travel holdall these might be double zips, hidden pockets, rubber-grip handles.

Give your copy a little lift

Lift letters are small note-like memos that enhance a sales message or reassure the reader about a purchasing choice. Often, lift letters are 'written' by someone other than the writer of the main letter copy. This creates an individual endorsement. For example:

> Dear Mr Jones
>
> Can't make up your mind?
>
> When I first looked through the Gardening Almanac I was amazed at the kind of detail that each entry went into. The illustrations are, to say the least, impressive. The technical data reveal fascinating facts that will help you get the most from your plants and flowers.
>
> Best of all, the price of just $99.99 means that you save $60 off the recommended retail price.
>
> Take it from me, if you only ever buy one gardening reference book in your lifetime, you should make sure it's the Gardening Almanac.
>
> Yours sincerely

The reply device

Like coupons in press advertisements, the mailing reply device needs to be clearly designed. Be sure to include details such as your fax number, email or telephone number. You could also consider completing a sample order form in handwriting. Always repeat the response incentive offer, if only in a couple of key words.

Consider including a YES and NO sticker for your reply device. This is a great involvement device that encourages the reader to select a sticker and then put it on the response device. Research shows that in the case of a free prize draw, if you offer people a choice of stickers, most people choose the YES sticker in preference to the NO sticker as that appears to influence their chance of winning in the draw. (Of course, this is not what happens.)

Alternatively, you could include a MAYBE sticker. This compromise retains the reader's interest and if you ask for a day-time number so you can follow the response up quickly with a phone call, you may be able to 'convert' a MAYBE to a YES. A MAYBE can also be passed on to other departments within the company who could offer the respondent an item that is more suitable for their needs.

Finally, try to include the powerful YES word within the copy for the reply device:

> YES – I WANT TO KNOW MORE.
> YES – SEND ME MY ALMANAC TODAY.

Twenty-eight creative mailing ideas

1 Envelopes with peel-off stickers

Stickers add intrigue and involvement. They are infinitely versatile. Peel them off and you can reveal part of the contents of the package. Why not give a sticker additional value by asking the recipient to use it on a free gift voucher?

Stick this onto the coupon inside and you could win a free holiday to Cairo.

2 Distinctive envelopes

Unusually shaped envelopes help make your mailing more distinctive. However, circles can be quite expensive to produce as they take up a lot of paper stock. Other possibilities are triangular-shaped envelopes, extra large envelopes and extra small envelopes.

3 Card decks

These are also known as 'postcard decks' or 'foil card decks'. You share a mailing with other advertisers, and all contribute special cards that fit in either a foil-type pouch or a clear plastic pouch. Your product details are presented in the form of a postcard. One side details the product whilst the other features a response device. A variation of this is a postcard that is distributed to relevant hotel and restaurant chains. Tourists pick up a complimentary postcard they can use and through doing so mail your message – usually featuring an interesting visual device – for you!

4 Video/CD-ROM/DVD mailers

Instead of producing a printed mail piece, why not produce a short video cassette or CD-ROM programme about your product or service? You can use the cassette/disk container to hold a response device.

5 The no-name mailer

Leave out the product name on the envelope. This works well when your product is financially sensitive or has already been mass-mailed several times. (I once had to do this for a credit card company that had previously been mailed to around 11 million households.)

6 The Jack-in-the-box mailer

Here the reader breaks open a seal – usually at the edge of the outside envelope. This reveals the leading edge of a piece of paper. The reader pulls the leading edge, which unfolds a concertina-type mailer in which each sheet is attached to another.

7 The door-drop mailer

Rather than sending a direct mail piece by using the post, you circulate it by using a letterbox distribution company, working door to door. The benefit of this approach is that you can be very precise about which households receive your mailing and you have greater control over timing its arrival.

8 The bangtail envelope mailing

In this case, you include a special envelope which features a perforated 'tail' of paper near the sealing flap that can be used as an order form.

9 Bill stuffer

You include a leaflet or separate letter along with your invoices or statements. This is a very cost-effective way of making bills more beneficial. If your budget doesn't stretch to a separate leaflet, you can use space available on the invoice or statement to highlight a creative message:

TOTAL NOW DUE $220
HAVE YOU APPLIED FOR YOUR PLUS CARD YET?
IT COULD SAVE $$$$s ON YOUR SHOPPING AT
SCOTSDALE NORTHSIDE – FOR FURTHER DETAILS
CONTACT THE
PLUS CARD HOTLINE ON 080012345

10 Birthday mailing

Write to someone on the occasion of their birthday or the anniversary of their first using or enquiring about your product or service. This is regularly used by insurance companies, who choose the anniversary of an insurance policy (e.g. a motor insurance policy) to remind the policy holder of the company's great deals so that they renew their contract:

> **12** MONTHS' ADDITIONAL PEACE OF MIND
>
> AT LAST YEAR'S PRICES.
>
> HURRY — YOU MUST RENEW YOUR POLICY
>
> WITHIN THE NEXT **11** DAYS!

11 Bounce-back mailing

Congratulations! You have successfully sold your product using direct mail. Now include a second special offer which is sent along with the product itself. For example:

> NOW YOU'VE BOUGHT A PENPOD — USE THIS COUPON
>
> TO *WRITE OFF* **50%** ON A PENPOD GIFT SET.

12 Member-get-member mailers

These are also known as 'MGM', 'Friend-get-a-Friend' or 'Introduce-a-Friend'. They are one of the most effective ways of enhancing your customer database.

The technique often relies on a small incentive-led leaflet that details an additional free gift to the recipient for recommending a friend. This can be strengthened by offering to provide an extra free gift if the friend signs up for a product or service:

> THIS GUIDE TO WINES IS YOURS **FREE**
>
> JUST FOR RECOMMENDING A FRIEND.

> THIS BOX OF SIX SPECIALLY SELECTED WINES IS YOURS **FREE**
>
> ONCE YOUR FRIEND STARTS TO ENJOY THE BENEFITS OF OUR CLUB.

Even if you don't have the budget to make a special incentive offer for an MGM, it is still worth your while to include space for a recommendation within a reply device.

13 Pop-ups

Pop-ups include anything from a pop-up letter to a pop-up coupon that places the order form directly into the recipient's hand.

14 Audio mailing

Audio mailings usually feature either pre-taped messages or pre-recorded CD discs. One audio fad was the use of pre-recorded microchips. When the recipient of the mailing piece opens the envelope, a hidden microchip connected to a tiny speaker inside the envelope is activated and a voice can be heard from inside the envelope!

Whatever kind of audio technology you use, take complete advantage of music, sound effects and a compelling story. As with video mailings, be sure to use the cassette box or CD-holder to include elements such as order forms or coupons.

15 Embossed membership cards

The technique of including a plastic credit card-type membership card – complete with the recipient's name embossed on it – was particularly popular during the 1980s. It can still be effective as a way to encourage custom and enhance personalization. For example:

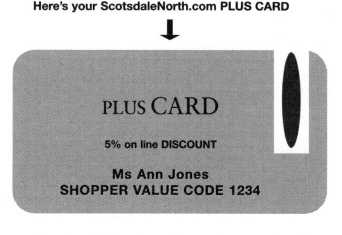

Here's your ScotsdaleNorth.com PLUS CARD

PLUS CARD

5% on line DISCOUNT

Ms Ann Jones
SHOPPER VALUE CODE 1234

Keep it safe, Ms Jones. The more you use it, the bigger your discounts.

16 Pre-mailer mailer

Also known as a pre-announcement mailer, this technique provides advance notification of a major mailing campaign. It works well when you want to announce something like a major prize draw:

> WATCH YOUR POST – THIS TIME NEXT WEEK
> YOU COULD BE A MILLIONAIRE!

Like birthday mailings, pre-mailers can be strengthened by including personalized details unique to the recipient:

> WE'VE ONLY SENT THIS NOTICE TO **23** PEOPLE IN QUEENSTOWN.
> YOU ARE ONE OF ONLY **4** PEOPLE IN YOUR ROAD WHO
> WILL RECEIVE IT – BY THIS TIME NEXT WEEK YOU COULD
> BE OUR NEXT MILLIONAIRE!

17 Keep up with the Joneses mailers

This is an example of database management working closely with copywriters. Assuming your product or service is mass market, check the geographical area that you intend to mail. Then produce a neighbours' list of all nearby residents who have previously purchased a specific product or service. This kind of list is called a 'cluster list'. Then:

> RIGHT NOW, YOUR NEIGHBOURS ARE MAKING
> GREAT SHOPPING SAVINGS WITH A PLUS CARD.
> WHY NOT JOIN THEM?

Dear Mr Jones	Dear Mr Jones
Last August you kindly purchased a picture messaging mobile phone from us.	Have you ever been at the wheel when, 'ring' 'ring', someone calls on your mobile phone?
As a valued customer, you can now take advantage of a hands-free car adaptor kit at 75% off the manufacturer's recommended retail price.	You can't pull over to a nearby parking lane. Even if you could, by the time you indicate and pull over the phone has stopped ringing.
All you have to do is complete and send the second half of this letter off to us today.	Boy, it's frustrating! Well now you can pick up that call without picking up the phone. Our free car adaptor kit is all you need. Simply complete the following and return it to us today. You'll even save 75% off the usual price.
We look forward to hearing from you.	Your name _____
Yours sincerely	Your mobile number_____
	Your credit card number_____
	Type _____
	Expiry date _____
	Signature_____
	Thank you.
	Yours sincerely

19 Cheque-book mailers

Cheque-book mailers feature a cheque-book type format in which each 'cheque' is a valuable voucher that can be redeemed for an incentive such as an additional entry into a prize draw or used against the purchase of goods.

The 'cheque stub' section of the book often incorporates text copy. Each page of text refers to that section's personalized 'cheque'.

20 Sniff and buy mailers

Scent strips are a cost-effective way of demonstrating, through the post, products such as perfumes. You can spice up a mailing such as a personalized letter by incorporating scent strips alongside the copy. The overall sensation (or scentsation!) is conveyed in a letter that you read and smell as you go along:

> YOU CAN SMELL THE SUMMER MEADOWS IN
> A SCOTSDALENORTH AIR FRESHENER.

21 Go green

Direct mail advertisers who wish to convey an environmentally responsible approach to mailings may print their entire mailer on recycled paper. This is a popular option for organizations such as charities or political parties. The downside is that recycled paper has a detrimental effect on print quality. The upside is that this effect can demonstrate that an organization isn't wasting its budgets on stunningly beautiful advertising – instead it is investing in helping needy causes. Ironically, recycled paper has been known to be more expensive to buy than ordinary paper!

22 Post and phone

This technique is another way to tease the recipient's curiosity. You send a simple mailing containing nothing more than a postcard. On it you feature an intriguing headline which directs the recipient to make a phone call – when all will be revealed.

Depending on your type of organization and the length of telephone message, this technique can be made even more cost effective by using a self-financing phone number such as a 0990 number.

A variation on this is to send an email with a message asking the recipient to watch their post (providing the email is not unsolicited). See also the Web-linked mailer, p. 182.

23 The overseas letter

Curiosity can be enhanced if you mail your piece from an overseas address. In certain circumstances, that may save on postal costs.

24 Fax mailers

Every office has a .com address. Remember that they nearly all
have a fax machine or software as well. By using it sparingly –
even asking for permission first – you can take advantage of it
to add immediacy and impact to your offer. Try to keep your
message on one page. Use large and bold typefaces and always
provide details of how you can be contacted.

25 Questionnaire mailers

Questionnaires help to test a market or build a new database.
They show existing customers that you care about their opinion.
They give you an ideal opportunity to contact customers and
strengthen the dialogue with them. You should write
questionnaires with simplicity in mind. Questions should be
clear, copy should be precise, terminology should be kept to a
minimum. Each question should require either one direct
answer or one choice from a pre-determined set of multiple-
choice answers.

Copy tips for questionnaires

- Explain why you are sending the questionnaire. Use a
  covering letter to explain why you are asking for a response.
  Reassure your respondent that answers are confidential. (If
  you intend to use the answers for other companies, give the
  respondent the opportunity to decline the option to share
  data with other organizations.) Consider the merits of
  rewarding answers with a free gift.
- Complete a sample question to show how the respondent is
  intended to answer the rest of the questionnaire.
- Don't put the cart before the horse. In other words, track
  your questions so that they first refer to a concept and
  gradually build up to a specific product or service that caters
  for a need.
- Try whenever possible to avoid open-ended questions. Here
  are examples of these:

  Why do you think ...

  Explain your views ...

- Include a 'Don't know' option. If you don't do that, the
  respondent who really doesn't have an opinion on a specific
  question may think that the question is too difficult and give
  up.

- Always tell your respondent that the questionnaire is not an intelligence test. There are no 'right' answers. The only thing being tested is your product or service.
- Don't cram too many possible answers into one question. Instead of:

> **TYPICALLY, HOW MANY OWN-LABEL PRODUCTS**
>
> **DO YOU BUY AT SCOTSDALENORTH.COM?**

ask about each of the product categories, one at a time, and then:

> **IN A WEEK DO YOU BUY**
>
> ONE ☐ TWO ☐ THREE ☐ CANS OF SCOTSDALENORTH VEGETABLES?
>
> **WHICH CAN OF VEGETABLES DO YOU BUY?**
>
> **MUSHROOMS ☐ CORN ☐ CARROTS ☐**

- If you have to be intimate – do so tactfully. Intimate or personal questions should if possible be avoided.

Instead of:

> **HOW MUCH DO YOU EARN?**

try:

> **IS YOUR INCOME BETWEEN**
>
> **£20,000 AND £30,000**   ☐
>
> **£31,000 AND £35,000**   ☐
>
> **OVER £36,000**   ☐

If you cannot avoid direct intimate questions, explain why you need to ask them.

Avoid:

> **HAVE YOU EVER HAD AN EXTRA-MARITAL AFFAIR?**

Instead ask:

> **IN ORDER TO ESTABLISH HOW OUR SERVICE CAN BEST PROVIDE**
> **CONFIDENTIAL COUNSELLING TO COUPLES, PLEASE ANSWER**
> **THE FOLLOWING:**
>
> **IN THE LAST YEAR, HAVE YOU HAD MORE THAN ONE SEXUAL**
> **PARTNER?**
>
> **YES ☐ NO ☐ IF YES, HOW MANY? 1–2 ☐ 3–4 ☐ OVER 5 ☐**

- Always include a pre-paid postage device – sealable and overprinted with the word 'Confidential'.

Refer also to *Teach Yourself Marketing*.

26 Prize draw mailings and competitions

Prize draw mailings and competitions add excitement and energy to a product or service offer. In the UK, these may be:

- Charitable lotteries.
- Draw for which no skill or purchase required; selection of a pre-determined number of tickets.
- Competitions calling for a fair degree of physical or mental skill or judgement, and with the proviso that a purchase must be made.
- Competition for which no purchase is needed, no payment is required, and there is no call for great skill or judgement.

So, ScotsdaleNorth could:
- Ask customers to make a purchase and enter a *competition* to:

> **IDENTIFY THE COUNTRY OF ORIGIN OF**
>
> **FOUR TYPES OF CANNED FRUIT**
>
> **AND COMPLETE A TIE-BREAKER**

- Ask any person to enter a hundredth anniversary *free prize draw* by completing a coupon and returning it by post. (No purchase needed.)
- Ask customers to purchase a *lottery* ticket for £1, with part of the proceeds going to a charity and a top prize of £20,000-worth of shopping (as long as the company was registered as part of a voluntary body giving proceeds to the charity and

followed the restrictions imposed by the Lotteries and Amusement Act).

- Ask anyone to play a shopping *game* and win a holiday (as long as the game was based on the rules for a draw and incorporated in the Gaming Act restrictions).

In copy terms, prize draws and competitions should lead with the big prize:

> **WE'LL PAY YOUR SHOPPING BILLS FOR LIFE.**

Are there any runner-up prizes? If so, list them. The more prizes, the more chances to win! And what's the total amount of prize money or prize value? Tell your readers:

> **ALL IN ALL, WE'RE GIVING AWAY AN INCREDIBLE**
> **$105,000,000 WORTH OF PRIZES!!!**

The bigger the figures, both in financial terms and appearance on the page, the better. You could also feature the big numbers on valuable-looking prize draw certificates.

Did you know?

One art director that I used to work with collected old bonds. He adapted the borders on each bond and used them to give an impression of value on prize draw certificates.

If there are any previous winners, give their names – with their permission. People like to see real people winning prizes. Always discuss how easy it is to enter and win.

Incorporate 'dream copy' into your text:

> Just think, this time next month you could be relaxing by the pool of the five-star Holiday Hut hotel in Dimona. Fancy a drink? Your bar steward will be delighted to serve you anything from a tropical Pina Colada to a long, cool and refreshing Tequila Sunrise.
>
> In the evening you can step out in style. We'll lay on a chauffeur-driven limousine that will whisk you and your partner away to the sensational Tangles night-club …

Or:

> What would you do if you won $20,000,000?
> Buy a mansion in the country? Ten Rolls-Royces?
> Your own light aircraft? ... Why not start up that
> business you've always promised yourself?
> Take a year-long cruise around the world ...

Always list your rules simply and clearly:

1 Entrants must be residents of the UK and over the age of 18, but not employees (or members of their families) or anyone connected with the draw.

2 All entries to be received by [date]. The draw for a Rolls-Royce Silver Shadow car will be made on [date].

3 Only one entry per person is allowed.

4 Entry to the draw is free. No purchase required. Proof of posting will not be accepted as proof of delivery. Responsibility cannot be accepted for lost or mislaid entries. Damaged or defaced entries will be disqualified. No correspondence will be entered into.

5 The winner will be notified by post. The name and area of the prize draw winner will be available after [date] to anyone sending a stamped self addressed envelope to [address].

6 No cash alternative will be offered.

7 The draw will be made by an independent body.

8 Entry to the prize draw is deemed to imply acceptance of these rules.

27 The IT card

This is a variation on point 14, including a CD-ROM as your company brochure (see p. 173). Instead of being a full-sized disc, the IT or multi-media card is the size of a credit card, yet fits into any standard CD-ROM player.

28 The Web-linked mailer

There are several options:

- You can simply send a postcard featuring your website address. Once readers have linked, all you have to do is keep them hooked on your site (see Chapter 12).
- You send out a free piece of software such as an electronic version of a notepad which the reader can type onto by using any PC. At the foot of each notepad 'sheet' is your URL. The reader simply clicks and connects automatically.
- You send out a complimentary Web connect card. The reader dials a special number (printed on the card) via a modem and connects to your site at no cost.

A word about catalogues

Shopping by post often features a catalogue of goods and services. The first-ever mail order business was incorporated on 15 September 1871 as the Army & Navy Co-operative. The society published its first mail order catalogue in February 1872. It had 112 pages and included goodies such as Ladies' Merino Drawers at 5s 9d a pair.

The rules of detailing everything about a product are particularly relevant for catalogue writing. Your style has to be direct. Captions relating to goods have to be benefits led.

Example from fashion catalogue:

(Picture of a blouse – close-up of buttons.)

> PRETTY COLOUR CO-ORDINATED BUTTONS THAT ADD
> AN EXTRA TOUCH OF ELEGANCE.

Explain how things look and feel and how they will make the user look and feel – or cook or read or write – better than ever before.

Example from fashion catalogue:

> NOW WARMTH NEEDN'T BE COMPROMISED BY STYLE.
> THESE BOLD CABLE KNIT CREW NECK SWEATERS ARE DURABLE
> ENOUGH FOR EVEN THE TOUGHEST SCOTTISH NORTH SEA
> CONDITIONS. YET THEY FEEL WONDERFULLY SOFT ON YOUR SKIN.

Copy needs to be complementary to the visual layout and style of the catalogue. It must be enthusiastic and personal, as if you were the shopper's companion. The companion in a shop would point to a special detail of something spotted; instead you include steps in captions throughout the catalogue's pages:

LOOK AT THIS ...

NOTICE THAT ...

Apart from highlighting aspects, this helps the general look of the page.

If you offer a credit facility, always include a small panel after each product description that shows how little needs to be spent over how long in order to buy the product.

Pages need to be highly accessible. Techniques include colour coding to differentiate between categories of item. You can also consider various forms of indexing including heavy board section dividers. You can incorporate extra details in boxes about the history of goods and size of clothes.

100% PURE TRIPLE-WEIGHT CASHMERE

YOUR CHOICE
OF COLOURS   MUSHROOM● MID GREY● TARTAN GREEN●
AVAILABLE SIZES S.M.L.XL.
Our direct price from Scotland:
            ONLY £xxx (UK & EEC)
            ONLY £xxx (OVERSEAS TAX FREE)
JUST QUOTE   CODE XXXX

Add interest by including background titbits about, for example, where a silk dress comes from. Or outline the manufacturing process behind an item:

THIS PEN HAS UNDERGONE 1000 PRODUCTION PROCESSES BEFORE BEING APPROVED.

Another method is to incorporate a testimonial from a happy user. Or include a guarantee panel.

Many catalogues also feature an introduction piece or letter. For this, follow the general rules of writing a direct response letter, with the copy acting as an all embracing guide that explains:

- What makes this catalogue so special.
- The effort that went into its production.
- The range within.
- The easy ways to order.
- Any credit facilities.
- Reiteration of the easy ways to order. (Shaded boxes or panels highlighting order hotlines, perhaps featuring a telephone salesperson, are a good idea to incorporate throughout the catalogue.)

Direct mail quick tips

- Direct mail builds customer relationships.
- Direct mail is a personal business.
- Good copy with bad targeting is wasted copy.
- Mailings need to inform.
- Mailings need to involve.
- Envelopes and copy should reflect a creative tone of voice.
- When appropriate use the words *free* and *you* in copy.
- Entice recipients to open an envelope *now*.
- Letters should be easy on the eye and simple to understand.
- Letters should feature multiple entry points.
- Letters should be personalized.
- Letters should be benefit led.
- Use the three Ws.
- Explain why someone should reply.
- Make replying easy.
- Make replying fun.
- Offer guarantees.
- Use postscripts.
- Feature relevant gadgets only.
- Consider different creative formats.
- Use leaflets to tell a fuller story.
- Use questionnaires to discover more about a prospect and enhance service to a customer.
- Use prize draws and competitions to add energy to a mailing.
- Know your aim.
- Get to know your prospects.
- Talk about them – not you.
- Focus on benefits.
- Get to the point.
- Keep it simple.

- Have a strong opening and theme.
- Be specific – not vague.
- Reflect the language of your brand.
- Offer believable arguments.
- Edit, edit, edit your copy.
- Ask for action.

Common sales letter mistakes

- Too chummy with reader (insincerity).
- Making clichéd statements.
- Too many features – not enough single-minded benefits.
- Bad-mouthing the competition.
- Making 'over-the-top' claims.
- Relying too much on the brochure.

Over to you

1 Write copy for three different types of zipper envelope.
2 Write a lead-in paragraph for a sales letter selling this book.
3 Write a lift letter from Hodder Headline urging people to buy this book.
4 Look at any example of direct mail and highlight the three Ws in the text.
5 Look in your wardrobe. Write a 60-word direct mail catalogue description for an article of clothing.
6 List six different ways to communicate 'free'.

07

direct mail and charity

In this chapter you will learn
- how to use celebrities
- how to develop charity copy tactics
- how to identify donors.

One of the most emotive uses of direct mail is the charity mailing. Although most charities are viewed as good causes, there are certain creative criteria which have been shown to be intrinsically motivating. These share the same key characteristics.

- Goal orientated – appeal for a specific tangible cause (e.g. human rights in China) or for the provision of an essential service (e.g. blood transfusion).
- For the helpless – appeals for charities associated with children, animals, the sick or handicapped; all regarded as good causes.

Kinds of donor

1 **The committed giver**

Gives generously/often. Decides carefully which charity/charities to support. Is concerned about social problems. May do voluntary work or know a disabled person. May have a religious commitment. Characterized by being a realist with an attitude to disability that is based on knowledge. As well as having a straightforward attitude towards giving help, not usually complicated by guilt feelings.

2 **The occasional giver**

Gives less often, usually when asked directly. Is concerned about social problems, but more passively. May do voluntary work or know a disabled person.

Characterized by an ambivalent attitude towards charities/disability, based on ignorance and guilt feelings – 'Should I be doing more?'

Both types of giver are sensitive to the point of resentment to high-pressure tactics.

What turns an occasional donor into a frequent giver?

- Change of lifestyle – often having children.
- Close contact with illness or disability.
- Maturing – becoming less self-orientated and more secure about their role in society.

What motivates people to give?

There are two main types of trigger:

1 **Direct behavioural trigger** – for example, pushing a collection box under someone's nose. This tends to cause an involuntary donation since it is often harder not to give than to give.

2 **Indirect behavioural trigger** – based on rational and emotional evaluation of the cause. A photograph of a sick child in an advertisement will cause the person to appraise the cause rationally before they are moved to contribute.

Both routes are important to help charities be more effective. The level of direct fund raising activity is as important as the indirect promotion of the charity's image and appeal.

Committed charity givers are likely to respond to a worthy cause, regardless of its relevance to them personally. In other words, they are willing to give to others in need.

Occasional givers are likely to be motivated by a personally relevant cause – in other words, they want to know what's in it for them (e.g. they may support safe sex information to limit the spread of HIV).

Attitudes towards charities using advertising and direct mail

Increasing competition in the charity market means that professional marketing of the worthy or good cause is becoming increasingly vital for survival. Charities adopt professional creative standards already used in the marketing of consumer goods. However, charity advertising, including direct mail, remains a sensitive area. Your copy should therefore recognize and respect the feelings of the reader. It is a waste of time to write copy that overdramatizes to such a point that some readers may be subjected to intolerable emotional pressure. Having said this, your copy should be realistic and may not always be pleasant. *Sympathetic realism* is permissible, *emotional blackmail* is not.

Flamboyant television or press advertising which clearly costs a lot of money may be perceived as a wasteful use of funds. When using direct mail, a good impression can be given by use of materials such as recycled paper and simple two-colour leaflets.

If one charity helps another through sharing the names of their supporters, that can save money in buying lists and improve responses. However, contributors to charities may object strongly to this and must be given an opportunity to refuse to have their details passed on.

Types of creative message and specific attitudes

Types of charity advertising can be broadly categorized.

1 **Shock/horror**
This type of copy message ranges from starving kids to frightening statistics. The first creative port of call for charity copywriters is often the horror story. This is not necessarily the best route to take. Overtly shocking visuals stimulate a high degree of negative reaction from even the committed giver.

2 **Case histories**
A charity often has stories to tell about how people have benefited from its help. A case history can be a very involving and interesting way to communicate activities. To do this it needs to:
a provide an emotive dimension (children are especially good for this);
b show how previous donations have helped transform a particular person's life:

> **$20** WILL GIVE THIS GIRL THE GIFT OF A BETTER LIFE

Use of personalities

Endorsement of a cause by a popular and respected personality not only increases the awareness of the charity, but also can add to the credibility of the cause. Obviously the choice of personality is an important consideration. Such perceived image will be representative of the charity itself.

Legacy-direct mail

This kind of direct mail often arises from the results of small-space advertisements placed near the wills and deaths columns in daily newspapers by those charities connected with the fight against terminal diseases (and with old age). For example:

> **1,000,000** CHILDREN KILLED EACH YEAR BY MALARIA.
> NO FLOWERS PLEASE.
> BUT YOU CAN MAKE A LEGACY DONATION TO **MALARIA NETAID**
> **www.malariahelp.org**

Tone

Neither an aggressive attack nor a feeble begging request for money is going to motivate someone to make a donation. This is especially true for the major charities, which must communicate an authoritative image to retain their level of credibility. Whilst it is important to show how reliant you are on donations, the tone in which you do so is crucial.

Dial 911 now!

With so many worthy causes and so much work to be done, day-to-day needs – however urgent – can overwhelm the potential donor. One creative way to overcome this is the Action 911 approach. This turns an ongoing crisis into an emergency. It can be achieved by concentrating on one aspect of a specific need. For example, the overall cause may be a particular country but your Action 911 approach can be shelter in that country:

> **$10** WILL SHELTER THIS CHILD FROM HURRICANES,
> FREEZING RAIN AND FROST BITE.
> TAKE ACTION. PLEASE GIVE TO THE
> EMERGENCY KOSOVO APPEAL TODAY.

Another way to use the Action 911 approach is to time your appeal to coincide with a 'giving' period of the year. Christmas is the firm favourite. You could also choose Diwali, Rosh Hashanah, Chinese New Year, Easter and so on. At the end of the last millennium, scores of Action 911 appeals were launched – especially ones associated with 'last-minute chances to be the first to give to …'.

We can't do anything without you

These creative messages explain exactly what the charity does and how it spends its money:

> **HERE'S WHERE <u>YOUR</u> DONATION GOES.**
>
> (Always ask for a specific sum of money.)
>
> **I WOULD LIKE TO HELP.**
>
> **(PLEASE TICK THE RELEVANT DONATION BOX)**
>
> ☐ **$25** WILL FEED A FAMILY OF FIVE FOR TWO WEEKS.
>
> ☐ **$15** WILL CLOTHE A REFUGEE FOR THE WINTER.
>
> ☐ **$10** WILL IMMUNIZE THREE CHILDREN AGAINST TYPHOID.
>
> ☐ I WOULD LIKE TO DONATE ...
>
> **THANKS FOR YOUR GENEROSITY.**

Notice that the largest sum was shown first and none of the sums is excessive. Also note the option for the donor to give a sum of their own choice.

Whenever possible, veer your copy towards helping people, not conditions. By all means use visual supports to show the scope of a problem, but centre both your copy and visual on individual cases within an overall problem. For example:

> **LUCY IS FIFTEEN YEARS OLD AND HOMELESS.**
>
> **£10** COULD PREVENT HER FROM MEETING MEN WHO
>
> ARE ALL TOO WILLING TO PART WITH **£10**.

Never make a request that makes the problem sound so vast that any donation would appear to be a drop in a bottomless ocean. Avoid this:

> EACH YEAR IT COSTS **$12** MILLION TO KEEP CHILDREN
>
> OFF THE STREETS.
>
> CAN YOU HELP?

moving pictures

In this chapter you will learn
- about the development of copy for TV
- how to attract viewers
- how to write direct response TV ads
- how to handle sex in TV advertising
- how and when to use TV celebrities
- how to use animation.

TV and cinema

Since the 1950s, television has played a major role in communicating sales messages. In the twenty-first century, thanks to WebTV and accessing streamed TV on mobile phones (via 3G technology), traditional television sets and multi-media consoles like games machines, this role will increasingly become more important. Digital networks have made the planet a smaller place in which sales propositions can be effectively communicated at a local level – globally. Irrespective of political borders, commercial broadcasting enables commercial messages to be transmitted across international borders, direct to the consumer.

The rapid rate of television penetration is amazing. From a creative copy view, there are two sides to growth. Originally, television copy was directed to vast mass markets. Copy detail specifics were kept to a minimum. TV copywriting still needs to be minimalist, concentrating on a single message. However, the mass-market approach is not always the right way to approach writing TV commercials. Here's why:

- Wider distribution of television signals creates greater demand for television sets.
- More viewers want more channel options.
- More channels mean more choice.
- Greater choice gives rise to higher levels of specialization.
- Specialization requires more defined targeting.
- Defined targeting means narrower markets.
- Narrow markets call for more specific copy.
- 'Tighter' copy speaks to smaller groups.
- Smaller, defined groups are more likely to be interested in the proposition.

So, on one hand the growth of television penetration and channel proliferation is breaking up the old mass-market benefits of TV advertising. Now it's tailored ('narrow-broadcasting'), so-called 'METV', in which you, the viewer, have the power to mix and choose from a smorgasbord of digitally enhanced, interactive channels. Which should you select?

Quick judgements are based on what the viewer initially sees as they zap channels (or, to use an Internet expression, surf) with a remote control. This results in:

1 TV commercials designed with attention given to the visual content rather than to word content. (At a glance, does this look interesting? Either yes, no or zap.)

2 Copy has to be trimmed down to the most basic information – viewers' attention span is quite short. A fairly elaborate picture takes 1.5 to 2 seconds to process. (That is the time in which the brain processes the words of this sentence.)

As viewers become more and more desensitized to TV, the task for copywriters to produce highly memorable TV commercials becomes increasingly difficult.

What makes people watch TV commercials?

Your mind constantly processes various stimuli. When that process is interrupted, the brain starts to concentrate on the source of the interruption. In the case of television commercials, when a sight or sound attracts attention, the pupil of the eye dilates. This in turn causes the lens to focus on the television screen. So a bridge is established between the viewer and the TV commercial.

This process of diverting the mind to one specific area of attention takes less than a second to establish itself. During that time, a decision has to be made about whether to allow the bridge to stand, enabling more detail from the source of distraction (i.e. the television commercial) to be processed; or to ignore the stimulus and go on to something more interesting.

With so many other possible distractions that demand attention from the viewer (such as an itchy hand or a hot cup of coffee that demands drinking), this process is virtually impossible to control. However, by understanding which stimuli are likely to arrest attention in the first place, it is possible to influence the viewer's propensity to becoming distracted by a television commercial.

The good news for a copywriter is that if the commercial is broadcast during a programme that is already of significant interest to the viewer, the chances are that they will not be distracted from the screen during a television break. Also, the sooner the commercial appears after the start of the break, the higher the probability that the viewer won't be distracted by something else.

Yo! You!

Possible routes to attracting attention include the following.

1 Material meanings

- Colours – vivid colours alert. Pastel colours pacify.
- Sounds – overtly loud or unusually muffled both stimulate interest.
- Movement – a moving object is often more 'moving' than a stationary one.
- Size – unusual sizes and shapes attract interest.
- Light – contrast stimulates.

2 Social interpretations

- Eyes – express feeling and depth (very good for close-up shots).
- Facial expressions – provide further details of emotions.
- Hands – accentuate key points.
- Posture – helps set the mood: casual, attentive, professional, laid back.
- Sexual undertones – incredibly strong attention distracters.
- Children or pets – bring out natural paternal or maternal protective instincts.

Now you've got the viewer's attention, pull the trigger

Once you have attracted the viewer's attention and constructed a bridge, you can begin to think about ways to make those images work with copy to trigger the right types of emotions for a product or service. To do this you must consider the way in which you present the basic attention stimuli. For example:

- Movement – animated.
- Size – huge shopping trolley.
- Sound – music.
- Behaviour – incongruent, novel or surprising.
- Hands – expressive.
- Face – animated.
- Posture – lively.

The television image could be of a tin of ScotsdaleNorth (traditional) baked beans pacing up and down in a shopping trolley singing to the tune of 'Please Release Me':

> PLEASE RELEASE ME, LET ME GO.
>
> YOUR KIDS WILL LOVE THE WAY I TASTE.
>
> AT A MERE 90 CENTS A TIN.
>
> VALUE MY FREEDOM,
>
> OR I'LL BE A HAS BEAN.

The commercial above ends with a mother removing the tin of baked beans from the shopping trolley and handing it over to an eager child.

This cheerful approach to selling baked beans sets off a wider and deeper range of psychological triggers. In this case the triggers could include:
• fun
• cheap
• cute
• children.

The viewer then processes this information and draws a conclusion: the product is fun to eat, cheap to buy and will keep the kids happy.

Each time you make a creative interpretation for a television commercial, as in all forms of advertising which help re-enforce a brand name, show the company logo either throughout the commercial (on the tin of baked beans) or at the close of the commercial, or both. In this way the viewer is stimulated to associate an image with the product. (Also refer to Chapter 2.)

Practical creative approaches

Now it's time to consider some popular creative TV genres. Unlike press advertising or direct mail, television – and, to a lesser extent, its cousin radio – is an entertainment centre. Your television commercial has to entertain as well as inform. Through doing so, a commercial acts as a catalyst for creative concepts to be embraced rather than endured.

The market pitch and 'how to ...' commercials

The sales style or spiel of an old-fashioned market tradesperson reveals great 'how to ...' TV commercial copy techniques. The trader shows you:

- What it does.
- How durable it is.

- What is for sale.
- How it compares with similar goods.

- Why he has to sell it *now*.
- Why you'd be crazy not to buy it.

- How cheap it is.
- What you should do to get it.

The sales spiel is confident. The trader will use enduring sales gimmicks – from throwing an unbreakable china plate on the ground to chopping a variety of vegetables with one simple cutting device. The customer is repeatedly shown the virtues of the product. One benefit rapidly follows another. It all culminates in an orgy of customer demands to buy this product *now*!

In just the same way, step by step, the 'how to ...' commercial explains how something can be done quicker, slower, easier, softer, cleaner, cheaper and so on. Nothing is left to speculation. Every aspect is assured. In the United States it is commonplace to put the market trader in a studio, give him television air time and get him to sell. The problem with this approach is that for a good sales pitch the seller needs time to warm up an audience until they are driven into a heated frenzy to buy, buy, buy!

One method of
- stirring up interest
- demonstrating a product attribute
- and stimulating sales in a limited time

is to use an unusual, even far-fetched demonstration.

Here is an example for PenPod:

VISUAL	AUDIO
Man sits in a demolition truck. He is about to swing the wrecking ball against the wall of an old building.	(Male, aged 35 plus, voice over (VO), very confident.) PenPod is the strongest, most reliable pen you can buy.
(Close-up.)	But don't take my word for it.

PenPod adhered to a brick wall. It is stuck on the bull's-eye of a painted target.	
Ball swings and hits the pen at full impact. The wall collapses.	(Sound effect (SFX).)
Man walks through the rubble and uncovers the PenPod. It is in perfect shape. He dusts it down, opens it and begins to write on a piece of paper.	Crash! Well that's all, write then.
(PenPod logo superimposed on the screen.)	You'd be lost for words without it.

The secret of writing a successful demonstration commercial is to put your product really through the mill. Defy speculation.

> BEFORE WASHING THIS T-SHIRT IN SCOTSDALENORTH BRILLIANCE POWDER IT LOOKED LIKE THIS. [GRIMY]
>
> NOW IT LOOKS LIKE THIS! [SHINY]

Proudly show off every detail. A working engine can be shown from inside. A plank of wood that's treated with fire-resistant paint can be shown being lowered and retrieved in one piece from the mouth of a volcano.

Get in the driving seat

Car commercials can embrace one or more of the following aspects:

- Show the car in action.
- Show someone driving the car.
- Show interior and exterior of the car. Exterior footage should feature the body highlights and the lines and curves of the vehicle.
- Show the type of person who drives the car.
- Show the type of person who typically drives the car driving the car.
- Concentrate on specific mechanical and technical enhancements – e.g. safety.
- Encourage you to test drive the car.

One of the most popular approaches is to show the car in action in a suitably dramatic landscape. Such commercials rely more on art direction than copywriting. Here, lighting, music and scenery take centre stage. The downside of this kind of TV commercial is that you can spend vast sums of money just searching ('recceing') for a suitable location before you get to film anything. Also you'll need to invest money in capturing the glamour: 16 mm or even 35 mm film is often chosen over video. This is because video does not usually capture colour tones as vibrantly as film does.

Special effects ranging from clever use of lighting to computer aided visual procedures are all well and good. Finishing touches such as film type, sound, set design, lighting, make-up, wardrobe and locations all come under the term 'production values'. The more time and effort taken over each production value, the more expensive the final presentation of the commercial will be.

Most special effects are inspired by music videos and cinema production effects. (Advertising usually follows trends – it does not set them.) However, no effect can ever replace a strong, single-minded message. Anything else distracts from the simple, big idea if you are not careful and is simply icing on the cake.

Did you know?

The first gay relationship commercial ever broadcast in the UK was shown during December 1995, for Guinness. It is a prime example of advertising following social trends rather than setting precedents.

Slice of life

Viewers identify with soap characters. As you have seen, television commercials take a sales message directly to the heart of a family home. They provide a great opportunity to introduce the viewer's family to a product's fictitious family.

The 'slice of life' technique helps establish a product or service as something that is accessible to ordinary everyday people. More importantly, showing the product being used by real people – people like the viewers – gives the product additional street cred.

Slice of life commercials can feature any person in a family:

- The kids
- Mum and dad
- Grandparents
- The kids and mum
- Mum, dad and the kids
- Grandparents and any of the above

Slice of life commercials can also feature:
- Friends
- Friends of the family
- Would-be lovers

As you are writing for everyday people, your dialogue should be written colloquially. Think of your copy as a transcript of conversation heard by eavesdropping on people in situations like these:
- at work
- at the dinner table
- watching TV
- at the bus stop
- whilst shopping and so on.

Subjects need to be based on everyday occurrences or (given acceptable creative licence) possible everyday occurrences. The best slice of life commercial campaigns have an ongoing theme that spins out across several TV commercials. For example:
- Will the girl ever get the boy?
- Will the kids ever appreciate their parents?
- Will he ever know it is she?
- Will she ever get promotion?

The slice of life scenario should revolve around the product – not vice versa. If you were, for example, to produce a slice of life commercial for a PenPod, the pen would act as an anchor point for the action.

First commercial:

Character B passes by the window of a shop selling a PenPod and daydreams about Character A, who is on business 1000 miles away.

Character A wants to write a letter to Character B and looks for a pen, but can't find one.

Beautiful Character C enters the scenario and offers to lend Character A her PenPod.

The first commercial ends leaving a question in the viewer's mind:

'Who is Character C?'

The end title reads:

Get the message with PenPod

Second commercial:

> Character B receives the letter from Character A and writes a
> love letter back to Character A.
>
> Meanwhile, Character C (who is at home) is seen writing
> something with her PenPod, signing it and then posting it.
>
> Character A receives a letter, opens it and smiles.
>
> Character B, in her location, smiles.
>
> Character C, in her location, smiles.
>
> The second commercial ends, leaving the question
> 'Who wrote what to whom?'
>
> The end title reads:
>
> Get the message with PenPod

And so on.

Intimate moments – handling sex on TV

You may have noticed that I included 'would-be lovers' in the
slice of life category of TV commercials. Television can
sometimes be considered as the eavesdropper's magnifying glass
on the world. It demonstrates – often graphically – what can be
achieved, given the right factors, in everything from business to
love, including sex.

> **Did you know?**
>
> Sex is sometimes presented as seductively alluring yet
> tantalizingly forbidden. The talk-show host Jerry Springer has
> banked a fortune on it. Politicians' affairs captivate world-wide
> audiences because of it. Sex sells. Pop star videos may feature
> glamorous divas who spread their reputation on it. Products that
> may be considered lavish, potentially bad for your figure,
> indulgent and so on all make great intimate-moment TV
> commercials.

When you want to bring in sex, ideal product candidates
include:
- ice-cream
- chocolates
- body care products like foam baths
- keep-fit equipment.

Sexual undertones can be really subtle yet powerfully effective. One common creative trick is to endow an inanimate object with a phallic symbol. For example:

- A woman snuggles up against a rolled-up towel and says how soft it feels against her skin.
- A model wearing luscious lipstick licks and then takes a long and sensuous bite into a ripe apple.
- A man caresses a bottle of aftershave with a female shape.
- A woman drinks from a stream of clear, frothy water cascading out of a long-necked bottle.

Another type of intimate-moment TV commercial is the secret sex approach. This can include an intimate confession about:

- Cleavage-enhancing bras.
- Sports and leisure activity supportive underwear.
- Leg-caressing tights.
- Passion-arousing perfume.
- Discreet sanitary towels that help you get on with your life.

The big star on the small screen

'I'm still as big a star as ever. It's only the screen that got smaller.'

(Gloria Swanson)

If you are going to hire a celebrity to endorse a product or service on television, first ask yourself who is going to be the real star of the production:

- The celebrity?
- The product?

If on the screen the star dominates the product, your creative message won't wash, so don't use the celebrity if there is a risk of that.

Did you know?

There have been many TV commercials that have made a star an even bigger celebrity. That's acceptable. But the product must not get forgotten somewhere along the road. Worst still, the new star's new image may mean that, several commercials down the road, the star's agent will demand more money. That makes a good case for settling all star appearances in writing before embarking on a long-term campaign.

As in testimonials used in press advertising (see 'Question headlines' on p. 77), write as the person would speak. If the star is really talented you may be asked to suggest an outline script and allow the celebrity to add the finishing touches. (This assumes you or your client is prepared to take a risk.)

A popular strategic creative option is to use TV stars rather than big-screen stars. Firstly, they usually cost less and, more importantly, they are more familiar visitors to the viewer's home as they are more often seen. Therefore they are more credible. Such stars may include soap opera players.

Stars needn't come from the show-business galaxy of glitz and glitter. Industry-specific 'stars' add extra credibility. Try these:
- A policeman endorsing a safety belt.
- A dotcom hero endorsing a website.
- A cook endorsing a food product.
- An author endorsing a pen.

If you really want to add public credibility to a product or service, you could always get ordinary people to endorse it. This approach makes a product appear practical rather than aspirational. One way around this is to feature ordinary people using the product and stars introducing the product to the ordinary person.

Creative techniques include:
- On-the-street interviews/doorstep interviews in which the star interviews people outside their homes about a specific product or service.
- Extreme close-ups of people discussing the product (known as 'Talking heads').
- Ordinary people acting like stars because of the glamour associated with the product in question. (One taste of ice-cream makes the housewife enter a fantasy world where she takes on the appearance of a well-known, sexy actress or singer.)
- Company directors demonstrating their own product and confidence in that product.

Animation

Animated characters are cute. They have been since the first English-language cartoon film appeared in 1906. The question to ask before enlisting the help of an animator is 'Just how cute is the image that you wish to convey?'

Cartoon characters can make:
- a weighty subject lighter
- a 'me too' item lively
- a toy more desirable
- a boring subject interesting
- a brand name person-friendly.

They can become the spokesperson for the brand. For example:
- Peter PenPod could be a talking, walking PenPod who introduces and demonstrates the product.
- The Fruities could be a pop band made up of ScotsdaleNorth fruit yoghurt characters.

Never become entrapped into writing an entertaining commercial that happens to sponsor a product rather than a sales commercial that is entertaining. Animated TV commercials should be uncomplicated.

Did you know?

The best animated characters are drawn with very human expressions. Indeed, the more you can incorporate exaggerated human qualities into a character, the more charming the character appears on screen.

Sound effects and music can make or break a piece of animation. Take as much care and spend as much time choosing suitable sound tracks as you do in choosing an animator. Music sound tracks can be parodies of existing pieces of music adapted to suit an individual piece of music. Parodies of 1950s–1990s music are especially popular.

Sung to Elvis Presley's 'Hound Dog':

(Animated dog, dressed in 1950s suit, singing to a can of dog food.)

You ain't nothing to a hound dog
Your meat is just brine.
You ain't nothing to a hound dog
Your taste is cheap brine.
Just hand back my Scotsdale
And I'll be doing fine.

(Spoken to camera – in Elvis's voice.)

You may step on my suedes,
but never mess with my meal, man.

Alternatively, you can feature extracts from existing mood-enhancing themes and songs.

I once adapted the original Addams Family TV series theme tune to promote the animated cartoon series of the Addams Family:

Title: Lurch sings   **Duration:** 30 seconds

Notes: Lurch sings the whole commercial to the Addams Family theme tune. Each scene enters screen from top to left, bottom, right and so on, in sequence.

Video	Audio
(cartoon channel logo) (animated explosion reveals action)	They're
Bear looks shocked and jumps out of picture (2 seconds)	kooky (SFX – bear in shock)
American presidential statues have a shock (3 seconds)	and they're spooky. (SFX – crumbling rocks)
All the family dancing (9 seconds)	You'll find them on the telly. So tune in, be there early
ID of all the family (2 seconds)	for the Addams Family.
Boy makes boggle eyes (2 seconds)	It's on the cartoon channel. (SFX – 'boing, boing')
Uncle Fester eats a chain (1 second)	Uncle Fester (SFX – 'crunch')
Lurch thumping his chest like Tarzan (2 seconds)	and me, Lurch,
Mr and Mrs Addams and Uncle Fester get groovy with electricity (4 seconds)	we'll welcome you to join us (SFX – electricity buzz) on the Addams Family.
Rain cloud appears and fills moat around the car (3 seconds)	If you think my voice is weird, (SFX – thunder clap) like a soprano with a beard,
Grandma cooking up a brew (4 seconds)	it's nothing as bizarre (SFX – bubbling stew)
Cartoon channel credits fall from top of screen	as the Addams Family. (Spoken to himself) With my musical talent, maybe I should get an agent.

When you write copy for a cartoon character, watch the clock. (Notice how the script for the Addams Family showed how long it took for each piece of action to be acted out.) In the case of a 30-second commercial, reduce your word count from 60–70 (usual for live action commercials) to 40–50 (right for cartoon commercials). This allows the cartoon to animate into life without being shackled by too many words. As with all television and radio commercials, act out your animated sequence to see if it fits within your allocated time slot.

Animation does not simply mean cartoons. You can consider animation as part of a live commercial to demonstrate the mechanics of a product, enliven a company logo or add emphasis to a sales message. For example:

- A housewife pours detergent down a kitchen sink and the plug hole animates into a smile.

Animation can also be used as a special effect. For example you could:

- Stretch a person's face in awkward directions, using part live action and part animation.
- Use stop frame animation to transform an ordinary scene into a Keystone Cops-style flickered image.
- Fly people on a magic carpet or even have them dance with an animated product.

The possibilities are endless.

There is one final advantage of animated commercials – especially those which feature cartoon characters. Sadly, a large proportion of the population have reading skills difficulties. This is because of many different factors, ranging from social, psychological and educational all the way to being new to the country. Like newspaper cartoon strips, animated cartoons help you get a message across simply and entertainingly.

The last laugh

Humorous copy on TV can give a fading brand a bit of shine.

Did you know?

Where possible, you should not apply overt humour to new brands as there is a danger that the humour will distract viewers from the sales benefits.

Viewers like to laugh. If you can make them laugh, hopefully they will pay greater attention to your message. Of course, if your humorous message is too hilarious, its overall effectiveness will be impaired. The viewer will spend too much time laughing at the gag rather than thinking about the product or service. On the other hand, a great joke can distract the viewer's attention from any arguments against making a purchase.

With so many possible directions it is not surprising that this type of commercial is one of the hardest to write. Even if you do get the gag right, there are only a finite number of times that you can broadcast the same joke. One of the main difficulties with managing humour for a TV commercial or even cinema commercial is that a good joke needs time to make an impact. Most TV commercials are 30 seconds in length. Seven of those seconds are taken up with establishing a scene and end-of-sequence logo branding.

Assuming you are convinced that a humorous commercial is the best way to sell a product or service, you have to consider what to base the humour upon.

A good gag with bite calls for:
• a well-structured plot
• an easily accessible set up
• an interesting character
• a precision-timed delivery
• and an unexpected punch line.
All in 30 seconds!

Did you know?

One of the best ways to look for something funny is to look at yourself. This is very hard. You have to observe your own frailties and shortcomings and list them, honestly – warts and all. Use the same technique on friends and family. You should eventually see a pattern of similarities emerging.

Use the most striking of those similarities to add dimension to a central character. Creating empathy with a character takes time. There are two ways to address this:

1 Borrow a character from a comedian, a comic strip or an amusing piece of animation.
2 Build a long-term campaign revolving around the central character.

Give the character a task which, try as they might, it seems that the entire world is ganged up on to foil. The problem is solved, thanks to a particular product or service. This helps create sympathy with the characters who are trying so hard to do something in order to make a point.

Video	Audio
Shop assistant builds a traditional pyramid of tins of baked beans – as an end-of-aisle sales promotion device	
She places the last tin on top of the pyramid	
The pyramid collapses	
She replaces the tin	
The pyramid collapses	
She replaces the tin	(Male Voice Over – MVO) NO ONE
The pyramid collapses	
She replaces the tin	BUT NO ONE CAN STOP
The pyramid collapses	OUR PRICES FROM FALLING
Graphic – animated ink stamp thuds onto the screen.	SCOTSDALENORTH PRICE SAVERS. GOOD FOOD HAS NEVER BEEN AT BETTER VALUE.
It reads:	
ScotsdaleNorth Baked Beans just 10p a tin up your high street on the Web	

Consider making your character talk to inanimate objects or treat awkward objects (such as something incredibly large like a grand piano, or tiny like a microchip, or absurd like a false leg) as if they were alive. You could place your character and product or service in an unfamiliar surrounding, such as:
• a different country
• a different time
• a different place
• a different planet.

You could also:
• mingle new technology with traditional ideas
• use upside-down logic (instead of hitting a nail in the wall, hit the wall into the nail)
• draw illogical conclusions from logical summations.

Consider introducing your character to other characters with peculiar afflictions, like a nervous twitch or a compulsion to squawk like a parrot – the stranger, the better. Consider exposing an unspoken social neurosis or depression. (However, keep it in mind that some of your viewers suffer from such a problem.)

Don't just settle for small problems. Give your character vast problems – exaggerate the predicament, exaggerate a solution, by finding the answer using the most convoluted of routes. If things have to go wrong, make them go disastrously wrong, allowing the product or service to act as the catalyst that saves the day.

Above all, remember that it's OK to see the funny side of life as long as that image insults neither the integrity of a product or service nor the viewer's instinctive perception of what is politically, socially and morally acceptable.

Video	Audio
Sombre, moodily lit room	(Psychiatrist)
In the centre is a psychiatrist	It's down to you.
He is talking to a patient	
(whom we can't see)	
The doctor sits on the edge of his large leather chair, looking concerned – obviously very involved with his patient's case	
Close-up of the psychiatrist, trying to reason with the patient	Things appear dark now. It needn't always be that way.
The psychiatrist stands up and walks to the other side of the room	You *really* have to want to change.
Close-up of the patient, who turns out to be an animated, branded light bulb	(Light bulb) OK already.
Titles appear on the screen – logo is a light bulb that a hand switches on; as the switch clicks so the words *Have you seen the light?* appear	(MVO) Brillo Lights. Have *you* seen the light?

TV you read

Once you have captured a viewer's interest, you need to retain it. One way of driving a message home is to turn a TV commercial into a graphic bulletin board. Instead of relying purely on a powerful image accompanied by memorable music and convincing dialogue, why not go all the way and add graphically designed titles that reinforce key benefits?

A PenPod TV commercial could show a beautiful actress in a romantic setting, writing with a PenPod. At the same time the dialogue (or voice over) could be saying:

The stylish way to write – right from the heart.

The superimposed titles could animate out of the apparent love letter, varying in shape and length, reading:

Through forcing the viewer to read text rather than just hear and watch images you are able to reinforce a key statement.

TV jingles

Contrary to popular belief, jingles are not meant to 'sing out' the end of a commercial. If that were their sole purpose, they would be self-defeating. Every jingle, no matter how melodious, would only serve as a sign to the viewer that it is time to lose interest in the commercial. All jingles, including radio jingles, provide instant recognition of a brand. In the case of radio, a jingle helps establish a brand logo and embellish it with 'sound' values. (See 'Music', pp. 226–7.) It is a musical reminder which combines the evocative pull of a musical score with the selling clout of a persuasive piece of copy. The craft of jingle composition may seem simple, even trivial. However, catchy jingles, like catchy headlines, are not easy to write.

A jingle has to:
- reinforce a product or brand name
- inform and add personality as well as amuse

> I'VE NEVER HAD A PEN FRIEND LIKE A PENPOD.

- make sense and at the same time rhyme

> IT'S THE ONE FOR ME – A WRITTEN GUARANTEE.

- summarize everything in one simple statement:

> GET THE MESSAGE ACROSS – PICK UP A PENPOD.

One of the product categories for which jingles are especially popular is toys. Jingles can have an important role in children's own play time. Each time a game is played, the child may think of the jingle associated with a toy character involved in the game. Even everyday tasks can be turned into play. Every time Mum or Dad serves the breakfast cereal, the child may think of a character in a TV commercial who uses the jingle.

Finally, a jingle should be enduring.

Did you know?

In the UK the Ovalteenies jingle was still going strong in the late 1980s – some fifty years after first being broadcast. The oldest American jingle that was still in use in the 1990s was first broadcast in the 1920s – for a cereal called Wheeties.

Get the picture?

Standard 35 mm or 16 mm film runs through a projector at 1440 frames per minute. A story board, which is a series of illustrated frames, helps capture the essence of the action shown in a piece of film. It is a vital tool to assist commercial directors with creative aspects such as lighting, mood, camera angle and general character positioning. It can show you or your client how the commercial will appear on the screen. However, there is a problem with story boards. There are many excellent artists who can show copywriters and art directors portfolios of different styles. Yet, unlike film or digital video, a story board can only capture the basic creative essence of a commercial, including shot continuity and the general flow of action. In order to accurately represent the entire (30-second) production, it would have to feature 720 separately illustrated frames! One version of a story board is called an 'animatic'. This is a crude animation of the commercial, sometimes used for research purposes.

Ask yourself whether you really need an expensive animatic or story board. If so, at what stage of the creative process? I recommend that you save a story board until you have settled for a typed TV script.

If you have to sell the commercial further, act it out. Read the script aloud, get colleagues to read parts. Titillate your audience. If you are selling the idea to a client, give the client the credit that they have an imagination – your job is to stimulate it.

Writing TV commercials requires you to play the commercial in your mind before committing it to paper. If you can capture what you see in your mind on paper, then you should be able to develop what's on the paper through discussion.

Once you have arrived at an agreed script, think about story boards, especially if you are going to sub-contract the actual production to a producer and director. Rather than dictate what you want – which restricts creativity – a story board will help provide you with peace of mind. What you originally played in your mind will be better understood by the person who has to put the image on the final version.

As for writing a script, please refer to the scripts that I have included in this chapter. Don't worry too much about technical jargon. If you like to use buzz words, the following list should be all you need to ensure that in terms of mechanics your final picture is seen and understood by everyone. If you want to describe a more complicated camera angle or technical aspect, do so in words – but never forget that a director should have the imagination to take your words and turn them into a moving experience.

Ad lib	Spontaneous dialogue – not scripted (ideal for on-the-street interviews).
Animate	To arrange an inanimate object or graphic in a way that, when seen as part of a finished film, gives the impression of movement.
CU	Close-up.

Cut	Change camera angle or scene.
Dissolve	Fade out of one picture or scene into another.
Editpoint	The point at which a scene change is planned.
Eyeline	The position of a subject's eyes on the screen.
Fade in	Brighten the illumination of a scene (usually at the start of a scene).
Fade out	Darken the illumination of a scene (usually at the end of a scene).
Freeze	Stop the action by freezing it in time.
FVO	Female Voice Over.
Lead-in	Initial words spoken by the VO at the start of the action.
MCU	Medium close-up shot – the person is seen from the chest upwards.
MS	Medium shot in which a person on screen is seen from just below the waist upwards.
MVO	Male Voice Over.
SFX	Sound effects.
Super	Superimpose one action or scene on top of another.
Track shot	Horizontal camera movement which zooms in or follows something.
VO	Voice Over.
Wipe	Change of scene from A to B, using a graphic device (e.g. scene B wipes diagonally across scene A).
Zoom in/out	Increase/decrease magnification of a subject.

If you are going to hand your script over to a director eventually, then you have two possible ways to write it:

1 If you are totally confident in the director's abilities, just write the dialogue and describe the action.
   • **Pro** – the director has the chance to enhance a production by giving the commercial an angle that you may not have considered.

- **Con** – are you seriously going to leave your 'baby' in another person's hands?

2 If you want to have greater control over the actual interpretation, also include the camera angles.
   - **Pro** – you know what you put down on paper will end up in the can.
   - **Con** – how would you like to have your creativity shackled and, more importantly, how do you think that will affect the final results?

Direct response television

Direct response TV commercials, like all direct response advertising, is cost quantifiable.

Did you know?

Financial organizations are leaders in DRTV. Commercials can be for anything from life assurance and saving plans to car insurance and home insurance.

In the UK, the original DRTVs (direct response TV commercials) lasted about two minutes. The copy style was usually led by demonstration techniques with a great deal of emphasis given to the response details. However, broader-stream advertisers who preferred repeated short, sharp 30-second commercials persuaded the TV networks to put a stop to these as all the best prime-time commercial spots were being lost.

The copy style of direct response commercials still tends to rely on the here's what it does and here's how you respond approach. Continuous graphics showing telephone numbers and website addresses are vital to reinforce the response mechanism. Weave the telephone number, email address and website details into the presenter's dialogue. By all means use clever techniques like talking telephones or music to give the response device even greater impact – as long as the technique doesn't distract from a clearly understood explanation of why the product or service is beneficial and how to get in touch:

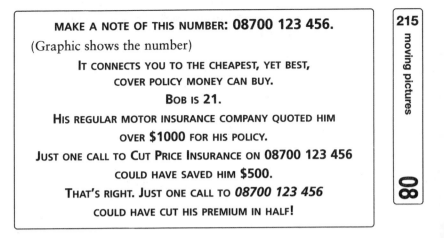

MAKE A NOTE OF THIS NUMBER: **08700 123 456.**

(Graphic shows the number)

IT CONNECTS YOU TO THE CHEAPEST, YET BEST,
COVER POLICY MONEY CAN BUY.

BOB IS 21.

HIS REGULAR MOTOR INSURANCE COMPANY QUOTED HIM
OVER $1000 FOR HIS POLICY.

JUST ONE CALL TO CUT PRICE INSURANCE ON 08700 123 456
COULD HAVE SAVED HIM $500.

THAT'S RIGHT. JUST ONE CALL TO *08700 123 456*
COULD HAVE CUT HIS PREMIUM IN HALF!

and so on.

The creative challenge in writing a DRTV commercial is to wake up the viewer to take some kind of action. A busy, all-singing and all-dancing commercial may lose its single-thought direction. Also if every DRTV commercial featured a presenter shouting or even singing a telephone number, the viewer would switch off the noise. A good DRTV commercial has to:

Demonstrate Stimulate Activate

This is achieved by combining a convincing message with a credible, not overtly pressurized setting. Target a specific audience and urge them to call a response number (particularly a DRTV ad for charity).

Beyond temptation

Based on the seven deadly sins, here are sure-fire ways to stimulate a response from your TV copy:

Sloth	Your product makes life easy, the viewer can do less hard work.
Greed	Why wait to boost your earning power?
Envy	Your friends will go green with jealousy when they see your brand new...
Gluttony	It's so low fat, you can eat as much as you like.
Pride	Display your collection with pride.
Lust	Wear this and drive your partner wild!
Vanity	You will look a million dollars.

I hope that entertained you – now, here's the bill

There's no denying it. Television can be costly.

You can get a commercial shown on regional terrestrial TV for just a few thousand dollars or even pounds – but it would be at the dead of night. Yet even that can compare favourably with a full-page national press advertisement covering a similar geographical region.

TV commercial costs are based on ratings, position, demographics and time. 'Rating' is another way of saying 'percentage of chosen type of audience'. If you want to attract (or reach) a proportion of housewives in South-East England aged 35+ in socio-economic group A1, you would want a rating of perhaps 90.

Timing depends on the time of day when a commercial is shown. Daytime television or very late-night/early-morning television is generally cheaper than prime-time television, when most viewers watch.

Then you have to consider the popularity of a programme and, more specifically, how popular a programme is with the type of person that you wish to reach. Finally, you have to consider the position within a commercial break that your commercial appears in:
• First during the first break?
• Last during the middle break?

And so on.

It is usually wise to purchase your TV time through a television air-time media broker, who has a large portfolio of clients. If you are particularly effective as a negotiator as well as being an effective copywriter and have a highly marketable product to advertise, you could get a very reasonable commercial rate. However, I would advise you against attempting this. It is far shrewder to direct your creative skills to raising viewers' interest by offering entertaining and compelling informative copy than to try to negotiate a higher viewing rate at a lower budget cost.

Before you worry about the cost of airing your celluloid or video masterpiece, you have to consider the cost of producing it. Remember, never let razzmatazz get in the way of a simple, single-minded idea. A straightforward single scene, employing one camera angle and one actor, may be just as powerful as an all-singing, all-dancing Hollywood-style production. Why not substitute for the dancers a couple of pairs of hands with little skirts tied around the fists and a face drawn on the back of each hand? Providing the creative treatment matches the style of product and the tastes of a market sector, anything goes.

Budget allowing, my suggestion is for you to recruit an independent producer who can negotiate on your behalf and 'marry' you with an appropriate commercial director – often easier said than done. (They will want to make the commercial one way whilst you may have other ideas.)

TV commercial advertising quick tips

- Commercials have to entertain as well as inform.
- Demonstration commercials work well with extreme examples.
- Special effects should enhance rather than distract from a single-thought message.
- People like people – 'slice of life' television is effective.
- Sexy commercials can turn guilt into desire.
- Although a celebrity may be a star in their own right, their appearance in a TV commercial is that of a guest – the lead vehicle remains the product or service.
- Animation can be cute. It must be relevant.
- Cartoons speak clearer if you make them say less.
- Never laugh at a product or service. Laugh with it.
- TV graphics of copy make messages more memorable.
- TV jingles should say 'buy me' rather than signify the end of a commercial.
- Story boards can only capture the essence of a commercial, not the soul.
- DRTV sells off the screen as you would sell off the page.
- DRTV commercials should strongly feature a response telephone number supported by a Voice Over that repeats the telephone number.
- If you produce a DRTV commercial, be sure that you have the ability to handle the response.
- Unless the creative message is about a product that is already well established – such as cost-effective car insurance – generally speaking, the longer the DRTV commercial, the greater the chance of a good level of response.
- TV airtime costs can be expensive. Satellite TV stations may be more cost effective than terrestrial ones.
- In terms of creative costs, a very simple yet effective commercial featuring computer graphics of a telephone number could be produced for well under £20,000. The more complex and sophisticated a commercial, the more it costs – and the higher the value of the promotion.

Over to you

1 The brand-new Pastiche 200 series car has a sun roof that when open disperses rainwater away from the car so that driver and passengers always remain dry – whatever the weather. Write three TV commercial treatments in script or story board formats which advertise this useful feature.

2 Write a 20-second TV commercial that encourages motorists to be extra nice to traffic wardens during a special 'Hug a warden' week.

3 Write a 60-second dialogue between two housewives discussing a new kind of washing powder that helps them iron out creases.

   a Keeping all the essential parts of the dialogue, cut the script down to 30 seconds.

   b Keeping all the essential parts of the dialogue, cut the script down to 20 seconds.

   c Keeping all the essential parts of the dialogue, cut the script down to 10 seconds.

4 From your own choice of pop singles, adapt a lyric to sell a PenPod.

   a Without changing any lyrics, choose two well-known songs that could be used to convey the right atmosphere and message for a PenPod TV commercial.

   b In no more than fifty words for each, describe the action of the two commercials devised in 4a.

5 List six different ways to write: CALL NOW ON 0500 123 123.

6 Video two TV commercials, then rewrite the commercials, conveying the same messages without dialogue, using just vision.

7 List eight different ways to write: NOT AVAILABLE IN THE SHOPS.

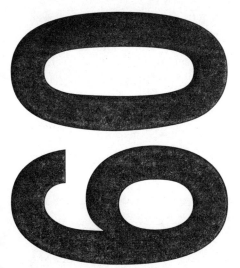

09

listen to this!

In this chapter you will learn
- how to turn a casaual listener into an avid supporter
- how to use music with copy
- how to choose a voice over
- how to use and choose sfx.

Unquestionably, television broadens the mind. (Up to its screen width.) Radio, on the other hand, can stretch the imagination far more effectively. You can listen to the radio just about anywhere, whilst TV demands you are visually as well as audibly connected. Radio is portable, intrusive and accessible. People listen to radio in all kinds of places:

• living room
• bedroom
• kitchen (over 72% of listeners have their set on in the kitchen)
• bathroom (over 27% of people listen to the radio in the bathroom, rising to 43% for ages 15–24).

The percentages above come from RAJAR (Radio Joint Audience Research Limited), which is jointly owned by the BBC and the Association of Independent Radio Companies.

In addition, people listen:

• in cars (17% of commercial radio listeners who are part-time or non-working women listen in the car between 9 a.m. and 12 noon)
• when preparing to go shopping (25% of female main shoppers say that they are likely to be listening to the radio when planning what food to buy).

So a radio commercial is heard by ordinary people doing ordinary things like eating – a good opportunity to target a snack food – or shaving – a good opportunity to target a shaving product ... Your audience is there. As long as your copy is realistic, accessible and believable you can be certain that when your copy 'talks' your audience will hear.

Academic research has shown that '[Radio] as a secondary medium accompanying its users while they are engaged in primary activities, can infiltrate their view of the world in a way which is all the more powerful for being half-conscious' (*Understanding Radio* by Andrew Crissel, published by Methuen).

In the UK, one-third of households have five or more radios in their homes. During the late 1990s, research carried out by CIA Sensor asked: 'If you were marooned on a desert island, which ONE of these things would you want to have with you?:

• A radio that works?
• A subscription to your favourite magazine?
• A subscription to your favourite national newspaper?'

You can guess the most popular answer.

Radio can bring a listener closer to a product or service:

(MVO)

The nib on this PenPod is so smooth that the ink (Whooooah!) slides down and through it effortlessly.

(SFX – MVO brushes himself down)

So giving a smoother, more professional finish to everything you write.

The first thing to do when writing a radio commercial is *not* to write for the listener. Use your copy to 'paint' evocative visual images, not just to present interesting sounds. There is absolutely nothing that the eye can see that the mind cannot 'see' even clearer. You have a powerful arsenal of creative weaponry at your disposal to hammer home a picture. These include:

1 **Choice of VOs** – young, old, male, female, rich, poor, indifferent, professional, zany, serious, happy, sad … and so on. (Unlike TV what the VO looks like is irrelevant. It is what they sound like in the mind that is important.)

2 **Sound effects (SFX)** – a good SFX can add humour and drama and, above all, 'show' a minute yet essential detail that builds tension and delivers credence to your commercial.

Would you like to 'show' the listener a shopper choosing something from a superstore? Here is an example:

(FVO – young Mum type, thinking to herself)

(SFX)

(Busy ScotsdaleNorth store)

Hmmm. Dave wanted something special for dinner tonight … Fisherman's Pie only $1.50. Not bad.

(SFX)
(Places pie in trolley.)

Hmmm. Something to wash it down? Ah, this looks like the job – ScotsdaleNorth's own-brand Muscatel just $5.99 a bottle. That should do nicely.

As for desserts … (giggles to herself) Well, I don't think that even ScotsdaleNorth can take off what I have in mind this evening.

(MVO)

ScotsdaleNorth. Good food, terrific value.

Instead you can 'show' the listener the shopper at home:

(SFX – busy meal time at home,
TV in background, general household pandemonium)

(Very young son)
Mum! Mum! What's for dinner?

(Husband)
Hello, luv.

(Very young son)
Mum! Mum! Sue won't let me play with the football.

(Young teenage daughter)
Hi, Mum, any chance of getting this blouse done for the disco
tonight?

(MVO – warm, friendly)
At ScotsdaleNorth we appreciate that busy mums lead busy lives.

(Mum)
The answer is, 'Wait and see', 'Good day at the office?',
'How many times are you going to wear that thing?'

(MVO)
So we've created the healthy Meal Maker range. Each tasty meal is
nutritionally balanced, with only the freshest of ingredients. Just pop
a Meal Maker in the microwave and, within minutes, you can serve
up a little masterpiece.

(Teenage son)
Not bad.

(Dad)
Mmm

(Daughter)
Maybe the diet should start tomorrow.

(Dad)
Watch it, you two!

(Friendly MVO)
Meal Makers for ScotsdaleNorth.
Perfect meals in minutes.

Delve deeper, turn up the creative volume

Radio has often been considered as a very poor and distant relation to TV. Personally, I think that whilst DRTV is one of the most dynamic ways to measure a creative campaign as well as the most sustainable way to nurture client relationships, radio is one of the most exciting opportunities for pure copywriting.

But does it work? For one piece of research an advertising agency invited over 300 housewives to test out a new ironing product. Whilst they were ironing, the agency made sure that a radio was being played in the background – ostensibly to make the atmosphere informal. In fact the purpose of the exercise wasn't to test the iron, but the power of radio.

The housewives later recalled a specific radio commercial that was played while they were ironing – right down to the brand name and details of what was said about the product. Significantly, creative treatment played a major role in recall.

Listeners are loyal and, compared to many other media, targeting is incredibly sharp – apart from very early crude experiments, such as in 1925 when Selfridges sponsored a fashion talk from the Eiffel Tower. In the early days of radio there were only three commercial stations in the UK:

- London Broadcasting Company (the first, which on 8 October 1973 transmitted the first commercial, a 60-second spot at 06.08 for Birds Eye Fish Fingers)
- Capital
- Clyde in Scotland.

Did you know?

The first radio commercial in the world lasted ten minutes. It was transmitted in New York by Station WEAF and advertised apartment space.

Now, hardly a year, sometimes hardly a month, goes by without another specialist radio station entering the airways. You can target anyone from a jazz enthusiast to a newshound by choosing your station and your programme. And the more stations there are, the greater the choice for the listener.

As you have seen from the commercial for ScotsdaleNorth, radio is a medium that allows you to describe a thought as well as an action. It is ideal for the kind of commercial that delves deep into a narrator's psyche. For example:

(MVO – grumpy, slightly zany)

What kind of a name is PenPod? Pen, pod. I can see it now. Hot summer's afternoon, big farm. Lots of strawberries. Lots of girls picking the fruit.

(SFX – summer day in the background)

Girls. She's nice. 'Hello … (Hmm) … How's it going?' she asks.

'Oh, fine,' I reply. 'Lovely day for it. Look I've picked hundreds and hundreds of ripe pens off the pod.'

'That looks tasty,' she replies.

Then one thing leads to another. I take her name.
She asks for my number … Ah yes. PenPod.
Fruity if you ask me.

(MVO 2)

Get it off your mind and down on paper with PenPod.

Delivering the message

It's not good enough to ensure that your radio commercial is heard. Your audience has to listen to it. Radio is ideal for conveying complex information. Just tune into a Talk Radio show – there is news, weather, sports, traffic updates, guests talking about different subjects. Like all messages, as long as your creative message is single-minded, radio will deliver it direct to the consumer's mind.

As with television, it is vital that you use your first few seconds to attract the listener's attention. Address your audience. Make your commercial lead into or out of a scheduled announcement. You could use a weather forecast:

(SFX – hot summer's day)

(FVO)

Weather like this is something to write home about.

Your forecast from PenPod.

> (During a Top Thirty pop music chart show)
>
> (Male rapper)
>
> Yo! Listen up. You can get a pack of
> 12 Colas from ScotsdaleNorth at a price that's
> as cool as it is refreshing.
>
> (SFX – opens a can of Cola and drinks)
>
> Ah. (Wipes his lips.) Who said you can't be tops if
> you're not number one?

Always consider link sentences:

> **WANT TO KNOW MORE? LISTEN TO THIS ...**
>
> **BUT THAT'S NOT ALL ...**

A good radio commercial is like a good old-fashioned chat between friends. One piece of news or gossip naturally follows another. As radio is so personal, people draw individual conclusions about what you say. They judge your message very subjectively, rather than allowing others to interfere with the one-on-one radio-listening experience.

Time for a commercial break

Proven creative listener-grabbing devices include music, SFX and scripts that are read quickly. By digitally compressing a commercial radio recording, you can speed up the commercial by as much as 15% without having a detrimental effect on its quality. That means you can literally squeeze thirty-eight seconds of scripting into thirty seconds. In the United States, tests have shown that this creative technique delivers up to a 40% improvement of aided recall over commercials read at normal speeds.

Another attention-grabbing technique is to record the commercial at a slightly higher volume than normally required. This method is also commonly used in TV commercials.

Radio commercials are considerably cheaper to produce than TV commercials. This means that longer-length commercials are more affordable. A normally spoken radio commercial allows for about seventy words in thirty seconds. One minute gives you about 150 words. However, depending on the mood of the commercial, you could easily double those figures (for a quickly spoken, 'Hurry, hurry, hurry' type of delivery) or halve that figure (for a slow, seductive commercial that makes the listener savour every single moment).

I once heard that the only accurate way to time a commercial is to measure the script in syllables – up to five = one second. However, I believe that the only way to time a radio commercial accurately is to buy a stop-watch!

Another radio attention-grabber is the question teaser:

> **WHERE CAN YOU BUY OVER 3 HOURS OF SOUL MUSIC FOR JUST £19.99?**

> **WOULDN'T YOU WANT LESS TIME ON YOUR HANDS? WITH OUR GENTLE ANTI-WRINKLE HAND-CREAM, YOU CAN.**

Three varieties, one flavour

Commercial radio is usually broadcast on either the AM or FM frequency. Most people nowadays listen on stereo FM, with an increasing number enjoying the clarity of digital. However, there are many stations that don't offer a choice, so you may find that your ideal target audience can only listen on AM (mono). When producing a radio commercial by all means listen to the results in the studio on an impressive sound system, but also insist on hearing how it will sound on a small transistor radio.

Music

Please refer to 'TV jingles' on pages 210–11. If you do choose to use music (and why not? – most radio stations are built on music) make sure that you have permission to use a track.

It's no good featuring the Beatles' song 'Paperback Writer' for a PenPod commercial if you can't afford the music rights. You may decide to parody a relevant track. Instead of 'Paperback Writer', you could feature the words 'PenPod writer'.

Whenever you write a lyric, make sure the words and sentences are short. Radio relies completely on sound. A simple sentence that can be understood first time is always preferable to a more complicated, longer version.

Perhaps you have decided to go for securing the rights for a piece of music. Once you have done that, you have to budget for the air play royalties. A great idea could end up costing a great deal. There are companies who will take publicly available music (known as public domain music) and edit it into usable 5- or 10-second segments (known as pre-recorded needle-drop music). You can also purchase existing music in commercial chunks from specialized commercial music libraries.

There are two schools of thought about music parodies.

1 **Pros**

- Teenagers and housewives listen to radio music so they will appreciate musical commercials.
- You can vary lyrics and even styles.
- You can vary singers.
- Music can evoke a time and mood.

2 **Cons**

- What is 'in' today is 'out' tomorrow.
- Music parodies are a poor excuse for an unoriginal creative idea.
- The royalty costs may be more than the increase in sales generated by the campaign.

Involve your listeners – it's to their advantage

Ensure that your creative idea is single-minded. Don't let complicated production enhancements get in the way of an easy-to-grasp message. Your brand name should be repeated throughout the commercial and, of course, listeners should be told how to get hold of the product or service – either by phone or in person.

If you want to make a special offer, consider setting a time limit for it as you would with direct mail:

THIS FRIDAY AT 5 P.M., WE'RE CLOSING THE OFFER FOR GOOD.

Notice 5 p.m. rather than simply Friday. This adds even greater urgency. The shorter your deadline, the higher your response. Make it 5.35 p.m. and you'll add even greater urgency. (As in TV, it's the small details that help build the bigger picture.)

You can also consider celebrity endorsements – especially radio presenters. This is quite common in the United States where presenters discuss products or services during the course of programmes. Such disguised endorsements are not allowed in the UK. However, you can still use the presenter during an obvious commercial break. As with all forms of dialogue copy, make sure that your copy sounds real and that what is said reflects how the presenter would normally speak.

One way around the UK radio regulations is to make your commercial part of a broader promotional package. It could be part of a competition to win a major prize. Competitions are always in demand by breakfast DJs looking for new ways to stimulate their early-morning listeners to get up and go without encouraging them to stand up and leave.

One of radio's greatest strengths is that it encourages listeners to participate in activities:

LISTEN TO THIS, THEN RING THIS NUMBER.

Any promotion featuring interactive ideas like a vote line or a quiz, a music dedication and so on, is going to increase interest and response. Studies show that 27% of local radio listeners physically interact with the station in some way – they phone in, have a dedication read out, enter a competition, attend a road show.

ScotsdaleNorth.com could run this kind of promotion. For example, the breakfast DJ could give away £100 worth of shopping vouchers every day for a week, as part of ScotsdaleNorth's centenary celebrations. This could be reinforced with a ScotsdaleNorth commercial.

Radio production

Some of the greatest fun you can have as a copywriter is in a radio commercial production suite. Unlike television, it is usual for copywriters to direct as well as write an entire production. Just as in TV you give the director the credit that they have the imagination to enhance your commercial, so in radio you should credit the actors with the ability and talent to take an idea and make it sound sweeter to the ear.

I am always impressed by the versatility of radio Voice Overs. One good actor can deliver in excess of seven distinctive voices – saving you time and the cost of employing lots of actors for one script. Once I asked an actor to deliver a line in twelve different ways. He obliged, brilliantly performing the line:

What, are you joking?
I've *really* won a hundred thousand pounds!

His accents included:
- Indian
- Welsh
- London
- Arabic
- Irish

- Scottish
- Deep South
- Israeli
- Spanish

Now try the line yourself!

Make sure you have enough scripts for everyone. Tell the actors everything about the product. Who's going to buy it? Why would they want to buy it? What did you have in mind when you wrote the commercial? A good actor needs a sound brief to make words work. Give all the help they need, down to advising them about emphasis of key words in the script:

- What, are you joking? <u>I've</u> really won a hundred thousand pounds!
- What, are you joking? I've really <u>won</u> a hundred thousand pounds!

It is accepted that radio commercials can be produced quickly. This is useful if you want to make an important announcement at short notice or to capitalize on the latest news story. However, whenever possible, you should plan your commercial with enough time to get the best Voice Overs and research the most relevant creative enhancements such as music, jingles and sound effects.

If a commercial lasts thirty seconds, you should allow for a minimum of two hours in the studio: half an hour for recording and the rest for production. Ideally, book three hours. If the commercial is complicated or requires more than three actors, this may need to be increased to even longer.

Radio commercials quick tips

- Write a mind picture, not a sound track.
- Concentrate on a single thought.
- Target your audience.
- Allow your copy to talk one to one.
- Consider capitalizing on a radio spot – e.g. the weather, a particular type of programme.
- Consider writing two radio commercials for one commercial break – one that leads into the break and one that leads out.

- Consider making your advertisement part of a broader promotion such as an on-air competition.
- SFX builds interest and reinforces believability.
- Don't overwrite a commercial. If you have to describe a detail, let an SFX provide it.
- Radio is cost effective. Consider producing two versions of a commercial – this avoids people getting bored with hearing the same thing and can be used as a form of creative testing.
- If you need longer than thirty seconds to convey a message, use longer (and vice versa).
- Choose your Voice Over to reflect your product and its audience.
- Involve your audience.
- Repeat the product name throughout the commercial.
- Radio is intimate – speak directly to your listener, in the bath, in the garden, in the car, at work.
- Write as people speak.
- Capitalize on the trust and faith which people have in radio.
- Use music prudently and watch costs.
- Voice Over actors can be incredibly versatile.
- The more time you take over recording your commercial, the greater the energy you can expend into ensuring it features high production values.
- Pre-plan all jingles and music.
- Remember that, unlike TV audiences, listeners zone in to programmes rather than zapping past commercials.
- As more people work at home, they look for company by using the radio – so the medium becomes ever more important. Plan for emerging markets.
- Radio is like direct mail that you post in someone's ear and gets delivered to their mind. Target your copy and you'll be on the right wavelength.

Over to you

1 Write a 30-second radio commercial advertising the power of radio.
2 Adapt a well-known lyric from the Top Thirty to sell a packet of ScotsdaleNorth washing-up powder.
3 Look around your room. Now match six products to six possible locations where people could listen to the radio.
4 Write a five-second sponsored introduction from Directions to a programme about food.

further media to consider

In this chapter you will learn
- how to write for posters
- how to write for transit posters
- how to target your poster copy.

Posters

Keep the message simple. That's the best advice for outdoor poster sites. Unless a poster appears in an area where people are virtually forced to stare at it (e.g. a railway station platform), there is precious little time to get a message across. Instead, think about producing a fast-to-read, easy-to-grasp piece of creativity that relies on blanket exposure rather than intimate targeting. That can be harder than you think. Brevity can lead to banality. Writing four words instead of a long sentence that says the same thing is incredibly difficult. Winston Churchill knew this. It is said that he would spend ten times longer writing a few well-chosen words than preparing a lengthy speech.

Typically, posters are seen by drivers in traffic. As roads become more and more congested, the poster audience becomes greater and, while stuck in traffic, people have longer to read advertising messages. That leads to another benefit of posters: apart from informing, they can turn a drab tarmac environment into a colourful and entertaining landscape.

Poster copy – including copy for in-store posters, which are usually A2 size – needs to be blatantly obvious. There's no point in writing something lengthy (except in situations where the reader has nothing other to do than to read your message). Take outdoor posters. Owing to their physical size and positioning, most posters are designed to be seen from distances in excess of 150 feet. If a motorist is passing a poster that is 250 feet away whilst driving at 50 miles an hour, they will have less than three seconds to take in its message.

Graphics can be lavish as long as they are not overcomplicated. Also, there is a safety argument for not overdistracting a driver's attention. For example, a poster featuring a naked woman hitching a ride with the headline

Don't goggle at me, watch the road!

may be an interesting way to promote driving safety, but it may have the reverse effect from what it is trying to communicate!

Three features of an effective poster:

1 Intriguing headline.
2 Dynamic complementary graphic.
3 Strong company branding using logos.

Often poster copy is too short to sell a detailed commercial message. Being road-side commercial signs, posters can remind people about a larger campaign on TV, in the press or on radio. Poster copy can be a shortened adaptation of a TV, radio or press advertisement or creatively different, yet part of a single-minded campaign. Posters can also be used as the sole medium to convey a message direct to the buying centre of a community.

Unlike TV, radio or the press, posters do not rely on editorial content. No one can zap out posters with a TV remote control. No one can skip pages. No one can turn a poster off. Because they have no editorial background, posters are only as effective as their creative message and location.

Ever since the first poster appeared in 1866, the medium has been an integral part of the environment. People often take posters for granted, so creativity has to work hard to get noticed. However, because posters are part of the everyday environment, when messages are read and appreciated the advertised product or service takes on the kudos of something that is part of everyday life and therefore a community commodity. Here are some creative ideas.

Good posters make people think.

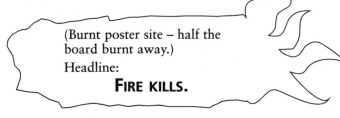

(Burnt poster site – half the board burnt away.)
Headline:
FIRE KILLS.

Good posters often make people laugh.

POSTERS ARE *SEXY*
(THIS ONE'S TOPLESS)

Good posters get to the point.

> ## £35 TO GO IN *SEINE*
> ### (FLY TO PARIS AT CRAZY PRICES)

Good posters are unsubtle.

> (Picture of car suspended in the air over a road, figures
> and words painted below it on the tarmac.)
>
> ## $12,500
> ### ON THE ROAD PRICE

Good posters make a dull journey stimulating.

> Poster 1:
> (Picture of housewife carrying lots of shopping in a
> superstore, looking directly at the 'camera', in shock.)
>
> ### THIS IS A HOLD UP
>
> Poster 2 – 50 yards down the road:
>
> (Same housewife, smiling as she shops on line at
> ScotsdaleNorth.com.)
>
> ### THIS ISN'T

Good posters offer a different interpretation.

> Poster showing two pictures:
> Computer and PenPod
> Headline:
>
> ### One of these Word Processors
> ### will never let you down.

Targeting your message with posters

Many copywriters assume that posters are purely for the mass
markets. This is not always the case. Posters can be targeted by
carefully placing them in key locations. For example, if you

want to attract business people you could consider placing a poster along a main business traffic route.

> (A super-sized poster for ScotsdaleNorth glue – three cars actually stuck to the poster.)
>
> Headline:
>
> ### STUCK IN TRAFFIC.

You can also target by area:

> (Poster featuring a picture of new ScotsdaleNorth superstore covered by a gigantic curtain.)
>
> **OPENING SOON**
>
> ## QUEENSTOWN'S BIGGEST EVER SUPERSTORE

Next stop – start buying

Transit posters on buses and trains allow you to write longer and more detailed copy. It doesn't matter if the passenger doesn't read all your message the first time. Like all poster advertising, the medium relies on sustained and broad coverage rather than a one-off impact.

Some of the best transport advertisements take full advantage of the environment in which they appear. Copy can discuss commuting to work by bus or train. The poster can be designed to utilize the shape of, for example, a double-decker bus. Use coach or bus front, back and side poster messages to talk directly to drivers. For example:

> (On the back of a bus, to be read by motorists.)
>
> Headline:
>
> **FOR THE LATEST TRAFFIC NEWS TUNE IN TO TRAFFIC FM**

Or:

> **FOLLOW ME TO THE NEWEST SCOTSDALENORTH SUPERSTORE**

Posters are fun to write and create. You can smash holes through them:

You can suspend things from them. You can make them move. Some poster contractors offer revolving poster faces that feature slats like blinds which revolve one after another to display different advertisements. The blinds can be controlled to revolve in one direction and then another in a timed sequence. PenPod could feature a series of revolving blinds to give the impression of a hand-written line of ink that grows longer and longer, developing into the headline copy.

You can use posters on buses and coaches to spread the message all around town.

Posters quick tips

- Keep copy short.
- Utilize shapes and surroundings.
- Think nationally, write locally.
- Let visuals do half the talking.
- Take longer to keep copy shorter.
- Amuse, attract and arrest.

Over to you

1 Write an in-store poster for a High Street printer promoting 25% off printing charges.
2 Write a transit poster promoting alternative transport to cars.
3 Explain how you would design a poster for the blind.

11

Yellow Pages and trade directories

In this chapter you will learn
• how to write a directory ad.

Yellow Pages

Yellow Pages are ideal creative platforms for businesses targeting consumers at home. Their success has spawned specialist business-targeted directories which feature similar page layouts. The key thing to remember when writing copy for *Yellow Pages* is that you need impact.

Some editions of *Yellow Pages* are printed on paper that does not make photographic images showing fine details a sensible option (unless these are printed on more suitable paper material and bound into the publication). So, use big, bold graphics and typefaces. Always feature a line of copy that explains what your (or your client's) company offers. For example:

ACME PRINT
LOW COST PRINTERS. HIGH QUALITY PRODUCTION.

Make your contact address details clear and easy to understand:

CALL QUEENSTOWN 98 98 98

Leave sufficient 'white space' to separate your advertisement from the many others on the page.

As in recruitment advertisements, use borders to add greater emphasis to your advertisement as well as to help establish a creative advertising style.

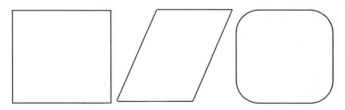

Consider the use of freephone telephone numbers to enhance response. If you are advertising in more than one directory, you could also feature a special code to gauge the effectiveness of each advertisement.

A modern equivalent of *Yellow Pages* is a Web page such as www.yell.com., or other listing services which use cable.

With *Yellow Pages* you can utilize the publisher's own national advertising to enhance your product or service, so you can feature your local advertisement as part of a greater national local services awareness campaign. On your van you can paint 'Find us in Yellow Pages'. This adds regional credibility and gives a potential customer the option to go home, open the local *Yellow Pages* and read your advertisement. (Mind you, they will also spot everyone else's advertisement. As yours will be remarkably well written, that shouldn't be a problem!)

Finally, *Yellow Pages* can be used as a source of distribution. You can have an insert that is delivered with each new edition. (See 'The door-drop mailer', p. 171.)

Other directories

It seems that just about every industry sector has its own specialist trade directory. More often than not, there are several trade directories for a sector. Paper quality ranges from absorbent to high quality art paper. Before you decide to advertise, I recommend that you contact the relevant industry's official trade association and ask which directory is best for a specific trade.

If you are offered a free line advertisement in a directory or if your budget doesn't stretch to a display advertisement, find out how many words you can feature within your space. This is how best to use four lines of copy:

1 In the first line summarize what you offer.
2 In the second summarize your specialities.
3 In the third line guarantee your offer.
4 In the last line, provide contact details.

For example:

ACME COPYWRITING
[ADDRESS]
AWARD WINNING STRATEGY-LED COPYWRITING AND CREATIVITY.
SPECIALIST IN THE WEB, BROCHURES, VIDEOS, RADIO
AND SALES PROMOTION.
PROVEN RESULTS, PROVEN VALUE.
CALL QUEENSTOWN **98 98 98** NOW.

If you are writing copy for a very small business, it is worth considering using a special telephone number exclusively for use in trade directories and other forms of advertising. Of course, you should always feature strongly the business's Web address. These tactics enable you to avoid publicizing private contact details and you can gauge the level of response without having to feature a code within the advertisement. If you or your client works from home, you should carefully consider whether or not to feature your address details:

Address featured?	Pros	Cons
Yes.	People can write to you.	Everyone – including possible weirdos – has your address.
No.	Your private details stay that way.	Your business could seem a bit shady.

The choice is yours.

Directories quick tips

- Be bold, be brash, be direct.
- Use distinctive borders.
- Always describe your product or service area.
- Include an offer or guarantee – e.g. 'No fees for initial meeting'.
- Always feature your Website address.
- Make full use of any of the publisher's own national promotions.

12

the internet

In this chapter you will learn
- how to identify typical surfers
- how to plan your site
- how to deal with Web protocols
- how to use Web 'action' words
- how to take advantage of Web rings.

The Internet – its origins

> **Did you know?**
>
> In 1969 the American Defense Advanced Research Projects Agency wrote a computer program that enabled researchers based at various locations (four to be precise) to communicate with each other. Thus, Darpanet was created. As the years passed, so the network of computers able to use the Darpanet system grew. By 1972, thirty-seven computers (or 'nodes') were on-line. Users started to exchange much more than research material. Each had their own electronic mailbox. Darpanet had a change of name to reflect a change of agency – it became Arpanet.

The network grew. The defence agency became concerned that too many people could access sensitive information, so in 1983 a new network was established – Milnet. Technology continued to develop and more US government agencies became interested in the system. NSFNET was created to connect educational locations together. By 1987 so many people were using the system that its original purpose (a means for sharing academic research) was overtaken by a much broader function and a network of people world-wide.

Today the Internet is a vast interconnecting international web of different computer networks including academic networks, governmental networks and private commercial networks, all of which use a universal data communication system (called a protocol) such as TCP/IP. Part of the so-called Information Superhighway, the Internet is accessible to everyone, from school children to nuclear physicists.

Advertisers have used the Internet from its very early days. Initially, they found it ideal to sell information technology items such as software. Now, with so many different types of surfers, it is the fastest growing area in the world for advertisers of all kinds. By the close of the last century dotcom commercials on US television accounted for over 90% of TV channel advertising revenue.

The Web today

Did you know?

It took 38 years for radio to attract 50 million listeners, and 13 years for television to attract 50 million viewers. In just four years the Internet has attracted 50 million surfers. Every four seconds, a further eleven organizations establish a Web presence. By 2005, West European e-commerce should be worth $260 billion. World-wide more than 500 million people will be surfing the Web, from Teeny Techies (aged 6–16) to Silver Surfers (aged 50+).

Soon the world will be divided into the Web content rich and the Web content poor. Those who are not part of the digerati (the dotcom surfer elite) will be seriously disadvantaged.

Who's on the Web?

My company, Gabay (www.gabaynet.com and www.theworks.co.uk), has identified distinctive types of surfers who can be targeted by dotcom copy.

1 Dotcom colonists

They:
- spend a lot of time on the Internet
- are high users of WWW retail sites
- have strong recreational orientation, with a disdain for chat-like social role-playing or sexual flirtation
- are mostly males with a wide spread in age and low household incomes
- are ideal for Web culture content and editor's choice selections.

2 Progressers

These:
- approach the Net as a resource for the pursuit of personal and career interests
- have lots of personal email accounts and email list subscriptions
- are frequent users of on-line or Internet classified ads
- are male and younger than the Internet population as a whole
- are ideal for personalized on-line services.

3 New.commers

They:
- are recent Webbies, mostly drawn or put on-line for work reasons
- wouldn't pay for Internet access if it weren't free
- rarely use on-line or email support services
- generally perceive themselves as having better things to do than become Net experts.

4 Mouse masters

Their qualities are:
- the most active Internet users
- more than 80% have been on the Internet for three or more years
- nearly all are males, with a median age under 30
- average to high household income
- ideal for Web-marketing sophisticated technical information, 'beta' test software, authoring tools, computer and software industry conferences and trade shows, and other computer-related products.

5 Party animals

They:
- are highly sociable
- typically experiment with on-line social play such as chat rooms
- are on average aged under 35 with medium to low household income
- because of youth and modest income are probably not lucrative for many on-line businesses.

6 Career surfers

They:
- charge almost all their on-line activities and computing to their employer
- mostly have more than two personal email accounts
- limit time on the Internet to essential work
- hate on-line misconduct
- are ideal for editorial information summaries, particularly within research or industry categories, and printable information.

7 Nice 'n' eazees

They:

- are comfortable on-line, active on the Internet, leisure orientated
- are happy to pay for Internet services
- typically have two or more email accounts
- are the oldest Internet segment in age
- are the highest subscribers to on-line services, and the highest users of mail e-catalogues and World Wide Web retail sites.

The nice 'n' eazees fit well in the categories of the new jet-set trendies – the so-called 'Net-Set'. These surfers, who include Milleniuls (born after 1982), not only know what to buy but where to buy with ease on the Web.

8 Scouts

These:

- seek specific information searches, communications and document sharing
- are impatient to learn the Internet via trial and error, often ending up doing so to get things done
- hate IT jargon
- resent having to separate Web content wheat from chaff
- rely on directories, especially those with recommendations
- are willing to pay for relevant information services
- are key for Web culture and 'Best of' editorial sections.

Did you know?

Estimates of the number of surfers vary. In the mid-1990s world-wide, there were only around 30,000 sites on the Web. At the start of the twenty-first century there were in excess of 800 million pages.

Designing your site

Designing your Web pages can either be done by using programs such as Dreamweaver or left in the hands of a specialist Web designer. Either way, aim to make your site simple to access and easy to navigate. Streaming software such as RealAudio and Flash lets you use features like on-line radio and video. However, only consider them if they add to an overall positive dotcom surfing experience. Whatever you do, try to achieve more for your site than simply design a Web version of an existing brochure. Offer a one-to-one media experience, bringing your brand as close as a surfer's screen. Allow the surfer to explore interactive aspects of your brand which they wouldn't achieve through simply reading traditional marketing material.

Tips for planning your site

Buy a roll of plain wallpaper and flow-chart your site. Start with the first page. Indicate the number of featured pages, varying the text throughout the site. Show links to other sites (i.e. Hypertext links). Never offer too many links per page. Consider a permanent site flow chart on each page.

Back to the drawing board. You may want a rough layout of each page in detail, or an electronic draft version of your site. If so, be sure to colour code each page leading to and from a specific navigational link. **Be warned:** Sites tend to grow in content according to the amount of time you spend building them. Time, especially when dealing with Web designers, is money. So agree everything on paper before committing yourself to a Web publishing stage.

The simpler your site, the more visitors you'll receive. Every time you add a plug-in (enhanced program such as on-line video) you potentially lose a customer who does not have the appropriate technology or, if connected to a company intranet, is not allowed to use such technology.

Never be tempted to squeeze additional last-minute material into your site, especially after the initial contents have been agreed. This will lead to nothing but heartache as you will exceed your budget and may well compromise the integrity of your site's design.

Samples of website layouts

Basic website structure

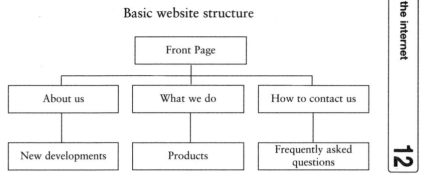

Basic customer dialogue site

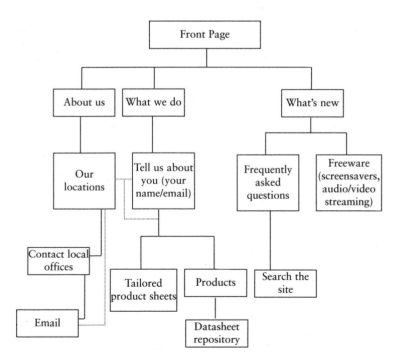

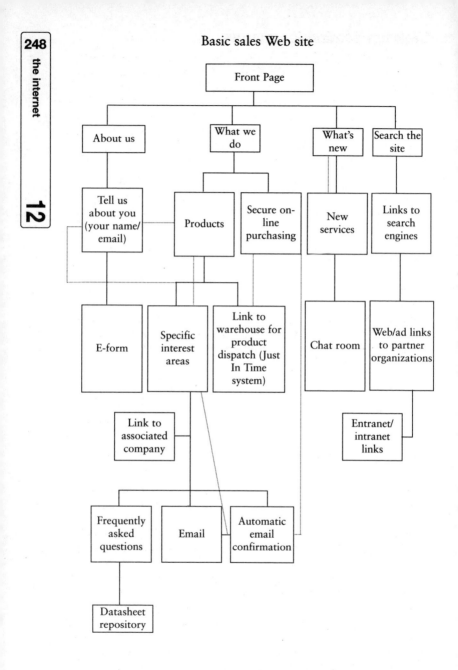

Basic sales Web site

Web application languages

The growth of Web technical languages is fast becoming the electronic equivalent of the Tower of Babel: Java, shockwave, XML and more. That's why I strongly advocate that a simple message in plain English should be your primary goal. The execution of that message is simply a Web coding interpretation that takes into account the speed of downloading the message, the technical ability to view that message and the degree of interactivity allowed by the prevailing technology.

The foundation for Web coding protocols is still HTML. This is used to produce the collection of documents (Web pages) that may be on computers which are quite literally countries apart but are linked using Hypertext to create the World Wide Web.

Did you know?

Hypertext was invented by Ted Nelson in the 1960s. It is a non-sequential matrix of information, creatively linked by allowing the user (or reader) to click with a mouse on a word or phrase. Through doing so, further details are found through either further text or perhaps an animated sequence that provides further explanation. Typically, Hypertext will link one set of copy to another within a different part of a document.

In my book *Successful Webmarketing in a Week*, I describe in detail the many marketing possibilities offered by the World Wide Web, which is part of the Internet. In terms of copywriting, the main thing to keep in mind is that the Web may at first seem purely a mass-medium tool but, upon closer examination, it is clearly the world's biggest direct marketing tool.

Unlike any other type of medium in which your strategic use of words, graphics and media selection draw your target audience towards your message, with the Web your audience gives you permission to communicate your message. This permission marketing is a direct reflection of the consumer's growing ability to discriminate between advertised messages and settle for their own choice of buying channel. Being global, the Web attracts local audiences with specific needs, yet the most popular language on the Web is English. Because of its international audience, Web English has to be precise, to the point and inviting. It is thought that surfers take no more than three clicks per page to decide whether or not to stick with a site. If your message is not sufficiently compelling, they simply click off.

Keeping surfers hooked

Make sure your words are given the space to breathe. Surfers read Web pages from the middle of the screen outwards. So plan your site accordingly. As a surfer's attention span is short, every word should be hard working. Linked together as paragraphs, your messages form a bridge of arguments that defend your brand positioning.

A common mistake that people make when writing dotcom copy is to incorporate Hypertext links into the middle of a sentence. This is a futile exercise. If they click on the link, your reader never completes your sentence. You quite literally waste your words.

It is essential that you keep your dotcom messages flowing. Avoid 'closed reading' by featuring link phrases which encourage the surfer to read further and longer, such as:
• But …
• However …
• So …
• Because …
• What's more …
• In addition …

Better still, use Web technology such as animated GIFS (pictures) to lead the surfer throughout your site.

Did you know?

Each day, the average person subconsciously hears or sees around 200 instructions. These range from 'Don't walk on the grass' to 'Buy one for the price of two'. We naturally filter out such messages; up to 20% of instructions are forgotten. That's why you need to avoid cyber noise: a confluence of dotcom messages whose force of delivery dissolves the thrust of a well-intentioned argument.

Getting the message read is down to the fundamental truths that have long been practised in traditional direct mail copy. It's a matter of AIDCA:
• Attention leads to Interest.
• Interest leads to Desire.
• Desire leads to the need to Convince your reader.
• Conviction leads to Action.

Paramount in this equation is Conviction. Unless you can convince your cyber audience about the value of your proposition, cyber-marketing copy becomes little more than marketing garnish on a plate piled high with hot air.

Today's digerati can see beyond the hype; they want the action. Give it to them.

Dotcom words and phrases

Tremendous	Plus	Free	Unbelievable
Money	Cash	Mega	Huge
Profit	Remarkable	Congratulations	Celebrate
Cool	Fast	Sparkle	Wicked
Evil	Saintly	Explode	Crème de la crème
Eternal	Sexy	Naked	Imagine
Truth	Revealed	Killer	Hurry
Promise	Guarantee	Urgent	Hello

The following dotcom copy phrases are often used as openers for emails, but they can double up in dotcom sites. You can add your own terms to the list. The key to success is to keep your message alluring, succinct and engaging. But remember, use this kind of language liberally to complement rather than replace a solid benefit-led proposition.

Read this before you have your first coffee break	Advanced notification	Does this sound like you?	Are you unshockable?	Hate work?
Want to meet your match?	Be honest – do you really need to read this?	Here's the advantage you've waited for	Save direct	Click here and save
Did you know?	Are you a yoosless spellehr?	Haven't we met?	Ask me a question	What we've been up to
You've just got to read this	I was once a sceptic too	I've heard of a great job for you	Are you mad?	I hate the Internet
Can you handle this?	In five minutes from now, your life will change for ever	Who says you can't have the best?	Start living here	Miss this – miss out

Official request	Look at this	This is not junk mail	Your name came up	Don't let your boss read this
This is not a scam	I've tried this and thought of you	What will they think of next?	Does this stimulate you?	Hold onto your hat
Be nice to yourself	Check this out –	I'm worried about you	Read this in private	

Copy often makes promises – like offering to write to someone, or promising to call. Once someone is on your site, they have made the moves – all you have to do is prevent them from moving on.

People read sites directly. There are no third parties involved. This is very much a one-on-one affair – from the screen to the surfer. That's why your copy should be highly accessible.

Open me quick!

To get noticed, legitimate email copy has to work harder than ever. There are four key motivators which encourage surfers to click emails open:

Money	A discount or means to earn more.
Ideology	An invitation to participate in a new concept or be part of a peer group.
Coercion	Join or get left behind.
Ego	You owe it to yourself – you're the best.

Of these, money, especially if it is written out numerically, works best.

Also, take the advice of email marketing guru David Chafley from Marketing Insights. He recommends your email has CRABS.

C hunk your paragraphs into blocks of no more than two sentences.

R elevance. Ensure your tone and style is appropriate.

A ccuracy. Check your facts and if possible drop jargon.

B revity. Get the message distilled into the first paragraph and make each bulleted item less than eight words.

S canability. Make headings, first words in paragraphs and calls to action stand out.

Getting closer to your surfer

A great way of getting closer to your cyber audience is to visit a newsgroup. There are thousands on-line. Each forum of surfers has specialized interests and some are interested in your organization's field. Through earning the respect of targeted newsgroups you can:

- understand your market's character
- gain a form of advocacy advertising ('newsgroupies' are the equivalent of the friends traditional direct marketing asks customers to recommend – the most powerful kind of clients money can't buy)
- with permission from the newsgroup controller, conduct informal research.

To find more information about writing for the Web visit www.gabaynet.com

Web rings

A Web ring is a collection of links with a common theme or interest which is actively sought by would-be customers by using search engines. To find one that's suitable for you go to www.Webring.org If you can't find one, you could always start up your own – and profit from inviting other sites to link to your site, widening your prospective audience. (Also search Google for BLOGs.)

Finally, spellcheck your site. Better still, get others to spellcheck it. Keep in mind this dotcom variation on the spelling verse I gave you earlier in this book:

> *I have a spell cite programme*
> *Its part of my win doze*
> *It plainly marks for my revue*
> *Ear ors I did knot no*
> *I've run this poem on it*
> *Its letter purr fact you sea*
> *Sew I don't have too worry*
> *My checker looks after me.*

Internet quick tips

- Feature your site IP address (URL) or email address on all company literature.
- Consider using other media to advertise your presence on the Web.

- Make sure that all technical hitches are sorted out before publicizing your site. Surfers don't appreciate being treated as guinea pigs.
- Make your site as interesting as possible – discuss latest industry issues, consider making your site an interactive game.
- Never overload graphics or colours.
- Download in layered stages using HTML.
- Market your site to search engines.
- Ask someone not associated with your company for views on what makes a good site.
- Make sure your site is relevant to your business.
- Substance rules over marketing sizzle – make sure your site features useful information.
- Always keep your site up to date and spellchecked.
- Don't make your site too complicated to navigate.
- Develop your changes according to site performance.
- Promote, promote and promote using traditional techniques such as press reviews.
- Although your potential audience is in millions, consider the Internet as a narrowcast medium which requires careful targeting.
- Read *Successful Webmarketing in a Week* for complete details.

You can learn more about writing copy for the Web by visiting www.gabaynet.com

13 press release copy

In this chapter you will learn
- how to structure your news release
- how to define the right kind of press release
- how to handle bad news.

News is what someone somewhere doesn't
want you to print: the rest is advertising.

William Randolph Hearst

Public relations

Strictly speaking, public relations is outside the remit of many
copywriters. However, for those writers who are freelance or
independent or have to cater for just about any type of publicity
writing, PR is an important tool.

PR is not free advertising. Its value far exceeds that. Good
public relations covers everything from staff communications
and product launches to handling bad news and a simple sign
by a roadside that apologizes for any inconvenience during
repair works.

> **Did you know?**
>
> According to the British Institute of Public Relations, 'Public
> relations practice is the planned and sustained effort to establish
> and maintain goodwill and mutual understanding between an
> organisation and its publics.'

In your capacity as a PR writer you have to act as the special
correspondent to every news medium who deals with your
client's interests. As such you have to appreciate the needs of the
press and the desires of your client – always a delicate balancing
act.

As a special correspondent you must understand how to make
an average everyday type of story newsworthy. You must be
able to present the facts of your story in a form that does away
with advertising hype and concentrates on interesting news
angles. You have to think like a newshound. You have to be
ready to track down all the elements of your story as well as the
markets who will be interested in printing either your version
directly or, more likely, their version as explained by you and
your press release. Finally, you have to show a sense of
responsibility to your client, the media and the truth. Nobody
will ask you for a second story if your first one was eventually
discovered to be nothing more than a cover-up or a pack of lies.

Get to know your media. As in advertising copywriting, you
need to know:

- which kind of publication features which kind of story
- which suit your needs
- how (in what style) they like a story explained.

For the purposes of this chapter let's concentrate on how to write a general news release and accompanying support material. This is the most basic form of PR writing and, as it is written from a broadly neutral stance, it offers the greatest attraction to the broadest media sources.

Every news story is divided into three essential components:

1 the headline
2 the lead
3 the body.

From a press release angle, think of the headline as a calling card between you and an editor. It announces in one or two sentences what you have to offer. For example:

> BRITAIN'S BEST LOVED RETAILER CELEBRATES **100** YEARS OF SERVICE.

Notice that the retailer's name was not featured – instead all the words were directed towards the subject features and benefits matter:

> BEST LOVED ... CELEBRATES ... **100** YEARS OF SERVICE.

Once you have cast your bait with a headline, you have to hook an editor's interest with a lead paragraph. Within no more than sixty words, your lead has to be sufficiently interesting and relevant for an editor either to read the rest of your press release or get a staff journalist to make further enquiries.

Leads are fact, rather than prose, led:

> SCOTSDALENORTH IS CELEBRATING **100** YEARS OF RETAILING IN THE UNITED KINGDOM. AS PART OF THE FESTIVITIES TO MARK THE EVENT, ON FRIDAY 8TH OCTOBER AT **7** PM, EACH OF ITS SUPERSTORES WILL FEATURE A FIREWORKS DISPLAY.

From a practical point of view, it is seldom possible to write a different press release for each publication. However, it is a good idea to target the story to a type of medium. In addition to giving you a theme for your story, that gives you assurance that when your lead is read it has a greater chance of working.

Here is the ScotsdaleNorth lead adapted for the popular press:

> **ON FRIDAY 8TH OCTOBER, THE SKIES ARE GOING TO BE LIT UP FROM JOHN O'GROATS TO LAND'S END. IT'S PART OF THE YEAR-LONG CELEBRATIONS TO MARK THE 100TH BIRTHDAY OF ONE OF ENGLAND'S BEST LOVED RETAIL CHAINS, SCOTSDALENORTH.**

The main components of a press release lead are:

• Who is doing:	Consider:
– What	– Who is it for?
– Why	– What do I need to say?
– When and, finally	– How will I flow the copy?
– Where?	– When will it be read?

Editors often take mere seconds to decide if the story is of interest or not. Avoid sending a press release which discusses something that has already occurred – editors work in the news business, not the history library.

Your press release should be tagged as an urgent matter. Consider including a FOR IMMEDIATE RELEASE notice or adding an air of privileged information: EMBARGO UNTIL (date).

Never use the word 'exclusive' unless the story really is exclusive to one publication. If you want to get round this, you can always make your story exclusive to one publication and after that 'special' for another publication. (Specials may be appropriate for local papers who would want a particular regional bias given to the story or trade publications which wish to discuss a specific business angle.)

Always include:
• the date when you sent the press release
• if very urgent, the time
• your contact details.

Next you move to the body of the release. There are various formulae for writing a coherent and logical product- or service-based press release. One of the best known is SOLAADS:

> Subject
> Organization
> Location
> Advantages
> Applications
> Details
> Source

We have already dealt with the first two on the list. Now you have to consider the main thrust of your press release.

1 Give further details of what's so different and new about the product or service. Who is likely to want it?
2 What are the benefits to the readers, surfers, viewers or listeners?
3 How best can it be used – what kind of problems does it address?
4 How does it shape up?
5 What does it feel like?
6 What does it look like?
7 How does it perform?
8 Who does the editor contact for further information?

Other types of press release

Your story may have nothing to do with materials or services. Often the best stories are the human interest angles. Essentially the format for such a release is similar to those for product- and service-based items.

(Show where the release comes from.)

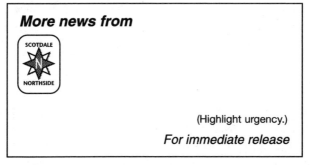

A strong headline, led by the person, features and benefits, *not* the company:

RALPH SOAMES SET TO TAKE SCOTSDALENORTH BEYOND THE FIRST DECADE OF THE 21ST CENTURY.

Not

SCOTSDALENORTH RECRUITS COMPUTER INC'S EX HEAD OF COMMUNICATIONS.

Feature a strong lead-in.

Non-indented first paragraph:

MARKETING AWARD WINNER RALPH SOAMES HAS JOINED SCOTSDALENORTH AS HEAD OF COMMUNICATIONS. 'IT WAS THE NATURAL CHOICE,' EXPLAINED SOAMES. 'THE COMPANY HAS THE RIGHT DISTRIBUTION CHANNELS AS WELL AS SPREAD OF BRANDS TO REALLY OFFER THE CONSUMER SOMETHING TOTALLY DIFFERENT FOR THE NEW MILLENNIUM. I BELIEVE THAT A CONTINUED TARGETED COMMUNICATIONS STRATEGY WILL HELP FURTHER REINFORCE THE COMPANY AS THE UNDISPUTED MARKET LEADER IN ITS FIELD.'

Next, include further details about his different approach to marketing and how it will affect the consumer.

Indented paragraph:

ONE OF SOAMES'S MOST FAMOUS MARKETING INITIATIVES WAS THE MOULD BREAKING LASTMINUTEBARGAINS.COM SCHEME THROUGH WHICH COMPUTER USERS COULD ORDER FMCG GOODS AT DISCOUNT PRICES DIRECT FROM THE INTERNET. 'I AM CURRENTLY LOOKING AT FURTHER WAYS THAT THE COMPANY CAN MAKE THE WEEKLY SHOP LESS OF A CHORE TO THE CONSUMER.'

Next, give more general information.

THIS YEAR SCOTSDALENORTH IS CELEBRATING 100 YEARS OF SERVICE TO SHOPPERS. SCOTSDALENORTH HAS 355 BRANCHES THROUGHOUT THE COUNTRY. ITS WEB DIVISION SCOTSDALENORTH.COM IS ALREADY ONE OF THE COUNTRY'S MOST POPULAR INTERNET RETAILERS. SPEAKING ABOUT MR SOAMES'S NEW APPOINTMENT, ROGER DALE, CHAIRMAN OF SCOTSDALENORTH, SAID, 'WE HAVE FOLLOWED RALPH'S CAREER CLOSELY OVER THE YEARS. WE ARE DELIGHTED TO WELCOME HIM TO THE TEAM.'

Conclude with a human interest angle and closing hook.

> **RALPH SOAMES (AGED 41) IS MARRIED WITH THREE CHILDREN. WHEN ASKED WHERE HIS WIFE MAKES HER WEEKLY SHOP HE ANSWERED, "WELL LET'S JUST SAY IT'S NOT A MILLION MILES AWAY FROM MY NEW OFFICE!"**
>
> **ENDS**

Some people prefer to mark the end of a press release by typing ########. If the press release must continue onto another sheet of paper, write '- more -' and head the following sheet with a suitable follow-on line. For example:

> **SOAMES JOINS SCOTSDALENORTH PAGE TWO**

Conclude with your contact details.

> **FOR FURTHER DETAILS**
> **PLEASE CONTACT Catherine Newman**
> **AT SCOTSDALENORTH PRESS OFFICE**
> **TELEPHONE 1234 5678**
> **FAX 1234 5678**
> **Email catherine@scotsnorth.com**

Even further releases

1 **Announcement release** – this is concerned with brief details about such subjects as a change of address or a new team member. Trade publications often feature short announcements on who's moving to what company. All that is usually required is a few lines of detail: who's moving from where to what position and with what responsibility.

2 **Background notes** – another kind of press release is a support piece – the background notes release. This is not usually for publication. It provides useful details about technical aspects or historical points related to the main release. Typically, background notes may feature previously published articles, research figures, brochures and company reports. In the case

of Ralph Soames, the background notes could include biographical details.

3 **Technical release** – this is often longer than the usual one-page, one-side main release. It does all the additional technical homework for an editor or journalist so they can write a complete and accurate account of how a particular product or service developed.

4 **TV or radio release** – finally, you may be required to write a special press release for TV or radio. If this is the case, you have to remember the points discussed previously in the sections relating to the broadcast media:

• Write as people speak.
• Sentences need to be crisp.
• Information needs to be distilled to its simple points.
• Wherever possible try to include at least one quote that encapsulates the entire message within ten seconds of 'talk time'. If that quote promises broader repercussions – all the better. (This type of quote is often called a 'sound bite' and is usually an edited highlight from a recording.) For example:

RALPH SOAMES HAS JOINED SCOTSDALENORTH. 'THIS IS ONE OF THE MOST EXCITING DEVELOPMENTS IN OUR ON-GOING COMMUNICATIONS PROGRAMME THAT WILL TAKE US INTO THE FIRST TWO DECADES OF THE 21ST CENTURY,' SAID SCOTSDALENORTH'S CHAIRMAN ROGER DALE.

RALPH SOAMES IS BEST KNOWN FOR HIS INNOVATIVE MARKETING WORK RELATING TO THE INTERNET. 'I AM PROUD TO HAVE BEEN PART OF THE TEAM THAT ESTABLISHED THE WEB AS A VALUABLE AREA FOR CUSTOMER TRAFFIC. I AM SURE THAT SCOTSDALENORTH'S AMAZING BRAND RANGE WILL SOON BE ENJOYED BY THE BIGGEST CUSTOMER BASE EVER SERVICED BY A UK COMPANY.'

If you wish to produce an audio release for the radio, find out what kind of format the recording should be on: reel-to-reel, DAT, MP3 or cassette.

Finally, always submit an accompanying letter with a broadcast release, explaining what the release is about, how it is relevant to an audience and where to contact you for further information.

When bad news is good news

The worst kind of news for a publicist is bad news. For example, a dead cockroach could be discovered in a tin of ScotsdaleNorth baked beans. A senior member of PenPod's management board could be exposed as a crook.

The first thing to accept is that the saying 'All publicity is good publicity' is a fallacy. Too many image-sensitive people have been driven to suicide by bad publicity for the saying to have any real credence.

There are three ways to deal with bad publicity. Here are the first two:

1 Deny the allegations

This is the most obvious course to take. However, there are times when the facts are weighted too heavily against your client to make any denial plausible. In this case you should resort to option 2.

2 Counter the allegations

This is the best option of all. Journalists want a news story. Give it to them. Only as well as one juicy bit of news, offer another, much more tempting morsel. This is a barter method and shows the journalists that you are on their side, helping them to get a good story – not a piece of tittle tattle – and above all to get to the bottom of what happened.

So, a dead cockroach is found in a tin of ScotsdaleNorth baked beans. Surely the *real* story is not about the company's public health checks but about who put it there in the first place. Offer a reward to find the culprit. The public's health is at risk. ScotsdaleNorth will leave no stone unturned to expose the culprits. Go further, announce plans to redesign tins so that they are tamper proof. Invite journalists to see the production line for themselves. Remember, *your client has nothing to hide*. If there is simply no way of avoiding adverse publicity, defend your cause by justifying your actions, showing the blatant regrettable victimization caused through the adverse publicity. Point out that it is a definite case of kicking a person when they are down.

If you must, face the music and be prepared to admit that a mistake was made. Then close the matter. People will respect you for it. Sometimes by prolonging a dispute you will make things worse. An early settlement can stop a one-off piece of sensational news becoming a much bigger problem that attracts greater publicity. Beware of what is sometimes called the 'David and Goliath syndrome', which occurs when the little guy shows up the big corporation.

So, where it is applicable to the situation, the big corporation may admit liability early on and then get on with other things – the fight is over. No further battles can emerge. There is no more news. The important thing is that a lesson has been learnt. The immediate, positive actions taken by the organization because of the experience can only benefit the consumer. You could take this further and, through doing so, gain extra news coverage by throwing down the gauntlet and asking the public for their opinion.

A lesson from the film industry

Deviating for a minute from the business world, this technique is often used by movie stars who are caught cheating on their partners. They may ask:

• Would you leave your partner if they had an affair?
• What would you do in my shoes?

Another avoidance technique for movie star couples who have hit the headlines is to allow a story to have a good run in the press, then get a key person to make a statement in a TV interview. The news of the up-and-coming statement will itself stimulate media interest. During the interview the person who cheated on their partner could apologize for their wrongdoing:

**'It was a one-off. I can only hope that they
will one day find it in their heart to forgive me.'**

Once the interview has been broadcast, the press can again be encouraged to ask their audience to comment.

The next step may be to get the aggrieved party to announce that they are so aggrieved because a wrong has been done that they just want to be left alone to 'figure things out'. About a month later, however, they come out of hiding and announce that love may yet bring them back together again. All this could lead to a tip-off to a press photographer that the couple are getting away from it all by taking a vacation at an exclusive tropical island. A photograph taken with a zoom lens, showing the couple walking hand in hand on a beach, is then published in the papers.

Soon publicity gets underway to launch the latest movie of one of the couple – or, even better, one about adultery in which they have joint starring roles. For guaranteed interest, a movie might star the wrongdoer and the alleged one-time extra-marital partner. Needless to say, whatever is most relevant will be a box-office success.

Back to the business world and the cockroach in the beans

Avoid direct advertising that attacks the parties attacking your client. This is a way to highlight a problem and turn it into a longer-term headache. If you have to advertise, produce only advertising that advises on any immediate risks to the consumer and demonstrates a positive response by your client:

WE'RE RECALLING OUR BEANS BECAUSE WE ARE RESOLUTE IN OUR PROMISE OF QUALITY

HAVE YOU RECENTLY PURCHASED A TIN OF SCOTSDALENORTH BAKED BEANS (BATCH NUMBER 12345)? IF SO, PLEASE RETURN IT TO YOUR LOCAL SCOTSDALENORTH STORE. YOU WILL BE GIVEN A VOUCHER WORTH £10.00 THAT CAN BE REDEEMED AGAINST ANY FUTURE OWN-BRAND PURCHASE.

THIS UNFORTUNATE ACTION HAS TO BE TAKEN DUE TO THE ACTIONS OF CRIMINALS WHO ARE BEING SOUGHT BY THE POLICE. SCOTSDALENORTH IS OFFERING A REWARD OF £50,000. IF YOU HAVE ANY INFORMATION THAT CAN LEAD TO THE CONVICTION OF THESE PEOPLE PLEASE DIAL 0800 123 123.

IN THE MEANTIME, WE HOPE THAT THE VOUCHER FOR £10.00 WILL MAKE UP FOR THE INCONVENIENCE CAUSED.

FOR GOODNESS SAKE – YOU CAN TRUST US.

If all that fails, the third way is still open to you:

3 **Sue**
Wherever possible, avoid this. It is costly, drags things out and highlights a problem. For instance, even if you have a good case, libel is difficult to prove. If, on the other hand, you are 100% confident that an injustice has been done, never be afraid to resort to law. It is, after all, there to protect your client's interests.

If none of the three strategies is an option, hire a professional publicist. Even a great copywriter like you can only achieve so much!

Press release quick tips

- Try to get all your facts onto one side of a sheet of A4 paper.
- Double-line space your text.
- Block your lead-in paragraph, indent the rest.
- Show where the news is from.
- Don't use capital letters to write a company name: ScotsdaleNorth, not SCOTSDALENORTH.
- Avoid underlining text.
- If there is more than one page of text use the word 'more' at the foot of the first page.
- Show the date of embargo or make your announcement on the day – news is now, not history.
- Time embargoes accurately to match a launch or special event.
- Write your story from the top down. Editors edit from the bottom up.
- Concentrate on facts, not flourishes.
- Show who to contact for further information and where.
- Avoid obvious hidden advertising for products or services.
- Don't try to create a story when there isn't enough to make it a story worth printing.
- Tailor the emphasis and style of a story to suit a media sector.
- Follow up a press release with a phone call. Does the journalist need any further details?
- Read and write your story as you think an editor would wish it to be received by their target audience.
- Double-check spelling.
- Use quotes only if they are relevant to the story.

Over to you

1 Write seven press release heading variations which announce that PenPod is launching a new pen.
2 Write a 200-word background autobiography.
3 Imagine you have been caught cheating on your partner. Devise a 12-point plan that would prove your innocence and have you coming out smelling of roses.
4 What does SOLAADS stand for?
5 Construct an advertisement from ScotsdaleNorth commenting on why a small section of the roof of one of its superstores caved in overnight – narrowly missing a pedestrian.

6 Write three short sentences that will encourage a news editor to read a press release about an industrial nail manufacturer who wants to announce a new length of nail that's being added to the production line.

I'M A COPYWRITER – STILL CARE TO JOIN ME?

THEN, BELIEVE IN YOURSELF, PRACTISE YOUR CRAFT.

PEOPLE WILL BELIEVE IN YOU AND YOU'LL GO FAR.

AND REMEMBER, A SIMPLE SENTENCE THAT CAN BE UNDERSTOOD FIRST TIME IS ALWAYS PREFERABLE TO A COMPLICATED, LONGER DESCRIPTION.

NOW GO OUT THERE, WRITE, SELL AND MEET THE DEADLINES

appendix

Making the jargon make sense

You will need to understand the language of copywriting. Here are some definitions. Terms in bold are themselves defined in a separate entry. See also pages 212–13, where you will find a list of technical jargon used for TV and radio commercials.

A/B split   The creative testing of two variations of one element in a direct mail package.

above-the-line   Originally referred to a form of agency remuneration; nowadays refers to **advertising** and **marketing** budget spent on TV, radio or published media. This concept has been superseded by through-the-line and integrated marketing, which offers a combination of above-the-line and **below-the-line** advertising.

account

1 A client of an advertising agency or promotions/public relations agency.

2 A general term used to describe a client's marketing affairs.

account executive   The person, usually at middle management or junior management level, who liaises between the agency and client.

account group   Agency team that works on an account.

ACORN   A Classification of Residential Neighbourhoods. This is a consumer-targeting system which provides a listed selection of residential property information.

adsterbation   Self-gratifying advertising

advertising   A planned and considered method of **marketing** that informs consumers about something and persuades consumers to do something, through doing so establishing a sales or marketing communication link between a service or product provider, its distributors, users and advocates.

advertising agency   A company that produces advertising and organizes advertising campaigns on behalf of clients.

advertising platform   The main benefits of facts to be conveyed through a piece of advertising.

advertising rate   The fee charged for time or advertising space in the media.

Advertising Standards Authority   The body responsible for overseeing public complaints about printed advertising.

advertising wedge   A product or service's leading benefit or feature that is highlighted within an advertisement.

advertorial   A combination of advertising and editorial style of copy to give the appearance of a pure piece of editorial. Often features the words 'advertising feature'.

advid   An advertising video tape often used by job and American college applicants as an electronic CV.

advocacy advertising   See issue advertising.

advt   Abbreviation for advertisement.

agency commission   The fee paid by the media to an agency for placing advertising.

American Marketing Association   Founded in 1936, it is recognized as the leading US association of marketing managers and teachers.

animatic   A semi-finished TV commercial usually presented in a rough animated format. It is often used for research purposes.

annual   Publication produced once a year.

answer print   The final print of a TV commercial for approval before broadcasting.

art buyer   A person employed by an advertising agency to commission creative suppliers such as printers and photographers.

art director   The person responsible for the visual concept design and execution, including graphical or photographic management, of a creative advertising project. Often advertising agencies team art directors with copywriters, thereby creating macro units of creativity – often supervised by a **creative director**. Where such team work occurs, generally creative ideas are jointly conceived.

artwork   The final creative execution of a piece of advertising material ready for print.

atomistic test   The research testing of individual parts of a design or advertisement.

author's alteration   A proof-reading correction made by a copywriter.

awareness A measurable capacity for people to recall a specific advertisement either when unprompted ('Can you name a brand of pen?') or prompted ('Have you ever written with a PenPod?').

back-to-back The broadcasting of commercials in a direct sequence.

backgrounders Public relation support material to aid journalists.

bait and switch advertising The now outlawed process of advertising a low-priced item in order to build customer traffic and then switching to selling a similar, higher-priced item.

bangtail An envelope designed with an attached perforated 'tail', used as a coupon or order response device.

banker envelope An envelope with a flap on the longest edge.

bastard size Special size of paper.

beauty shot A close-up shot of a TV or cinema advertised product.

believability The scale by which an advertisement is believed.

below-the-line **Advertising** and **marketing** budget spent on **promotions**, including direct marketing and sales promotions as well as those areas not dealt with in **above-the-line** advertising.

bill-me-later Payment charged once the goods have been received.

bill-stuffer Please refer to **statement stuffer**.

billboards American term for poster sites; known in the UK as **hoardings**.

billing
1 The fee charged to a client by an agency.
2 The net charge made by a media supplier to an agency; the gross charge less the discount given to the agency.

bi-monthly Publication produced every two months.

blind ad A classified advertisement which does not reveal the identity of a client.

blow-in card A loose reply card inserted into a magazine.

blurb
1 Basic product or service descriptive copy.
2 Short introductory copy on a book jacket that highlights, explains and enthuses about the text within the covers.

body type The typeface used in the bodycopy.

bodycopy The main text of a piece of copy.

border The perimeter line that distinguishes one advertisement from another on the printed page.

BRAD   British Rates and Data. A monthly reference source of media and advertising cost and circulation data.

brand   'A name, term, symbol or design (or a combination of them) which is intended to signify the goods or services of one seller or group of sellers and to differentiate them from those of competitors' (as defined by Philip Kotler, the author of *Marketing Management*).

brand association   The mental link between a specific product or service and its general category.

brand attitude   A consumer's opinion of a product or service.

brand differentiation   The ways in which a product or service is perceived to be different from its competitors.

brand image   The emotive 'gut feelings' conjured up by **advertising** or **marketing**, felt by the consumer towards a product or service.

brand loyalty   The ultimate aim of a brand manager – to secure the continued custom and product or service endorsement from a client.

brand switching   The act of changing from one brand to another.

BRE   Business Reply Envelope. A pre-addressed envelope from a mailer to be returned by a recipient.

broadsheet   Large-sized newspaper, as opposed to a small-sized tabloid.

broadside   The traditional name given to paper printed on a single side only.

brochure   A printed bound pamphlet (derived from the French word meaning to stitch, *brocher*).

bromide   A photographic print. (The world's first photographically illustrated advertisement was placed by the Harrison Patent Knitting Machine Company of Portland Street, Manchester. It appeared on 11 November 1887 and showed the company's staff near a display stand.)

buck slip   A US-dollar-sized piece of paper that announces an offer for prompt reply.

business press   Specialist press aimed at the business community.

byline   The name of a journalist responsible for a specific article or report.

campaign   A planned and co-ordinated sequence of **advertising, marketing** and promotional activities constructed to achieve a calculated result.

CAP   Code of Advertising Practice.

caption   Copy that describes a specific illustration or photograph.

centrefold spread   Centre spread of a publication, which can be opened flat to show large headlines and pictures.

CERP   Centre Européen des Relations Publiques, otherwise known as the European Federation of Public Relations Organizations.

character count   The overall number of typespaces in a piece of copy, including spaces between words.

Chartered Institute of Marketing   Europe's largest professional body for **marketing** and sales practitioners.

Cheshire label   A name and address label used as an alternative to a window envelope.

circular   A widely distributed piece of advertising material.

clean copy   An error-free piece of copy.

clean proof   An error-free typeset proof.

clip   A short piece of film.

club line   An unsightly first line of a paragraph at the foot of a page or column, with the rest of the paragraph being printed on the next page or column.

cluster   A group of people sharing a common interest or feature.

cluster analysis   A statistical method of sorting samples of people into clusters.

cognitive dissonance   A consumer's disappointment when there is a vast perceived difference between what is expected from a product and what it actually delivers. It can be avoided by stating clear product and service facts within copy and by featuring money-back promises or guarantees if the consumer is not completely satisfied.

cognitive psychology   A general approach to psychology stressing the internal mental processes.

coin rub   Please refer to **scratch off**.

coined word   A word created for a specific purpose.

cold lists   Lists of prospects which have not been previously contacted by a specific advertiser.

collectable   A one-off object or series of objects sold as limited editions using direct marketing techniques.

column inch   The unit of measurement for a standard newspaper or magazine column.

column inch rate   The cost of a column inch.

concertina fold   A paper fold which opens out in the form of the bellows of a concertina.

contact report   A written account of a meeting between a creative supplier or agency and their client.

contest   A sales promotion method that awards prizes to consumers who perform tasks such as completing a phrase.

continuity writer A person who writes programme publicity and information copy for commercial broadcasters.

control The standard by which quality is gauged. Direct mailers feature a control package that has proved the most effective of at least two mailings. All variations of a creative theme are measured against this control. The term is also applied to the most successful creative interpretation of an advertisement within a campaign.

controlled circulation The free distribution of a publication to targeted addresses.

conversion pack A direct mail piece that is meant to convert an enquiry to a sale.

copy approach The main theme or creative thrust in a piece of copy.

copy chief/head Senior copywriter with management responsibilities.

copy editor The journalist who approves and edits journalistic copy produced by reporters.

copy platform Creative rationale and description based on an agreed advertising strategy.

corporate identity Material representation through the **logo**, corporate colour scheme, uniform or **livery** of an organization.

cost per thousand The cost of an advertisement per 1,000 viewers or readers. Also known as CPM (Cost per Mille). To calculate, divide the cost of the advertisement by the circulation of the publication. In the case of TV or radio you have to take into consideration the time at which the commercial is broadcast.

cost plus An **advertising** execution produced at production cost + agency expenses.

counter card A point-of-sale notice highlighting a product name and price.

coverage

1 The geographical reach of a specific medium.

2 The declared parameters of a market.

3 The percentage of the audience within a market able to see an outdoor poster.

4 The total number of people or households, irrespective of location, that buy or receive a publication or see/hear a broadcast.

CPE Cost per Enquiry. The total cost of a mailing divided by the number of enquiries that it produces.

CPO Cost per Order. The total cost of a mailing divided by the number of orders that it produces.

creative director Employee of an agency who is responsible for the output or creative work and overall supervision and co-ordination of creative staff (or teams).

creative strategy A communications goal based on an intended result, product or service benefits and the data to support the marketing aim.

customer relations Public relations programme aimed at consumers using communication devices such as questionnaires, newsletters and after-sales support services.

cut off See **deadline**.

daily rate The fee for **advertising** space charged for all editions of newspapers published during the normal working week.

database A computerized pool of information from which selected data can be utilized.

deadline The latest time a completed advertisement or piece of copy can be accepted.

dealer listing A list that is included in a piece of copy, showing regional dealers who market a product or service.

dealer relations PR directed at commercial distributors of products or services.

demarketing The method of discouraging consumers from buying or consuming. For example, for a summer water conservation campaign: 'By all means splash out on the sun oil, but please conserve your water.'

demographics Classification of an audience make-up based on economic and social influences and conditions. Classifications can be segmented by age, sex, income and working status.

desktop publishing Computer-generated advertising and publications including newsletters, leaflets and press advertisements.

de-dupe The method of identifying and eliminating duplicate names from mailing lists. Once completed, the information is referred to as 'de-duped data'. (Please refer also to **merge and purge**.)

die-cut Paper or cardboard that has been cut to a specific shape.

direct mail The targeted sending of advertising and promotional items direct to likely consumers.

direct mail advertising A term to describe **advertising** or promotional material sent or distributed via a mailing system.

direct marketing A direct channel of distribution using any form of marketing communication that encourages a response and delivers a measurable result.

DMA   Direct Marketing Association. British professional body for direct marketing practitioners.

dirty copy proof   Copy with hand-written comments and amendments. (Opposite: **clean proof**.)

display face   Typeface designed for display-sized advertisements.

DMSB   Direct Mail Sales Bureau. An organization started by the Post Office to promote the use of direct mail.

donor list   List of people who have donated to a charity.

door-to-door   The **direct marketing** distribution of material by hand, usually to residential neighbourhoods.

double-decker   An outdoor poster in two separate tiers.

double-duty envelope   An envelope designed to be torn yet retain its return envelope features.

dummy   A mock-up sample of a communications piece.

dump bin   A point-of-sale item which carries products in a bin.

edit suites   Audio and video post-production facilities for editing purposes.

EDMA   European Direct Marketing Association.

electronic cottage   The term given to the home of a freelance copywriter, designer or person who uses computer technology to link their home with their clients.

embargo   Request to withhold press information until a specified date and time.

English creep   The spread of English as an international language. Over 345 million people use English as their first language and an extra 400 million use it as a second.

envelope stuffer   **Direct marketing** material enclosed in a **direct mail** piece already containing a business letter, invoice or statement.

exclusive   A press release or other kind of information written for one media source.

eye camera   A special camera used to measure visual stimulation and record eye movements of research volunteers when reading copy.

face

1 A specified set of typefaces belonging to a 'family' of typefaces.

2 The bare frontage of an outdoor poster.

3 A page which when opened naturally faces the reader.

4 The opposite page from a piece of copy.

family life cycle   This is in six stages:

1 Young single people.

2 Young couples with no children.

3 Young couples with their youngest child under 6.

4 Couples with dependent children.

5 Older couples with no children at home.

6 Older single people.

farm out   Subcontract work.

feedback   Data fed from consumers that helps managers to assess the overall performance of a product or service **advertising** and **marketing** campaign.

filler advertisement   An unbooked advertisement used to fill up blank publishing space.

flanker   Another term for a line extension brand, referring to a spin-off companion product to a successful brand name (e.g. Soft and Gentle Bath Foam could lead to a flanker, Soft and Gentle Shower Gel).

flat animation   Two-dimensional animation.

flier   Simple sheet of **advertising** material usually found in a mailing piece.

flush and hang   Text which features the first line of copy flush with the left margin and subsequent lines indented.

FMCG   Fast Moving Consumer Goods. Products which are meant to have short retail shelf life and high stock requirement based on a fast repurchase demand (e.g. soap, biscuits, butter).

fount   Alternative word for 'font', meaning a complete set of type of one style and size.

four-colour process   Colour printing featuring primary colours separated by a filter.

frankly I'm puzzled   Traditional style of direct marketing copy, which asks why the recipient has not responded to an offer.

free flier   An extra insert in a **direct mail** piece that offers a special gift for prompt reply.

free keeper   A low-cost item that the recipient of a mailing piece can keep at no obligation.

free newspapers   Typically, weekly local newspapers delivered door-to-door.

free ride   A cost effective way to save mailing costs by including a specific offer within a different mailing.

free-standing stuffer   A loose insert stuffed into a publication.

free trial   See **sample**.

freelancer   A self-employed person who works independently (e.g. freelance copywriter).

freepost   A Royal Mail service whereby the mailer finances the cost of postage.

frequency   The average number of times that a prospect is exposed to a specific advertisement during a specified period of time.

fuzzword   A seemingly defined word that actually confuses a piece of communication – in other words, elegant gobbledegook.

fuzzy sets   Psychologist's term for imprecise language that confuses the reader.

galley proof   The proofed copy text prior to being formatted into pages.

gatefold

1 A leaflet folded so that its two edges meet in the centre.

2 A multi-part insert or cover of a publication that has to be unfolded in order to be read.

generic advertising   An advertisement or commercial that highlights product or service benefits without mentioning a brand name or local outlets.

generic terms   Product descriptions such as 'cornflakes' which describe a product yet are not registered trade names. (One could have ScotsdaleNorth Cornflakes.)

ghost writer   A person contracted to write in the name of someone else.

glossy magazine   Publication printed on high-quality paper.

Greek   Also known as Latin – garbled text on a rough layout that represents the size and position where final copy will eventually sit.

guarantee   An advertiser's promise to a consumer.

guardbook   Portfolio of a client account's creative work.

gutter   Space between columns of text without a vertical dividing rule, or between pairs of pages.

hack   A hired writer who is probably willing to write about anything for any reasonable price.

hanging indent   First line of paragraph set wider than the subsequent lines.

headline   The largest display of text, setting a theme and agenda for the subsequent copy.

heart-stopper   A lottery card sales technique whereby a scratched card reveals all but one number in a sequence required to win a prize. This 'just missed' sequence of numbers usually encourages the purchaser to buy another card.

hidden persuaders   Relates to advertising techniques first described by Vance Packard in the 1950s. The term is sometimes used to describe the role of PR professionals.

hoardings   See **billboards**.

hotline A specially promoted telephone response line which encourages sales, provides information or acts as a form of customer contact service. (The world's first telephone helpline was introduced by the Samaritans on 2 November 1953.)

house agency An agency owned and/or managed by an advertiser.

house corrections Type errors noted and marked on a first proof before a proof is seen by a client.

huckster A bygone, insolent term for an account executive.

hype Overstated publicity.

hyphenless justification Justification of lines of text which avoids breaking words up over two lines.

iconic medium A medium such as TV or video in which images appear as reality.

idea bank A pool of creative ideas that are logged and referred to when required.

ideogram A graphic device that represents an idea or meaning.

illustrated letter A letter that incorporates some kind of illustration or graphic.

imagery Figurative language; the illustration and emphasis of an idea by parallels and analogies of different kinds to make it more concrete and objective.

impact The tangible effect that advertising has on an audience.

impressions The total number of exposures to a specific advertisement during a specified period of time.

in-ad coupon A coupon featured within a press advertisement.

in-flight magazine Magazine published by an airline and placed in the back of seats in an aircraft.

in-pack coupon A coupon that can be redeemed at an outlet.

in-pack premium A premium item offered free with a product.

in the can Completed radio, video or filmed commercial.

Independent Television Commission Deals with complaints about advertising on TV.

independents Privately owned and managed media companies or publicity and advertising agencies.

inquiry response mailing A mass-targeted mailing meant to generate enquiries rather than orders.

insertion An individual advertisement or commercial.

Institute of Direct Marketing Trade organization and educational body for **direct marketing** users, agencies and suppliers.

Institute of Public Relations British professional body for PR practitioners.

International Public Relations Association Senior professional body for PR practitioners around the world.

island position Advertisement surrounded by editorial.

issue advertising Sometimes called advocacy advertising. Used by an organization to discuss its views on topical issues.

jingle track Musical score for a commercial.

job sheet Standard agency administration form describing the expenditure on and progress of a client project.

joint promotion
> 1 A promotion promoting two companies; one features a product or service that supports another's product or service.
> 2 One company endorses another.

junk mail Unsolicited, poorly targeted mail.

key account
> 1 Important client of an agency.
> 2 Important retailer or distributor for a client.

key code Form of letter or numerical coding to measure effectiveness of a campaign.

landscape See **portrait**.

launch The introduction of a new service or product to a market.

layout Sketch or blueprint that shows the intended order of contents and visual styling of an advertisement mail piece, poster and so on.

lead Opening section of copy.

lead time The time gap between the creative concept and the final result.

LHE Left-hand edge.

LHS Left-hand side.

lifetime value The entire term value of a consumer to an organization. Typically the cost of acquiring a consumer is high. The longer the consumer remains loyal, the less the investment costs and so the greater the overall lifetime value.

lift letter A second letter within a **direct mail** piece designed to 'lift' response. (See also **publisher's letter**.)

list ad An advertisement listing more than one item (e.g. a series of records).

list broker An agent who sells databases of sales prospects.

list cleaning Removal of inaccurate data from a database.

list manager An agent for database lists.

list segment   Section of list chosen against specific criteria such as sex and job title.

literal   Error made by a typesetter.

live copy   Copy read 'live' on air.

live names   A term that describes active customers contacted through **direct mail** techniques.

live tag   'Live' message read on air to provide additional local information relating to a pre-recorded national commercial.

livery   Corporate design and styling on all forms of transportation.

logo   An abbreviation of 'logotype'. A particular shape, design or trademark that distinguishes an organization. Also known as a 'signature', 'sig' or 'sig cut'.

loose insert   Please refer to **free-standing stuffer**.

lottery   A sales promotion prize contest based on chance.

lower case   Small letters of the alphabet.

Madison Avenue   Generic term referring to the US advertising industry.

mail list seed   A 'planted' named recipient of a mailing list (a process known as 'salting'). Seeds are typically used to monitor the effectiveness and accuracy of a **direct mail** piece.

mail merge   Computer program that combines a database with copy for a mailing. (See also **merge and purge**.)

mailing list profile   The characteristics by **demographics** of a mailing list.

mailing list sample   An indiscriminate selection of names to test the response to a mailing list.

mailing list test   A random pick of names to test the effectiveness of a mailing list.

Mailsort   Term for pre-sorted discounted Royal Mail mailings.

mandatory copy   Legally required copy.

market atomization   Term used when each consumer is treated as a unique market segment.

market profile   A term to describe the **psychographic, demographic** and geographical characteristics of prospects.

marketing   The management process responsible for identifying, anticipating and accomplishing customer requirements profitably.

marketing department   An organizational department responsible for marketing either for profit or non-profit (in the case of a voluntary organization). Areas of marketing responsibility may include or be a combination of **direct marketing, sales promotion, advertising,** sales, market research, product development and planning and administration.

marketing director Employee responsible for co-ordination and approval of marketing programmes.

marketing mix The combination of promotion, price, product and distribution that creates the foundations of an organization's marketing agenda.

mass media TV, press and radio which reach a large proportion of the public.

media A collective term for cinema, press, radio and TV – also known as **mass media**.

media buyer An advertising agency employee who co-ordinates and negotiates media schedules.

media kit A sales folder containing information about a specific media publication, programme or resource.

media plan A proposal that details media budgets and recommended channels for an advertising campaign.

media speak Journalistic fad which is a corruption of the English language.

merge and purge Assimilation of different databases which also removes duplicated or unwanted information. (See also **de-dupe** and **mail merge**.)

mf. More follows. Marked at the bottom right of a press release when there is a continuation.

MGM Member-get-Member (or Recommend-a-Friend or Word-of-Mouth advertising). When a current customer recommends a product or service to a new **prospect**.

mini catalogue A shortened version of a larger catalogue, often featuring special seasonal offers.

mnemonic Symbol or acronym to aid memory.

mock-up A near-finished representation of a final creative execution.

mood music Musical track which helps establish a desired atmosphere.

morgue Ready written obituaries for VIPs.

multi-mailer One mailing containing several loose single promotional sheets.

music bed Musical background track.

musical logo A melodic corporate signature.

NABS National Advertising Benevolent Society. Highly respected British charitable organization for professionals working in the media.

news hole The amount of news space in a publication after advertisements have been placed.

newsletter Organizational journalistic-style publication that contains information of interest to members and associates of the organization. They provide a sense of belonging as well as an outlet for planned dissemination of management plans and member or employee developments. (The world's first recorded house journal was the *British Mercury* in 1710 – it was delivered three times a week to the homes of any of the insurance company's policyholders who subscribed.)

novelty format   An unusually sized or shaped mailing piece.

nth name   A **direct marketing** database technique that divides the total number of names in a list by a required number of 'test' names to produce a sample. For example, 10,000 'test' names chosen from a 100,000 overall total of names would result in every 10th name being selected for 'testing'.

offer   The terms and conditions under which a **direct mail** item or service is promoted.

on-camera narration   Narration delivered on screen by a presenter.

on-pack coupon   A coupon attached to the outside of a package.

on-pack premium   A free gift attached to the outside of a package.

one-stage/step   A promotion in which a sales cycle is completed in one step without any need for further follow-up by letter or telephone. (The **prospect** reads an advertisement and, on its strength, places an order for a product or service.)

open end

1 A recorded commercial with allocated space for a tag.

2 A programme produced with time for commercials.

3 A programme with no set time to end.

open-rate   The most expensive chargeable media rate.

opinion research   Research based on opinions rather than facts.

order card   A response card to complete and return by mail.

order form   A response form to complete and return by mail.

orphan   A stand-alone line of copy left at the foot of a page.

package insert   A promotional item inserted in a package.

package test   The evaluation of mailing elements individually or in their entirety.

page proof   The printer's proof of a completed page.

paid circulation   A publication that is distributed to people who have paid a subscription.

pamphlet   A leaflet that contains eight or more pages.

Pantone   Colour-matching system.

passive media   Media that require the viewer or listener to do nothing more than watch or listen.

paste-up   A camera-ready layout.

peak time Period which attracts the largest TV or radio audience figures.

peel-off label A self-adhesive label that can be attached to an order form.

penetration Another term for **reach**.

personalization The inclusion of a recipient's personal address details within a mail piece. (Research proves that personalization always increases response.)

piggyback A secondary offer included within a mail piece.

pitch A new business presentation.

planning The activity of predicting future events and using those assumptions to develop strategies that will help achieve the ultimate goal.

poco Brief for 'politically correct', sometimes used by feminists to refer to non-sexist language.

portfolio A case or folder of work.

portrait Upright page (opposite: landscape).

positioning A strategy that 'positions' a product or idea according to how a consumer perceives that product or service relative to competitive offerings from providers of similar goods or services.

PRadvertising Cross between advertising and public relations.

PPI Printed Postage Impression. The pre-printed Royal Mail licensed mark which typically appears on a **direct mail** envelope.

premium

1 A free item or an item offered as an inducement to test, trial and eventually purchase a product or service.

2 An extra charge for a special advertising position within a publication or as part of a broadcast.

presentation Formal presentation of creative and strategic concepts and proposals.

press clipping A published article of interest archived for future reference.

press officer PR professional who specializes in press relations. (Ivy Ledbetter Lee, a former New York financial journalist, was the first public relations consultant. He opened for business in 1903 and his clients included a circus, bankers and politicians. The first PR company in Britain, Editorial Services Ltd, opened for business in 1924. The first public relations officer in Britain worked for Southern Railway and was appointed in 1925.)

press pack A portfolio of information relating to a specific press release or announcement.

price-off A cut price strategy to encourage trial or increased usage of a product or service.

production department An advertising department that co-ordinates and supervises all aspects of technical creative production.

programming schedule A notification of programme times and dates which aids a **media buyer** when selecting TV or radio commercial time.

promotion A concerted **marketing** method to increase sales of a product or service, usually through using a **sales promotion** technique.

prospect A consumer who is likely to become a customer.

psychographics Classification of **prospects** according to lifestyle and personality traits.

publication date The date a publication becomes available to the public.

publicity still A photograph used for publicity purposes.

publisher's letter A **lift letter** from a publisher.

pull Printer's proof.

pull quotes The enlargement of the text of key quotations to give added emphasis.

pull strategy A method that invests in large **advertising** and **marketing** budgets to stimulate consumer demand and in turn encourage intermediaries to handle and promote a product or service.

push strategy A method to encourage consumer demand and stimulate intermediaries to stock a product.

Q&A Question and Answer. In print this usually takes the form of a panel of questions and answers which relate to technical aspects of a product or service. Q&A panels typically appear towards the back of a product or service brochure.

qualitative research Research designed to measure attitudes and perceptions based on kind or condition rather than on amount or degree.

quantitative research Research-based sample quantities based on amount or degree rather than kind or condition. According to AGB research in England, the key quantitative questions are:
- Who are you?
- What do you buy?
- Where do you buy?
- How much?
- At what price?
- When?

- What else could you have purchased?
- Where else could you have purchased it?

quarterly Publication published in a three-monthly cycle.

questionnaire A form featuring a sequence of closed or open questions to be completed and returned by a targeted respondent.

rate card A form detailing specified media **advertising** costs and support information.

reach The overall total percentage of targeted **prospects** in a specific area exposed to a specific advertisement during a specified period. (Also known as **penetration**.)

reader ad A copy-only advertisement that appears to be genuine news or editorial. (See also **advertorial**.)

reader profile A **demographic** classification of readers.

reader response The response of readers to an article or piece of **advertising**.

readership The total number of people reached by a publication.

redemption
1 The percentage of coupons or trading stamps that are cashed in.
2 The general cashing or trading in of coupons or trading stamps.

repeat mailing A mailed follow-up sent to the same list of names as a first mailing.

repositioning A planned **marketing** attempt to reposition a product or service within a market by changing features, price or distribution – or a combination of all three.

research director Agency employee responsible for the purchase and analysis of information that influences a **marketing** strategy.

response A planned reaction to a planned arousal.

response device Any piece of communication which accommodates a response.

response list List of individuals who have responded to a **direct mail** campaign.

retainer A fee that secures the ongoing negotiated exclusive rights to call from time to time upon a person's professional services, such as copywriting.

rhetoric The written and spoken language of persuasion. Also sometimes refers to a pompous style of language.

roll fold A way of folding paper – usually a leaflet – whereby each printed section is rolled around the next at the paper's edge fold.

rough   A brush-stroke layout indicating a general creative concept.

round robin   Traditional name for **direct mail** letter.

run of book/paper   Advertising space and location determined by a publisher rather than an advertiser.

run on   To continue copy on the same line rather than go to a new line.

rushes   Rough, unedited print of daily film footage.

sales promotion   'The range of techniques used to attain sales/marketing objectives in a cost effective manner by adding value to a product or service either to intermediaries or end users, normally but not exclusively within a defined time period' (Institute of Sales Promotions, definition).

sample
1 A group of individuals representative of a percentage of the population.
2 A complimentary portion or test quantity of a marketed product (also known as a trial offer).
3 A quantity of data picked from a total **direct mail** database.

scratch-and-sniff   A method of incorporating scent onto paper. When scratched, an impregnated scent panel is activated.

scratch off   A **direct mail** device (also known as **coin rub**) whereby a coin is used to scratch a coated paper to reveal a special message.

selective demand advertising   Advertising aimed to create awareness and provide information about a particular brand.

self-liquidator
1 A gift or premium which is financed by its offered purchase.
2 A sales promotion display provided to a retailer for a fee to the supplier or manufacturer.

sharpening   A cognitive process in which the information retained becomes more vivid and important than the event itself.

shelf life
1 The amount of time that a product can remain on a retail shelf.
2 The longevity of a product or service based on its popularity and demand.

shelf strip   A point-of-sale printed strip attached to the facing edge of a shelf.

shirt-board advertising   Advertising printed on the cardboard used to support laundered shirts. Popular in the United States.

sleeper   An unpublished 'seed' name. Please refer to **mail list seed**.

spokesperson   A person who endorses an advertised product or service.

sponsored programme

  1 A TV or radio programme that is partly financed by a named advertiser.

  2 Any event may be financially subsidized for **marketing** or **advertising** purposes.

statement stuffer   A small printed advertisement inserted in an envelope containing a bill. (Also known as **bill-stuffer**.)

stock   Music, art, graphics or photographs available from specialist libraries.

style book   Manual of approved corporate styling for ad design.

suit   Generic term referring to a non-creative employee of an advertising agency.

suspects   A consumer who may or may not become a customer.

sustaining advertising   Advertising that maintains consumer demand rather than increasing it.

sweeps   The months of November, February and May, set by a US TV rating service to establish the ranking of TV network shows. This sets the level of advertising rates for local stations.

sweepstakes   A **below-the-line** technique in which prizes are offered to participants on a random chance, no skills basis. An assumption is made that the technique will eventually encourage the consumer to buy a product (no immediate purchase required). A sweepstake condition requires that a sweepstake or prize draw is run according to a set of published rules.

take one

  1 Leaflets or pamphlets freely distributed via a sales promotional desk top or mounted dispenser.

  2 In the United States, an attachment to a transit advertising vehicle card. The take one is a coupon or information request sheet. It often incorporates an envelope or is part of a pad.

talking heads   A TV production featuring extreme head-and-shoulder close-ups of subjects discussing a specific item or area of interest.

talking shelf strips   A point-of-sale printed strip or item attached to or near the facing edge of a shelf which contains a movement sensitive electronic device. As the consumer passes, the device triggers a pre-recorded sound track which discusses the product. (Belgian advertisers have found that such devices may increase sales by 500%.)

target audience   The ideal prospective audience which would be interested in a specific product or service.

tear sheet   A page torn from a publication sent to an advertiser as proof of publication.

teaser campaign   A series of brief announcement advertisements which stimulate curiosity.

telemarketing   Market prospecting, selling, servicing and informing via the telephone.

television director/producer   A person employed to manage and co-ordinate the production of TV commercials.

test marketing   See **zone plan**.

thank you letter   A **direct mail** copy technique in which a customer is thanked for making a purchase or enquiry.

threshold effect   The stage at which the effectiveness of an **advertising** campaign can be seen to be working.

thumbnail   A miniature, rough layout.

tie-in promotion   A promotion which markets more than one product or brand.

time-sheet   A standard form to record the amount of time spent working on a client project.

tip in   A loosely placed publication insert. See also **free-standing stuffer**.

tip-on   A coupon reply card or sample glued by its edge for easy removal from a printed piece of advertising.

tombstone   Originally a Wall Street financial advertisement used in the USA for, among other things, announcing new stock issues. So called because the copy only provides the bare facts – the bare bones.

tone of voice   General attitude, expression or approach given to a message.

traffic building   An **advertising** communication that can include **sales promotion** or **direct marketing,** designed to encourage retail store traffic.

traffic department   The department within an advertising agency which co-ordinates the work flow of projects between departments.

treatment   The overall styling or approach to a piece of **advertising**.

trial close   A copy technique whereby the reader is asked for an order at an early stage of a **direct mail** letter. The copy then directs the reader to the coupon. This technique can be repeated several times during one direct mail letter.

trial offer   A special **marketing** offer, meant to encourage future consumer purchase, made within a particular period of time. See also **sample**.

TV shopping   Also known as shop-at-home. TV programmes or channels that are likened to shopping catalogues. (This area is also embraced by the Internet.)

Two-stage/step   A promotion in which a sales cycle is completed in two steps with a follow-up by letter or telephone. (The **prospect** reads an advertisement and, on its strength, applies for further details of a product or service.) See also **one-stage/step**.

ultra   Short for the 'ultra-consumer', who insists on purchasing the very best – regardless of personal income.

usage pull   The power of advertising to encourage individuals to purchase an advertised service or product.

USP   Unique Sells (or Selling) Proposition. The outstanding benefit or family of features which distinguish a product or service from the competition.

voice   Breadth of media coverage.

Voice Over   The voice of an unseen narrator or presenter.

voucher copy   A copy of an entire publication sent to an advertiser as proof of publication and position as agreed.

white mail   Letters sent to mail order firms which result in more paper work (e.g. complaints and enquiries).

white space   Unprinted space which gives greater emphasis to printed **advertising**.

window envelope   An opening or 'window' **die-cut** into a **direct mail** envelope which shows part of the contents of the mailing inside. The cut is usually covered by glassine, a type of transparent paper.

word spacing   The space between words in a line of justified type.

wraparound   A cover/holder which carries a mail order catalogue and supporting material such as sales letters and order forms.

X-factor   The undefinable aspect of a person or a company that can't be copied but brings success.

yes/no envelope   A response **direct mail** envelope which encourages readers to reply to an offer, irrespective of whether or not they intend to make a purchase.

yes/no stamp Similar to the **yes/no envelope** response enhancement device. Instead, a YES and a NO stamp are attached to a response device. This encourages customer involvement and gives a sense that the mailing is an 'active' item.

Z fold A method of folding paper such as a sales letter into three equal parts. The middle third forms the diagonal column of the letter Z.

zip envelope A **direct mail** envelope which is opened by pulling a tab.

zone plan A strategy to test a new product or service using **advertising** in a highly targeted small geographical area. Also known as 'test marketing'.

taking it further

Further reading

Christopher, Martin, Payne, Adrian, and Ballantyne, David, *Relationship Marketing*. Butterworth Heinemann, 1991.

Considine, Ray, and Raphael, Murray, *The Great Brain Robbery. Business Tips*. The Marketer's Bookshelf (Philadelphia), 1986.

Crissel, Andrew, *Understanding Radio*. Methuen, 1980.

Gabay, J. Jonathan, *Reinvent Yourself*. Momentum, 2002.

Gabay, J. Jonathan, *Successful Webmarketing in a Week*. Hodder Headline, 2000.

Gabay, J. Jonathan, *Teach Yourself Marketing*. Hodder & Stoughton Educational, 2003.

Hodgson, Dick, *Direct Mail and Mail Order Handbook*. Dartnell Press (Chicago).

Stone, Bob, *Successful Direct Marketing Methods*. Crain Books, National Textbook Company.

Further learning

ww.gabaynet.com

index